THE GREAT RESET

The Great Reset

2021 European Public Investment Outlook

*Edited by Floriana Cerniglia, Francesco Saraceno,
and Andrew Watt*

OpenBook
Publishers

https://www.openbookpublishers.com

Open Reports Series, vol. 10 | ISSN: 2399-6668 (Print); 2399-6676 (Online)

ISBN Paperback: 9781800643505
ISBN Hardback: 9781800643512
ISBN Digital (PDF): 9781800643529
ISBN Digital ebook (epub): 9781800643536
ISBN Digital ebook (azw3): 9781800643543
ISBN XML: 9781800643550
DOI: 10.11647/OBP.0280

Cover image: Photo by Sander Weeteling on Unsplash, https://unsplash.com/photos/iGDg_f_mlWo
Cover design: Anna Gatti.

Contents

The *Outlook* is the result of a joint effort by several economists belonging to a wide range of academic institutions and policy institutes; they all wrote in their personal capacity.

The work was coordinated by Floriana Cerniglia, Francesco Saraceno and Andrew Watt with logistical and financial support by CRANEC—Centro di ricerche in analisi economica e sviluppo economico internazionale, Università Cattolica del Sacro Cuore—Milano; Fondazione Astrid; OFCE-SciencesPo Paris and the Macroeconomic Policy Institute (IMK), part of the Hans-Böckler Foundation.

The authors are affiliated to the following institutions:

- Beijing Normal University, BNU (China)
- Bruegel (Belgium)
- Cassa Depositi e Prestiti, CDP (Italy)
- Consiglio Nazionale delle Ricerche, CNR (Italy)
- CRANEC, Centro di ricerche in analisi economica e sviluppo economico Internazionale, Università Cattolica del Sacro Cuore, Milan (Italy)
- Centre for Eastern Studies, OSW (Poland)
- Central Bank of Chile
- Central European University—CEU (Hungary)
- Environmental Change Institute, University of Oxford (United Kingdom)
- European Investment Bank, EIB
- European Policy Centre, Brussels
- Environmental Change Institute, University of Oxford (United Kingdom)
- Fondazione Astrid, Rome (Italy)
- International Monetary Fund, IMF
- Katholieke Universiteit Leuven (Belgium)
- Luiss School of European Political Economy, Università Luiss Guido Carli, Rome (Italy)
- Macroeconomic Policy Institute—IMK (Germany)
- Neoma Business School (France)
- Observatoire français des conjonctures économiques, OFCE-SciencesPo, Paris (France)
- Paris School of Economics (France)
- The Global Climate Forum (Germany)
- The Vienna Institute for International Economic Studies—wiiw (Austria)

- Universidad de Cantabria (Spain)
- Scuola di Scienze Politiche 'Cesare Alfieri', Università degli studi di Firenze (Italy)
- Università degli studi di Bari (Italy)
- Universidad Loyola Andalucía, Seville (Spain)
- University of Vienna (Austria)
- Vistula University, Warsaw (Poland)
- Warsaw School of Economics (Poland)

Acknowledgements

As this report goes to print, we want to express our gratitude to those who made our work possible: first and foremost, to all the chapter authors, who in general respected the deadlines, and interacted with us and with the referees. The result is a collective volume that has a consistent message throughout.

We also sincerely thank the heads of our respective institutions: Alberto Quadrio Curzio, President of CRANEC, Franco Bassanini, President of Fondazione Astrid, Xavier Ragot, President of OFCE-Sciences Po, and Sebastien Dullien, Director of IMK. Their support and encouragement are the reasons why this report exists. Their help was essential in securing financial and logistical support and even more importantly: they put the issue of public investment at the centre of their respective institutions' scientific projects well before the pandemic brought painfully to the fore the need to appraise the theme of investment.

We also thank Giovanni Barbieri from CRANEC for his efficient editing of the volume. Last, but not least our gratitude goes to Alessandra Tosi of Open Book Publishers, who smoothly managed the refereeing process of the report, and adapted to the new constraints posed by the COVID-19 crisis.

Floriana Cerniglia
Francesco Saraceno
Andrew Watt

Authors' Biographies

Giovanni Barbieri is a Research Fellow at Cranec (Centro di ricerche in analisi economica e sviluppo economico internazionale) at Università Cattolica del Sacro Cuore. He holds a PhD (2017) in Institutions and Policies. He previously worked as Adjunct Professor of History of International and Commercial Institutions at the University of Palermo (D.E.M.S., Italy) and project researcher in the Kone Foundation Project "Regional Challenges to Multilateralism", based at Tampere University, Finland. His main expertise is in international political economy (IPE), in particular the problem of uneven deveolopment and the new challenges posed by rising countries to the current global governance scheme.

Andrea Brasili is a Senior Economist at the EIB (Luxembourg) where his research interests are both micro (firm level) data analysis and macroeconomic developments, in particular those related to fiscal policy. He received his PhD in Public Economics from the University of Pavia (Italy). Before joining the EIB, he worked in the private sector (in Italian banks and asset management companies) as a research economist, still collaborating with academia.

Floriana Cerniglia is a Full Professor of Economics at Università Cattolica del Sacro Cuore (Milan) and Director of CRANEC (Centro di ricerche in analisi economica e sviluppo economico internazionale) She is the Co-Editor-in-Chief of EconomiaPolitica, Journal of Analytical and Institutional Economics. She received her PhD from the University of Warwick (UK) and her research interests are in Public Economics and in macroeconomic policies. She has published in leading international journals and she has coordinated and participated in a number of peer-reviewed research projects.

Giuseppe Coco (PhD, Exeter, MSc York, BSc Firenze) holds the Chair in Economics at the School of Political Science 'Cesare Alfieri' in Firenze, where he has been the Director of the Master in International Relations. He is Advisor to the Fondo Nazionale Innovazione, a member of the Scientific Committee of the 'Corte dei Conti' Alta Scuola di Formazione, and a member of the Scientific Commitee of the ASTRID Foundation. He has previously held the positions of Head Economic Advisor to the Minister for the Mezzogiorno (2016–18) and Vice Prime Minister (2015–16); Visiting Research Fellow at City University, London (2009–11); Member of the Simplification Unit (2004–09), and Senior Economist in the Prime Minister's Office in Italy (1999–02); and Lecturer in Economics at the University of Exeter, UK (1997–99). He edited two recent volumes on the development of the Mezzogiorno with Laterza and Il Mulino. His research has also been published in the Journal of Banking and Finance, the Journal of Money, Credit, and Banking, and the European Economic Review.

Adam Czerniak is Director for Research and Chief Economist at Polityka Insight and Head of the Institutional and Political Economics Department at the Warsaw School of Economics. He holds a PhD in Economics. Until 2012, he worked as a banking economist. Previously, he cooperated with the World Bank and the FOR Foundation; he was also a Ronald Coase Institute scholarship fellow. He authored dozens of publications in the fields of economic sociology and institutional economics, and on the varieties of residential capitalism within the European Union. He is the Polish representative to the European Master in Official Statistics Board (term 2021–23).

Luigi Durand is currently a Senior Economist in the Monetary Policy Division of the Central Bank of Chile. His research interests are in international macroeconomics with a focus on capital account policies. His previous work experiences include the IMF, the Independent Evaluation Office of the IMF, and the ECB. Luigi received his PhD in Economics from Johns Hopkins University in 2020. He also holds a MA in Economics from Johns Hopkins University and an MSc in Economic and Social Sciences from Bocconi University.

Raphael Espinoza is a Deputy Division Chief at the IMF, where he has worked on a variety of countries, including the UK during the Brexit negotiations, Spain during the euro area crisis, and the Dominican Republic during its 2009–10 IMF programme. He has also been a Lecturer (Assistant Professor) in Economics at University College London (UCL), where he was the Director of the Centre for Studies of Emerging Economies and a financial stability expert for the central banks of Peru and Colombia. He previously worked on the US subprime crisis as an economist for the ECB. He has written extensively on fiscal policy, monetary policy, and financial stability, including in two books published by Oxford University Press.

Lieve Fransen has been a Senior social and health policy Advisor for a range of different institutions, businesses, and think tanks since 2015. She recently organised major events on implementing the SDGs with private sector and is one of the co-authors of the ground-breaking Prodi report on investing in social infrastructure. She is a medical doctor specialising in global public health and social policies worldwide. She has a PhD in social policies from Antwerp and is the author of many scientific and policy publications. Dr Fransen has had a distinguished career which includes roles as Public Health Advisor to the Ministry of Health in several countries and Director for Social Policy for the European strategy for 2020 and the European semester in the European Commission until May 2015. She launched the Social Investment Package and the recommendation for investing in children in 2013, and has previously been a member of the G8 social impact investment task force and social innovation in the EU. Dr Fransen has considerable recognised experience in external relations and European policies and institutions, and worked extensively with the UN and the World Bank, as well as with private sector entities and investors. She has previously been the founder of the Global Fund for aids, malaria, and tuberculosis, and was the chair of the board representing the donors. She is now a well-recognised policy maker at senior management /director level in the EU in different departments of the European Commission, including Development, Trade and External Relations, Communication and Political Reporting, and Social Affairs and Employment.

William Gbohoui is an Economist at the International Monetary Fund, where he has worked on several countries including Burkina-Faso, France, Indonesia, and Luxembourg. He holds a PhD in Macroeconomics and Public Economics from the University of Montreal, where he has also been a Lecturer. He has written research papers on a wide range of topics covering quantitative macroeconomics, public finance, fiscal policy, inequality, and the labour market in the euro area. He has also contributed to books on economic integration and trade, published by the International Monetary Fund and Palgrave Macmillan.

Pierre-Yves Geoffard is a Professor at the Paris School of Economics, directeur d'études at EHESS, and directeur de recherche at CNRS. His academic work focuses on the economic analysis of health and healthcare systems, health policy, and socioeconomic inequalities in health. His most recent book to be published (with Jean-Pierre Couteron, Jean-Felix Savary, and Yann Bisiou) is *En finir avec la guerre aux drogues* (Esprit Frappeur, 2021).

Mario Holzner is an Executive Director at wiiw. He also coordinates economic policy development and communication with a focus on European economic policy. He has recently worked on issues of infrastructure investment in greater Europe, proposing a European Silk Road. He is also a Lecturer in Applied Econometrics at the University of Vienna, Department of Economics. He obtained his PhD in Economics at the Vienna University of Economics and Business in 2005.

Carlo C. Jaeger is Co-Founder and Chairman of the Global Climate Forum, leading GCF's Green Growth research process. He holds a Professorship at Beijing Normal University (BNU) and was Professor for Modelling Social Systems at Potsdam University in Germany and chair of the research domain 'Transdisciplinary Concepts and Methods' at the Potsdam Institute for Climate Impact Research.

Atanas Kolev is Principal Advisor at the Economics Department of the EIB. He has worked on a wide range of topics related to investment and investment financing at the firm-, sector-, and economy-wide levels. He has been an organiser and contributor to the annual economics conference of the EIB on topics like economic and social cohesion, investment in the energy sector, adaptation to climate change, public investment, and infrastructure investment. Atanas Kolev is currently a coordinator, reviewer, and economic editor of the EIB annual investment report. He holds an Economics PhD from Universitat Autònoma de Barcelona.

Raffaele Lagravinese is a Senior Lecturer of Economics at the University of Bari (Italy). He holds a PhD in Economics from the University of Bari (2011) and a Master's Degree in Economics from the University of Roma Tre (2007). His main expertise is in the areas of Urban and Regional Economics, Health Economics, and Economics of Education. In the past, he has been a Visiting Scholar at the University of York (2009–10), the University of Cambridge (2013), and London School of Economics (2016). In 2016 he became was Adjunct Professor at Brunel Business School of London.

Diana Mangalagiu is a Professor at Neoma Business School, France and the Environmental Change Institute, University of Oxford, and Adjunct Professor at Sciences Po. She has a dual background in natural sciences (PhD in Artificial Intelligence, Ecole Polytechnique, MSc Physics) and social sciences (MSc Sociology, MSc Management). She has over two decades of research, teaching, and advising experience in sustainability, long-term planning, risk governance, and articulation of environmental and economic policies in corporate and public policy settings, addressed through modelling, stakeholder-based inquiry, and foresight approaches. She authored numerous scientific articles and books in fundamental and applied areas, co-founded the Initiative for Science, Society and Policy Dialogue and co-chaired the pan-European Environmental Outlook of the UNEP. She is a scientific board member of the Integrated Risk Governance Project, SEI Initiative on Governing Bioeconomy, and expert for IPBES. She leads advisory, research, and development projects with national and regional governments, companies and World Banks, and OECD and UN agencies.

Adolfo Maza is a Associate Professor of Economics (Accredited as Full Professor) at the University of Cantabria. Prof. Maza received his PhD degree in Economics in 2002. Later on, he completed a postdoctoral stay at the University of Berkeley. His main areas of research include regional economics, economic integration and globalisation, the labour market, migration, and energy economics. He has published more than seventy papers in various international scientific journals, most of them included in the Journal Citation Report (JCR) database. He has also participated in quite a few international congresses and meetings. He was awarded the "Young Researchers Prize" by the Spanish Regional Science Association. He is the Coordinator in Spain of the Erasmus Mundus Joint Master in Economics of Globalisation and European Integration (EGEI). Finally, he has acted as a reviewer for numerous scientific journals, as well as for international funding agencies such as the *National Science Foundation (USA)*, the *Austrian Science Fund, and the Czech Science Foundation.*

Mathieu Plane is a Deputy Director of the Analysis and Forecasting Department at the OFCE Research Center in Economics, Sciences Po, Paris. He is in charge of economic forecasts for the French economy and works on economic policy issues. He has written several articles in scientific journals and has participated in several reports for public institutions. He teaches at Sciences Po, Paris and at the University of Paris Pantheon-Sorbonne. He was, in 2013–14, economic advisor to the Ministers of Economy, Industry, and the Digital Sector. He speaks and writes regularly in the media. He has recently published, in collaboration with other authors of the OFCE, *Margin Rate and Investment in the Export Sector: A Comparative Analysis between France and Germany*, *The Wave of Recovery: Economic Outlook for the French Economy 2021-2022*, and *French Economy 2022* by Éditions La Découverte, Repères collection.

Sebastian Płóciennik is Professor of Economics at Vistula University. He received his PhD from the University of Economics in Wroclaw. In 2013–21 he was head of the European Union Programme and the Weimar Triangle Programme at the Polish Institute of International Affairs (PISM) and in 2003–09, researcher at the Willy Brandt Centre for German and European Studies in Wroclaw. Between 2015–17 he was Co-Chairman of the Board of the Foundation for Polish-German Cooperation (FWPN). His research focuses on the German economy and economic integration in Europe, as well as types of capitalism. He has lectured at the University of Wrocław, ABiF Vistula, and universities in Germany, USA, South Africa, Canada, South Korea, and India.

Romano Prodi was born in 1939. He is a Full Professor of Industrial Economics at Bologna University. From November 1978 to March 1979, he was Minister of Industry. From November 1982 to October 1989 and from May 1993 to July 1994, he held the position of Chairman of the Institute for Industrial Reconstruction (IRI). From 1996–98 and from 2006–08, he was the Italian Prime Minister. From 1999–2005, he was President of the European Commission. He was Chairman of the UN-African Union High-Level Panel for Peacekeeping in Africa from July 2008–10, and was Special Envoy of the Secretary-General for the Sahel from October 2012 to January 2014. From 2009–13, he was Professor at Large at Brown University, and from 2010–15, Professor at CEIBS (China Europe International Business School) in Shanghai. He is now President of the Foundation for Worldwide Cooperation.

Edoardo Reviglio is Head of International and European Projects at "Cassa depositi e prestiti" (CDP), Rome. He is an Adjunct Professor of Economics at LUISS Guido Carli in Rome, and President and Faculty Member of the International University College of Turin. He has previously been a member of the Council of Economic Advisers of the Italian Ministry of Economy and Finance. He is one of the co-authors and chairmen of the Working Group on Finance of the Prodi report on investing in social infrastructure. He has considerable recognised experience in academic and policy research, and represents CDP in international institutions (UN, G20, G7, OECD, EU), working extensively with them. He is on the Board and Scientific Committee of several think tanks at national and international level. He received his BA, Summa Cum Laude, from Yale College, was Senior Fellow at the Department of Mathematics of Yale University, and was Research Associate at the Department of Mathematics of Imperial College, University of London. He is the author of many scientific and policy publications. His fields of interest include public finance, banking and finance, law and economics, and economic history.

Debora Revoltella has been Director of the Economics Department of the European Investment Bank since April 2011. The department comprises thirty economists and provides economic analysis and studies to support the bank in defining its policies and strategies. Before joining the EIB, Debora worked for many years on CESEE, was first in the research department in COMIT, and later worked as Chief Economist for CESEE in UniCredit. Debora holds a PhD in Economics and has also worked as Adjunct Professor at Bocconi University. She is a member of the Steering Committees of the Vienna Initiative and the CompNet, an alternate member of the Board of the Joint Vienna Institute and a member of the Boards of the SUERF and the Euro 50 Group.

Katja Rietzler is Head of the Unit of Fiscal Policy at the Macroeconomic Policy Institute (IMK), part of the Hans-Böckler Foundation. She holds a PhD from the Freie Universität, Berlin. Among other topics, her research focuses on fiscal issues of the municipalities, the German tax-system, public investment needs, and fiscal rules. In addition, she is responsible for the IMK's macroeconometric model. As an expert she regularly participates in parliamentary hearings on issues such as tax legislation, annual budgets, or the debt brake and its implementation.

Désirée Rückert is an Economist in the Economics Department of the European Investment Bank, where she is involved in the EIB Investment Survey, a large-scale survey of corporate investment activities. Her research interests are in digitalisation, start-ups, and applied public economics. She holds a PhD in Economics from Cologne University.

Francesco Saraceno is a Deputy Department Director at OFCE, the Research Center in Economics, Sciences Po, Paris. He holds PhDs in Economics from Columbia University and the Sapienza University of Rome. His research focuses on the relationship between inequality, macroeconomic performance, and European macroeconomic policies. He has published in several international journals. In 2000–02 he was a member of the Council of Economic Advisors for the Italian Prime Minister's Office. He teaches international and European macroeconomics at Sciences Po, where he manages the Economics concentration of the Master in European Affairs, and in Rome (Luiss). He is Academic Director of the Sciences Po-Northwestern European Affairs Program. He is a member of the Scientific Board for the LUISS School of European Political

Economy and formerly of the Confindustria's Scientific Committee. He advises the International Labour Organization (ILO) on macroeconomic policies for employment and participates to IMF training programs on fiscal policy.

Jochen Schanz is a Senior Economist at the European Investment Bank. After a PhD in game theory at the European University Institute, he worked at Lehman Brothers, the Bank of England, and the Bank for International Settlements on monetary and financial stability. At the European Investment Bank, he focuses on public investment and human capital.

Mouhamadou Sy is an Economist at the International Monetary Fund. Prior to the IMF, Mr. Sy worked at the Office of the President and at the Macroeconomics Policy and Research Department of the African Development Bank (AfDB). Before joining the AfDB, he worked at the French Prime Minister's Economic Policy Planning Office in Paris with a focus on international macroeconomic issues. His work to date in policy publications and peer-reviewed journals covers a wide range of topics related to international finance, macroeconomics, and public finance. He holds a PhD from the Paris School of Economics which won him the prize for the best thesis on "Monetary, Financial and Banking Economics", awarded by the Banque de France Foundation jointly with the French Economic Association. He also holds a BSc in Econometrics from the University Paris XII.

Jonas Teitge is a Researcher at the Global Climate Forum, where he is part of the Green Growth research process. He obtained a Diploma in Economics from the University of Potsdam with a focus on Econometrics, Quantitative Methods, and Macroeconomic Modelling in 2011, and joined the Global Climate Forum directly after. The focus of his research is centred around the impact of climate policy measures on economics in general, and the prospects of the European Green Deal in particular. To study those questions, he has specialised in agent-based computational modelling and is designing and calibrating economic models that also take the impact on the climate from environment resource carbon emissions into account.

Reinhilde Veugelers is a Full Professor at KULeuven (BE) at the Department of Management, Strategy and Innovation. She has been a Senior Fellow at Bruegel since 2009 and a Senior Non-Resident Fellow at the Peterson Institute for International Economics since 2020. She is also a CEPR Research Fellow, a member of the Royal Flemish Academy of Belgium for Sciences, and a member of the Academia Europeana. From 2004–08, she was on academic leave, as advisor at the European Commission (BEPA Bureau of European Policy Analysis). She served on the ERC Scientific Council from 2012–18 and on the EU-RISE Expert Group advising the Commissioner for Research. She is a member of VARIO, the expert group advising the Flemish minister for Innovation. She is currently a member of the Board of Reviewing Editors of the journal *Science* and a co-PI on the Science of Science Funding Initiative at NBER.

José Villaverde is a Full Professor of Economics (University of Cantabria). He received his PhD degree in Economics from the University of País Vasco. He has been a Visiting Professor at many universities in Denmark, England, Taiwan, China, United States, Belgium, Chile, Poland, Czech Republic, Ecuador, and Argentina. The scope of his current research interests encompasses international and regional economics, economic integration and globalisation, and the labour market. He has authored several books and published more than 150 papers in refereed journals. He has also participated in many international congresses and meetings. He has acted as a consultant for the World Bank and the European Commission. He has also served as a reviewer for numerous scientific journals in the field of economics.

Antilia Virginie is a Research Assistant at the European Central Bank. She received her MSc in Economics from University College London and has previously worked in the Economic Studies division of the European Investment Bank.

Andrew Watt is Head of the European Economic Policy Unit at the Macroeconomic Policy Institute (IMK), part of the Hans-Böckler Foundation. He holds a PhD from the University of Hamburg. His main research fields are European economic and employment policy and comparative political economy, with a particular interest in the interaction between wage-setting and macroeconomic policy. Recent work has focused on reform of the economic governance of the euro area, emphasising the need to coordinate monetary, fiscal, and wage policy in order to achieve balanced growth and favourable employment outcomes. He has served as advisor to numerous European and national institutions, including the European Commission, the European Economic and Social Committee, and Eurofound.

Katharina Weber is a Research Assistant at the School of Public Policy of the Central European University (CEU). She holds a degree in law (LLB) and is currently pursuing her Master's degree in Public Policy. Her research interests include economic and environmental sustainability with a focus on circular economy and adaptation aid for climate change.

Christoph Weiss is a Senior Economist in the Economics Department of the European Investment Bank. He received a PhD in Economics from the European University Institute. His research interests include firm dynamics, labour economics, development economics, and applied microeconometrics.

Muhammad Usman Zahid is an international development practitioner currently engaged as a project manager with the Centre for Economic Research in Pakistan. Trained in public policy, international development, and economics, he received his Master's from the School of Public Policy at the Central European University. His Master's thesis focused on the use of evidence in policy learning, with a focus on political economy of the policy-making process. Usman's research interests encompass political economy, development, and governance. Up until 2021, Usman worked with the World Bank to improve agriculture extension services and productivity in Pakistan, while previously he has been engaged with the Government of Pakistan in the health and education domains, implementing projects that have aimed at improving access to public health as well as increasing educational outcomes in public schools in the Punjab province.

Maximilian Zangl holds a Master's Degree in Public Policy from the Central European University. His background is in International Relations and Management, while his research interests focus on environmental and governance policies. He has been a research assistant at Webster Vienna Private University.

Preface

This edition of the *European Public Investment Outlook* was written after the most dramatic moments of the COVID-19 pandemic but still during times of considerable uncertainty.

Still, European policymakers seem to have learnt the lessons of the mismanagement of the sovereign debt crisis: thus, the pandemic and its awful impact on European economy and society resulted in a strong momentum for the European Union in tackling the challenge of economic recovery through the adoption of, in some cases, unprecedented fiscal policies. These include the activation of the Stability and Growth Pact general escape clause, a temporary easing of the rules on state aid, and economic stimulus packages, which are financed through the issuance of long-term European sovereign debt securities.

For the first time the taboo of a significant creation of European sovereign debt seems to have been overcome, unveiling the strong appetite of global financial markets for investment in European sovereign safe assets.

The result—even if cast as a one-off step—marks an epochal turn from the "fiscal austerity plus national reforms" approach to a "European Public Capital spending plus national reforms" approach, embedded in the ambitious Next Generation EU programme. The issue of "Eurobonds" by the European Commission is also a crucial step for financing the investment of Next Generation EU.

For the first time, likewise, it was thus possible to verify the beneficial effects of a convergent synergy between fiscal policies and monetary policies, a synergy which was, for a long time, evoked and hoped for by many authoritative exponents of economic science, as well as by the former president of the ECB, Mario Draghi. In fact, the combined action of the European Commission's expansionary fiscal policy and the European Central Bank's accommodative monetary policy has strongly helped to contain the dramatic effects of the epidemic crisis on the economy and on employment, and has also, *inter alia*, contributed to avoiding tensions on national sovereign public debts, albeit whilst the latter were consistently increased by the measures adopted by all European governments in order to face the epidemic emergency, mitigate its impact on households and businesses, and support recovery.

A main difference with respect to the 2020 edition of this *Outlook* is that, in 2021, European Public Investment has gained a significant European element through the financing mechanism of the Recovery and Resilience Facility (RRF), associated with

    https://doi.org/10.11647/OBP.0280.14

the EU 2021–27 budget. With €672.5 bn, this is by far the biggest item in the Next Generation EU package, which totals €750 bn, 5.4% of 2019 European Union GDP. This macroeconomically significant and shared approach to public investment is an important innovation.

The format of the 2021 edition of the *Outlook* remains the same as in 2020. The *Outlook* goes to the heart of the subject of public investment, taking two complementary angles. The first is to identify public investment trends and needs in Europe and in selected countries, addressing the initiatives taken by European governments to tackle the COVID-19 related recession and to sustain and rebuild their economies. The second is the analysis of key domains where European public investment is needed to build a more sustainable Europe, such as transportation, climate change, digital transformation, social infrastructures, formation of human capital, etc. Both sections shed light on the impact that the Recovery and Resilience Facility is likely to have on overall public investment and thus on the overall macroeconomic structure of the European economy.

Taken together, the two parts show the value of public capital both within European countries and as a European public good. Public investment is a tool aimed at different goals: innovation, sustainable growth and high-quality employment, education, social cohesion across European regions and countries, and the fight against climate change. While there are some trade-offs between these objectives, they can largely be treated as complementary, with single projects achieving multiple goals.

Three welcome innovations are taking place within the EU as part of the Next Generation EU initiative:

1. for the first time in the history of the EU there is a massive, shared, and coordinated action at the European level to finance public investment and to boost EU economic growth, with no concerns about specific single-country fiscal constraints or deficit-spending limitations;

2. the choice and planning of investments are left to the political decisions of the individual member states, but the European Union seeks to orient these choices by linking them to a model of sustainable development based on social, gender, and intergenerational equity, environmental sustainability, and the systematic use of digital technologies;

3. with the aim of recovering Europe's strategic autonomy in global competition and of repositioning the continent on a path of long-lasting, balanced, and sustainable development, the disbursement of European financial resources is linked to the approval and implementation of important structural reforms, but for the first time the European constraint is associated with the allocation of the resources needed to finance the reforms and mitigate their short-term impacts; together, reforms and public investment could create the conditions for a boost of private investment.

A crucial issue remains, for the moment, unsolved: the new European policies to support public (and private) investment (and the related instruments) have so far been conceived as exceptional and temporary. How can they be made structural and permanent? This is the question underlying the debate on the Stability and Growth Pact reform and on ways to make the NGEU programme permanent, on the development of a common EU fiscal policy, and on the creation of a European Debt Agency. These are matters, perhaps, for the next *Outlook*.

This 2021 *Outlook* was coordinated by Floriana Cerniglia (Cranec), Francesco Saraceno (OFCE—Sciences Po), and Andrew Watt (IMK—Hans-Böckler Foundation) in a complex environment. The authors of the different chapters of the *Outlook*, from various institutional backgrounds, collaborated in an admirable way, enriching their perspectives from different countries. These "diversities" valuably contributed to the quality of the *Outlook* and made the message emerging from this volume even more significant.

Franco Bassanini
Sebastian Dullien
Alberto Quadrio Curzio
Xavier Ragot

Introduction

Floriana Cerniglia, Francesco Saraceno, and Andrew Watt

Recent weather-related catastrophes have underlined the urgent need to stem climate change. Together with the massive economic and social impact COVID-19 has had on our lives, they have forced the issue of public investment to the centre of the public policy debate. The dire condition of public capital in most advanced economies was exemplified by the widespread unpreparedness of healthcare systems in facing the pandemic. That is why most commentators (amongst whom the editors of this volume) welcomed the fact that from the beginning, while doing whatever it took to minimise the health and economic effects of the pandemic, European countries quickly moved towards ensuring a robust post-COVID recovery, in the hope of avoiding mistakes made ten years earlier.

The Next Generation EU (NGEU) programme, nested in the EU budget, was agreed upon—after some difficult negotiations—relatively quickly, and is centred on the creation of a Recovery and Resilience Facility (RRF) aimed at financing investment for economic recovery. As we write these lines, most national recovery plans have been approved by the Commission and the Council and the first instalments of grants are being disbursed. This is not the place to discuss the novelty of the programme, or whether it truly constitutes a Hamiltonian moment, a founding act for a Federal Europe (on this, see Saraceno 2021 and Watzka and Watt 2020). What matters for our purposes is the fact that NGEU is a massive effort towards financing public investment across Europe, especially in countries currently facing fiscal constraints, and creating the incentives, through reforms and complementary infrastructure projects, for a renewed boost of private investment.

Of course, the comeback of public investment in the policy debate is not related solely to the pandemic. The Global Financial and Economic Crisis of 2008—and in Europe the disastrous experience of the subsequent euro crisis—challenged three decades of consensus in macroeconomics centred on a limited role for macroeconomic policy and, within that limited role, a strong emphasis on monetary policy (Saraceno 2017a). The financial crisis, the liquidity trap, and the zero lower bound forced governments to resort to providing their economies with massive support, *de facto* taking fiscal policy off the backburner. That, in turn, revived the debate on the effectiveness of fiscal policy. The whole "rethinking macroeconomics" discussion revolved around the

https://doi.org/10.11647/OBP.0280.15

size of fiscal multipliers (e.g., Gechert and Rannenberg 2014), the return of the policy mix, and the long-term impact of macroeconomic policy (Fatàs and Summers 2018). Public investment was at the centre of this debate. On the one hand the crisis put in the spotlight the degree of degradation of public capital, including in the highly productive advanced economies (DIW 2013), while on the other hand, the importance of public investment as a stabilisation tool, its impact on potential growth, and the crowding-in effects on private investment gradually became the new consensus in the theoretical and empirical literature (Le Garrec and Touzé 2020). The most visible result of this renewed interest in public investment is the famous IMF World Economic Outlook chapter on public investment (IMF 2014), which highlights that the high productivity of public investment in a situation of depleted public capital stock, together with all-time low levels of interest rates, has turned public investment into a "free lunch".

European policymakers, entangled in their obsession for fiscal discipline which permeates the Maastricht architecture, have until recently been largely impervious to the rethinking macroeconomics debate raging in academia and the international policy institutions. The old consensus was the background, justifying the combo "austerity plus reforms" that led to the self-inflicted second recession in 2012–13 and a decade of soft, disappointing growth. Some policymakers did pay lip service to the need for public investment to sustain recovery (one example being the widely quoted Jackson Hole speech by then ECB President Mario Draghi in 2014), but this necessity was carefully framed within the need for fiscal discipline as a priority for governments, and the respect of the very same fiscal rules that had yielded procyclical fiscal policies and curtailed public investment. Thus, it is not surprising that the Juncker Plan, the 2014 post-crisis EU flagship investment programme, supposedly a pillar for economic recovery and sold to the EU citizens as a boost to public investment, was in fact little more than an (underfunded) public-private partnership.

The first edition of *A European Public Investment Outlook* (Cerniglia and Saraceno 2020) and the project to transform this publication into a permanent observatory on public investment in EU countries was born out of frustration regarding the state of the public investment debate in Europe. By gathering high-ranking academics and policy institutions to discuss the role of public capital in boosting potential growth, we aimed to show that, provided European policymakers managed to shrug off their old mindset, a public investment push would be not only feasible, but also highly desirable. In fact, the first part of the 2020 *Outlook* showed that, despite the lip service given to the need for public investment, following the sovereign debt crisis it had become the first casualty of austerity policies in the Eurozone (including in its largest economies).

The first edition, published in 2020, was mainly written before the COVID-19 pandemic. Nevertheless, the authors of the *Outlook* collectively (and in a decentralised manner!) took the stance of considering public investment in a broad sense as any addition to the stock of material and immaterial public capital. Alongside classical, bricks-and-mortar infrastructure investment, the authors highlighted the need to invest in social capital, education, health, social cohesion, and R&D.

The policy reaction to the COVID crisis hinted that the frustration with the European debate might be becoming less justified. While many of the old reflexes are still present, the swift response to the pandemics, and more importantly the relatively quick agreement on the Next Generation EU investment plan, suggest that European policymakers might have learnt from the mismanagement of the sovereign debt crisis.

A major difference to the 2020 *European Investment Outlook*—and indeed to any past discussion of public investment in EU member states—comes in the form of the Recovery and Resilience Facility: national fiscal policy is no longer the overwhelmingly predominant driver of public investment across all EU member states. While in the past, EU funding via the structural funds has been an important element of public capital spending in some countries during certain periods, for the first time, by means of the RRF, the EU is financing public investment in macroeconomically relevant orders of magnitude (even considering that they are spread over a multiannual timeframe) across member states.

The total volume of spending that will eventually take place under the RRF is still subject to uncertainty. The facility is divided more or less equally into a grant and a loan component. While all member states will tap their grant allocation, it is not yet clear to what extent they will take up the offer of EU loans (among the largest economies, so far only Italy did); they can decide to do so at a later date. That said, the total potential volume of the RRF is €672.5 bn, of which €312 bn consists of grants and up to €360 bn of loans. This is by far the biggest item in the overall Next Generation EU package which totals €750 bn, measured in 2018 prices; this represents 5.4% of 2019 GDP.

The required funds are raised by the EU Commission on financial markets. The bonds have been in strong demand from investors. This is rightly considered a major step forward in the EU integration process. This will be the case, in particular, if it proves possible to expand the EU's own resources—as all the EU institutions have, in principle, agreed should happen—so that the debt service will be made out of EU rather than national resources. The debt service schedule will run from 2028–58.

In spring 2021, member states had to submit recovery and resilience plans to the European Commission detailing their spending plans. These had to be in line with country-specific recommendations addressed to them in the course of the European Semester process. In addition, there is a requirement for 37% of the project expenditure to be targeted at climate-protection measures and 20% related to digitalisation. Following Commission approval, the Council greenlights the disbursement of funds to individual member states. Initially 13% of each country's allocation was available to kickstart recovery; these resources were transferred to member countries in August 2021. The remaining funding is made available in stages, depending on the achievement of agreed milestones. Disbursement is planned to be completed by 2026.

The RRF has a strongly redistributive component, favouring countries with below-average per capita GDP—thus working similarly to the cohesion funds—but also those whose economies were hit hardest by the pandemic; there is therefore also a strong stabilisation component and a fair amount of risk-sharing, a real novelty in EU policymaking. Consequently, the contribution of the RRF expenditures to total public spending varies considerably between member states. The national chapters in this *Outlook*—for France, Germany, Italy, Poland, and Spain—provide detailed accounts of the national plans and the priorities the different countries have set.

A recent analysis by the French Treasury (Bénassy-Quéré 2021) compares national discretionary stimulus measures with expected allocations under the RRF. In countries such as Greece and Italy or Croatia and Romania, RRF spending dwarfs the national stimulus measures. For Nordic countries or Austria, on the other hand, the macroeconomic significance of RRF spending is limited. In terms of public investment, though, RRF spending, which is more medium-term in nature, will be more important than this comparison suggests, as national stimulus measures were often focused on short-term income support. Precisely assessing the investment content of RRFs is difficult—and arguably somewhat arbitrary given that, as noted earlier, the definition of public investment is a matter of debate—but is expected to be high; see the first chapter in this report.[1]

An early study of the impact of the RRF, looking only at the grants component and assuming that all measures took the form of public investment, estimated a significant impact to annual GDP, of the order of 0.3 pp in each year of the programme (Watzka and Watt 2020). This average concealed a substantial spread across countries, with the hardest-hit member states benefiting from a considerable boost to output and employment; in Greece, for example, the boost was more than 1% of GDP per year. A more recent study by the European Commission (Pfeiffer, Varga, and in't Veld 2021) focuses on the spillover effects between countries. (It also goes beyond the RRF to consider other spending programmes within the overall Next Generation EU package.) A country-by-country assessment neglects the fact that countries also benefit from the support given to neighbouring countries with which they have close trading relations. The authors estimate that this spillover effect adds, on average, one third to the impact of RRF spending. This proportion is higher in countries where the direct impact is lower. In the main scenario, EU GDP after three years is 1.5% higher than without the NGEU programme.

This European Investment Outlook, like the first edition of 2020, is organised in two main parts. Part One assesses the state of public investment in Europe as a whole (Chapter 1) and in a specific group of countries: France (Chapter 2), Germany (Chapter 3), Italy (Chapter 4), Poland (Chapter 5), and Spain (Chapter 6). The common thread of these chapters is to update the data presented in the prior edition, and provide a description of the policy response to the COVID-19 crisis and of the respective economic recovery plans as part of NGEU.

---

1   The RRF has, alongside spending measures, a structural reform component which may prove important for raising potential output in some countries but is not assessed in this report.

Chapter 1 by A. Brasili, A. Kolev, D. Revoltella, and J. Schanz highlights that wide public investment gaps have opened in the European Union over the past couple of decades despite a recent uptick in 2019 and 2020. Increasingly ambitious targets for the digital and green transition have contributed to these gaps. The EU Commission estimates that an additional annual investment of about €350 bn is needed to meet the current 2030 climate and energy targets. In the EIB's Municipality Survey, two thirds of respondents see gaps in climate change mitigation and adaptation, 47% in digitalisation, and 46% in transport. The pandemic offers the opportunity to "rebuild better". Public investment is the focus of member states' Stability and Convergence Programmes and of the Recovery and Resilience Facility. Exceptionally low interest rates and the ECB government bond-buying programme make it easier to fund these expenditures. They create a window of opportunity in which governments, through wise investment, can gradually shift their debts onto sustainable paths. Governments should, however, recognise that these benign conditions are not the new normal and can quickly change. Hence the authors emphasise the urgency to make the best use of the EU funds to strengthen economic growth.

Chapter 2 by M. Plane and F. Saraceno traces the trend of public investment and public capital in France since the 1970s, summarising and updating the analysis of the chapter from the previous *Outlook*. Compared to other OECD countries, both the level of public capital and the quality of infrastructures in France are high. But the trend has not been favourable. Gross public investment has been on the decline for years, and net public investment has seen an even greater drop, becoming negative: the depreciation of public capital is not compensated by new investment. The net worth of public administrations is still positive but has suffered a significant fall and reached a worrying low point. Indeed, since 2005 public debt has grown faster than public capital. A recovery in public investments only began two years prior to the COVID-19 crisis, with an increase of nearly 14% between the end of 2017 and the end of 2019 (linked to the electoral cycle of municipal elections). A partial reverse in public took place after the municipal elections. Furthermore, the crisis linked to COVID-19 led to an unprecedented dip of nearly 10% in public investment during the first half of 2020 compared to the last half of 2019. Overall, public investment contracted by 4.1% in 2020. It is in this context that the French government unveiled, in September 2020, the contents of its recovery plan of €100 bn over two years, part of which (€40 bn) is financed with funds from the Next Generation EU programme. Like all other major EU countries (except for Italy), France chose only to access RRF grants. Out of the €100 bn, around €36.7 bn will be dedicated to public investment. This is quite considerable, but certainly inadequate to complete the modernisation and the greening of the French economy. Once the worst of the pandemic passes, the emphasis must return to national fiscal policy.

K. Rietzler and A. Watt, in **Chapter 3**, begin with the analysis of the German situation presented in last year's edition of Outlook and describe the role of public investment and public capital stock since German reunification, demonstrating that public investment has been insufficient for more than a decade. The country needs massive public investment in a number of fields to modernise its infrastructure and ensure that Germany meets its own climate policy goals. This year's chapter looks at the most recent developments and presents an analysis of public investment across policy fields and activities at different levels of government. The authors focus on the massive stimulus package, which the German government launched in summer 2020—the so-called "Konjunktur- und Zukunftspaket" (stimulus and future package). They assess the investment content of the package and the progress made in its implementation. They summarise the German Recovery and Resilience Plan (Deutscher Aufbau und Resilienzplan, DARP) as part of the EU's NGEU programme, noting the substantial overlap with the domestic stimulus plan. Finally, recent simulations with the National Institute's Global Economic Model (NIGEM) are presented, which show that under the current financial conditions, a significant credit-financed public investment initiative is compatible with a reduction in the debt-to-GDP ratio. The authors conclude that, while nobody knows when the pandemic will finally end, the debate on post-crisis fiscal consolidation is in full swing in Germany and a key issue in the autumn election to the Bundestag. Some political positions in support of rapid budget consolidation are incompatible with the enhanced investment and more ambitious climate policies which Germany, and the whole of the EU, need.

In **Chapter 4**, F. Cerniglia and G. Barbieri take up the case of Italy, which, of all the EU countries, has suffered the most from the coronavirus pandemic, causing a contraction of its GDP unparalleled since WWII. The authors assess the measures taken by the Italian government to tackle the economic fallout caused by the pandemic. The year 2020 was a turning point for public investment in Italy, thanks to the widespread conviction that a robust socioeconomic structure, capable of resisting exogenous shocks such as those caused by the pandemic, could be constructed with a thorough and consistent policy, comprising tangible and intangible public investment. The authors have updated the data on public investments in Italy from the previous *Outlook* (Cerniglia and Rossi 2020). Public investments, which declined from 3.7% to 2.1% from 2009 to 2019, gained a slight momentum. In 2019 they went up to 2.3% of GDP. During 2020, notwithstanding the slowdown due to the pandemic in the first half of the year, public investment increased again and the investment-to-GDP ratio climbed to 2.7%. In the south of Italy investment expenditure still remains stagnant. The National Recovery and Resilence Plan (PNRR)—presented by the Italian government at the end of April 2021—is an ambitious plan (more than €200 bn, of which €191 bn is from the Recovery and Resilience Facility) and identifies six main missions (digitisation, innovation, competitiveness, culture and tourism, green revolution and ecological transition, infrastructure for sustainable mobility, education and research, social inclusion and cohesion, and health) and three transversal priorities: decreasing territorial, gender, and generational inequalities. Southern Italy is considered one of the most economically depressed areas in the EU, and 40% of the PNRR's "territorialisable funds" (i.e., €82 bn) will be allocated to the south, which accounts for 34% of the national population and only 22% of Italy's GDP. Overall, there are encouraging signs of strengthening both the planning of public investment and redefining the regulatory framework, which has made public investment in Italy a slow, cumbersome, and ineffective process. However, one of the elements to which greater attention should be paid in the following months is the governance of the PNRR, as well as the decision-making process at all levels of government.

In **Chapter 5** A. Czerniak and S. Płóciennik analyse the Polish case. First, it must be emphasised that high GDP growth and accelerated structural changes in Poland's economy after joining the EU have been largely driven by public investment. Nearly three decades of constant and relatively high economic growth have made it possible for Poland to partially catch up with the level of development of the most advanced European economies. To continue this positive trend, Poland must fulfil several requirements including a stable demography, a higher degree of innovation, more efficient infrastructure, and a better supply of public goods, like healthcare. Remaining on the convergence path requires further increases in expenditure, especially for energy and digital transformations. The chapter analyses what prospects exist for increasing the scale of public investments and indicates the most promising areas of state activity. The chapter analyses the National Recovery Plan (Krajowy Plan Odbudowy, KPO), which foresees a public investment increase of around €87 bn. The authors point out some of the risks linked to the existing plan: a polarised political landscape and uncertainties linked to the implementation of some of the current reforms.

In **Chapter 6** on Spain, J. Villaverde and A. Maza update last year's data and focus on the key characteristics related to the evolution of public investments in Spain from 2000 to 2020. In 2020, due to a more relaxed and counter-cyclical policy stance from Brussels, the investment effort grew by 2.6%, and its 2020 level of investment is larger than the 2000–09 average. They also assess what Next Generation EU funds can imply for public investment for Spain. For the 2021–26 period, the EU has approved a disbursement of up to €140 bn, about half in direct transfers and the other half in loans. As pointed out in the Spanish RTRP (Recovery, Transformation, and Resilience Plan), the investment foreseen, with its cumulative nature, will make it possible to reach a public investment effort of around 4% of GDP; this will not only imply closing the gap with the EU average, but also means that net investments will be positive for the first time since 2011. According to the authors, the arrival of EU funds will provide a big push for the economy, helping it to become more modern, productive, resilient, and competitive.

The second part of the 2021 edition of *A European Public Investment Outlook* focuses on the challenges caused by the pandemic and the pillars of the Next Generation EU investment plan. The chapters on digitalisation (Chapter 10), energy and green transition (Chapters 11 and 12) and territorial cohesion (Chapter 13) mirror the NGEU priorities (that in turn follow the workplan of the Von der Leyen Commission, which took office in December 2019). The chapters on healthcare (Chapter 8) and education (Chapter 9) contribute to the debate on the need for social capital, an aspect that the pandemic has cruelly highlighted. It is worth mentioning that the researchers working on the *Outlook* start from a broad definition (i.e., both tangible and intangible) of public capital: a chapter on social capital was already included in the first edition of *Outlook*, written before the pandemic.

The underlying theme of the entire study is the impact of public investment on GDP and on private investment. In this year's edition we decided to dedicate a specific chapter on multipliers (Chapter 7) written by L. Durand, R. Espinoza, W. Gbohoui, and M. Sy. This chapter confirms that public investment stands out as an instrument for boosting growth. Not only can it raise economic activity in the short-term, it can also increase the productive potential of the economy by expanding the capital stock and thus improving productivity. This is especially important for countries seeking to support their economies through crises while simultaneously boosting long-term growth and protecting their fiscal space (IMF 2020). This is the situation many advanced economies face as they kickstart their economies after having shut them down in an attempt to prevent the propagation of COVID-19.

Prior to Keynes, conventional wisdom believed that an increase in public investment would lead to an equivalent decrease in private investment so that the level of aggregate output would remain unchanged: this so-called Treasury view of crowding-out underpinned the idea that deficits should be reduced in order to trigger confidence and private investment.

However, the chapter shows that the Keynesian view, according to which public investment crowds-in private investment by boosting short-term growth and triggering positive expectations, has quite strong empirical support. A few examples of the literature are provided and the results of a meta-analysis are reported. The authors discuss some of the conditions that can lead to strong crowding-in. Moreover, they assess the EU structural funds and Recovery Fund and discuss, in light of the recent literature, whether the EU Recovery Fund is likely to crowd-in private investment and which private activity in the sectors will be most hit by the fallout of COVID-19.

P.-Y. Geoffard in **Chapter 8** discusses healthcare. In a broad sense, any healthcare intervention that improves patients' health may be qualified as an investment. Good health, a major component of individual welfare, could also increase labour supply, especially at an older age, and labour productivity. In this sense, health is a key component of human capital. However, the author points out that such an approach raises many issues. Not every good or service that improves welfare can be qualified as an investment. Many treatments can alleviate pain, and improve or restore the autonomy of the patient, without increasing their future productivity. The value of healthcare cannot be reduced to the effect it may have on future production. Hence, in this chapter the author focuses on a narrower definition of health investment as the current expenditures that may improve future health. Such a definition encompasses disease prevention, human capital investment in healthcare and long-term care labour, and capital expenditure in healthcare.

The issue of investing in education is considered in **Chapter 9** by L. Fransen, R. Prodi, and E. Reviglio. One among the many heritages of the pandemic is the impact of digital distance learning and tele-education during COVID-19, along with the urgent need to transform current education and learning models, and to invest in physical and intangible infrastructure for the future based on new needs and growing digitalisation. These evolutions show up in recent data on capital expenditures in education in the EU, as well as in the likely change of the Stability and Growth Pact, especially regarding social investment and infrastructure. The new expansionary policy that is taking place within the EU will increase the supply of "safe assets", which includes financial instruments for social and green infrastructure. Another point of interest in this dynamic is the role of multi-lateral and national promotional banks and institutions in becoming new "market makers" by increasing "patient capital" going into the real economy. Finally, the InvestEU programme and Next Generation EU (NGEU) fund both have the potential to impact on investment in education.

Turning to the chapters that mirror the spending priorities established by NGEU, in **Chapter 10** D. Rückert, R. Veugelers, A. Virginie, and C. Weiss tackle the issue of digital technologies and digital transformation, as the COVID-19 crisis is likely to play a dual role in the adoption of digital technology. On the one hand, the crisis has led to a wider recognition of the importance of innovation and digital transformation. According to the 2020 results of the EIB Investment Survey (EIBIS), the majority of firms in the EU and the US expect COVID-19 to have a long-term impact on the use of digital technologies. On the other hand, many firms have experienced a fall in revenues and liquidity during the pandemic. This may force firms to focus on short-term survival strategies, leading them to delay or cancel investment projects. The chapter uses EIBIS data on more than 13,000 companies from the 27 EU countries, the UK, and the US. EIBIS monitors firms' use of various advanced digital technologies, allowing them to capture the digital adoption rates and assess the impact of digital transformation on different economies. In 2020, EIBIS also asked firms about their future digital perspectives. First, the authors identify four corporate digitalisation profiles based on firms' current use of digital technologies. A substantial share of non-digital firms do not consider investment in digital transformation as an urgent priority, even beyond the COVID-19 crisis. This share of "persistently non-digital" firms is larger in the EU than in the US, in particular small firms. Second, results show that dynamics along the digital divide matter for firm performance and employment. "Persistently non-digital" firms are less likely to create new jobs, and tend to pay lower wages and invest less in the training of employees. They are also less likely to invest in innovation activities. Finally, looking at the major obstacles to investment perceived by firms in the EU, the findings suggest that addressing barriers to skills and digital infrastructure should also be a priority for policymakers. Similarly, addressing the regulatory burden and its associated uncertainties should be high on the digital policy agenda.

The EU has committed to reducing greenhouse gas emissions by at least 55% compared to 1990 by 2030, and being climate neutral by 2050. The 2030 reduction goal cannot be reached without a massive expansion of renewable energy generation in Europe, requiring annual investment of around €150 bn. This is the main concern of **Chapter 11** by C. Jaeger, D. Mangalagiu, and J. Teitge. The authors argue that the unprecedented EU response to the COVID-19 crisis could contribute to the indispensable stream of public investment by nearly €50 bn annually, and specifically to the investment flow needed for renewable capacity expansion. The authors discuss three challenges that need to be tackled. First, to reduce unemployment and counter the dangerous divergence in the Eurozone, Italy, Spain, and the other main recipients of EU funds, need, among other things, to prioritise the construction sector and digitalisation, rather than generating power from renewable energy. Second, the present EU support will decrease in two years and end in three, and countries will have to begin paying back in 2028, before they can generate a reasonable return. Finally, inevitable setbacks will require new solutions that go beyond the present plans. Therefore, an EU public investment flow for renewable generation needs to go beyond 2023. Effective demand in high-unemployment countries needs to be prioritised while renewable generation is expanded in countries with available national resources. Last but not least, a variety of European regions should be supported in the spirit of experimentalist governance rather than being forced into a "one size fits all" approach. With these three strategic components, the European Green Deal can be implemented as the historical mission that it was conceived as.

The EU goal to be climate neutral by 2050 includes a target 90% reduction in greenhouse gas emissions caused by transport (EC 2019). The transport sector alone accounts for around 25% of the global carbon (CO_2) emissions and more than half of the global demand for fossil fuels (IEA 2019). In **Chapter 12**, M. Holzner, K. Weber, M. U. Zahid, and M. Zangl discuss this theme, building on a previous study, and propose the construction of a European Silk Road, including a high-speed rail network extending almost 11,000 kilometres, with a northern route from Lisbon to Uralsk on the Russian-Kazakh border, and a southern route from Milan to Volgograd and Baku. The focus of the contribution in the *Outlook* is on an assessment of the emission reductions achievable with a line from Lyon to Moscow. Setting out their assumptions for various parameters, they determine the GHG emissions of constructing and operating an HSR network, and provide an estimation of how many tonnes of CO_2 could be saved as compared to road and air travel, over a life cycle of sixty years. The results suggest that, in addition to economic benefits, the CO_2 savings are very substantial.

As in the previous edition of the *Outlook*, a chapter has been dedicated to the EU's cohesion policy, given its decisive importance in the EU budget. G. Coco and R. Lagravinese show in **Chapter 13** that the EU is a significant contributor to public investment in every member state, but not all cohesion expenditure translates into investment. The authors try to disentangle the investment component by looking at the policy themes for the 2014–20 programming period. On an EU scale, they find that 67% of programmed expenditure is investment in a statistical sense, while 7% is in human capital development. However, there are large differences among member states in the share of the investment component, probably explaining the heterogeneity in the estimated impact of cohesion policy among the member states. Moreover, they tackle the issue of the cohesion policy's ability to increase overall investment at the regional level. They compare investment at the NUTS2 regional level, normalised to regional output and to the national level of the same variable, by isolating a group of regions that have been the largest recipients of the cohesion fund over time. Here again they find significant heterogeneity in the results. While in some countries, underdeveloped regions have been able to raise investment (as defined above) beyond the national level, in others (notably Italy and Greece) this has not occurred. This could be considered as an indirect signal of a lack of additionality of cohesion policy in the public investment component. According to the authors, it is important that Eurostat develops a measure of public investment at a regional level to allow for a direct assessment of this issue.

The EU is not a federal state; therefore, it is not surprising that member states were at the forefront in combating the pandemic. For the same reason, the fastest way to channel European resources towards investment was to borrow jointly and to finance national investment plans through the Recovery and Resilience Facility. At the same time, investment in public goods with a strong cross-border component, such as healthcare or transportation networks, should naturally have a genuine European dimension (Creel et al. 2020). Among the priorities for the medium term, European policy makers should therefore think about possible ways to implement EU-wide investment projects. A European Debt Agency (Amato et al. 2021), establishing a permanent borrowing capacity, could be complemented by a European investment agency capable of designing and implementing European investment projects. Such an agency would need to be very carefully crafted to guarantee the accountability typical of fiscal policy by national governments. Some form of oversight by parliament and the Council in determining (or at least validating) investment projects would certainly make the procedures more cumbersome, but that seems unavoidable.

It is clear that, while waiting for a system to genuinely implement European public investment, European support for public investment via the RRF/NGEU can only be a complement to, and never a substitute for, effective and sustained national public investment. One of the consequences of Europe's fiscal framework—notwithstanding declared intentions to the contrary—has been to curtail public investment. In particular, countries coming up against one of the fiscal rules pertaining to (structural) deficits or debt levels have been forced to cut back on spending. In the short run the easiest option, economically and politically, is simply to not implement planned, new investment projects.

At the start of 2020 the EU Commission launched a process to evaluate and revise its fiscal rules, which in any case have been suspended until 2022 due to the pandemic. It is vital that, as part of the reforms, effective measures are put in place to protect and promote public investment. For this reason, many reform proposals include some form of "golden rule", i.e., the principle that, while (cyclically adjusted) current spending is balanced, governments may—indeed, should—borrow to finance productivity-enhancing public investment (e.g., Dullien et al. 2020; Creel et al. 2013; Saraceno 2017b). While there is currently considerable momentum behind such a stance in principle, the devil is very much in the detail. Critics fear that, given the difficulties in arriving at an economically satisfactory, easily operationalisable definition of public investment, a golden rule would open the floodgates to higher public borrowing. Most proposals, therefore, either have a quantitative upper ceiling (as a share of GDP), operate with a restrictive definition, or impose some form of "double-lock", i.e., prior EU-level approval of specific investment spending. This will certainly be a subject of intense political discourse in the coming months as the debate on economic governance reform heats up once again after, hopefully, economic conditions begin to normalise. Whatever solution is finally reached, protecting national public investment from being squeezed by injunctions from Europe's fiscal rules is vital if European countries are to sustain the public investment needed to dynamise their economies and face the challenges of climate change in particular.

Europe faces serious challenges in maintaining its position in the global economy, in the face of competitive pressures both from developed partners, such as the USA, and from other powers, some with authoritarian systems of government, of which China is clearly the most important. Major steps forward will be required if Europe is to attain the "strategic autonomy" in a variety of fields which is necessary to meet that challenge. Among these, the measures described in this *Outlook* which are needed to strengthen public investment at national and European levels are by no means the least important. In the new global scenario, completely different from the time in which the Maastricht order was designed, the European Union needs to redefine its mission, identifying with greater precision and selectivity the areas in which to concentrate its common activity in the face of the new global competition. All this is essential to avoid single European countries, including the major ones, from sliding into a condition of global weakness and even marginality in various sectors. Putting emphasis on planning and implementing large European public investment projects (or missions) is not just a matter of growth *tout court*; it instead means thinking in a new global geopolitical context and about the role of Europe in that context. Once the pandemic is over, we do not believe we can return to the *status quo ante*. To think this would mean underestimating both the depth of the transformation that the current crises have impressed on the world economy (including mainstream economic thought) and the impact of the new post-pandemic geopolitical configuration, marked by a radicalisation of the confrontation between the US and China.

References

Amato, M. et al. (2021) "Europe, Public Debts, and Safe Assets: The Scope for a European Debt Agency", *Economia Politica*, *in press*, https://doi.org/10.1007/s40888-021-00236-6.

Bénassy-Quéré, A. (2021) "A Good Read for the Summer: the National Recovery and Resilience Plan!", *Direction générale du Trésor*, 16 July 2021.

Cerniglia, F. and F. Saraceno (eds) (2020) *A European Public Investment Outlook*, Cambridge: Open Book Publishers, https://doi.org/10.11647/obp.0222.

Creel, J., P. Hubert, and F. Saraceno (2013) "An Assessment of the Stability and Growth Pact Reform in a Small-Scale Macro-Framework", *Journal of Economic Dynamics and Control* 37(8): 1567–580.

Creel, J., M. Holzner, F. Saraceno, A. Watt and J. Wittwer (2020) "How to Spend It: A Proposal for a European Covid-19 Recovery Programme", *ec*72 (June).

Dullien, S., C. Paetz, A. Watt and S. Watzka (2020) "Proposals for a Reform of the EU's Fiscal Rules and Economic Governance", *IMK Report 159e*. Düsseldorf.

Fatás, A. and L. H. Summers (2018) "The Permanent Effects of Fiscal Consolidations", *Journal of International Economics* 112, November: 238–50.

IMF (2014) "Legacies, Clouds, Uncertainties", *World Economic Outlook*, October.

Le Garrec, G. and V. Touzé (2020) "Le Multiplicateur d'investissement Public: Une Revue de Littérature", *OFCE Working Paper* 28/2020 (December).

Pfeiffer, P., J. Varga and J. in't Veld (2021) "Quantifying Spillovers of Next Generation EU Investment", *European Economy Discussion Paper* 144, July 2021.

Saraceno, F. (2017a) "Rethinking Fiscal Policy: Lessons from the European Economic and Monetary Union", *ILO Employment Working Paper* 219, August.

Saraceno, F. (2017b) "When Keynes Goes to Brussels: A New Fiscal Rule for the EMU?", *Annals of the Fondazione Luigi Einaudi* 51(2): 131–58.

Saraceno, F. (2021) "Europe After COVID-19: A New Role for German Leadership?", *Intereconomics* 59, March/April: 65–69.

Watzka, S. and A. Watt (2020) "The Macroeconomic Effects of the EU Recovery and Resilience Facility", *IMK Policy Brief* 98, October 2020. Düsseldorf.

PART I

OUTLOOK

1. Public Investment in the Pandemic— Europe at a Glance

A. Brasili, A. Kolev, D. Revoltella, and J. Schanz

Introduction

Wide investment gaps have opened in Europe after a long period of subdued government investment and increasingly ambitious targets for the digital and green economic transition. By 2016, EU government investment had declined to a twenty-five-year low of 2.8% of GDP. Since then, it has recovered only marginally. Without large public and private investments, the economy cannot reap the benefits of digitalisation nor adapt to climate change. According to the EU Commission, about €350 bn of additional investment is needed annually during 2021–30 relative to the previous decade if 2030 climate and energy targets are to be met.[1] Survey data also confirm sizable investment gaps. In the European Investment Bank's (EIB) Municipality Survey, two thirds of respondents see gaps in climate change mitigation and adaptation, 47% in digitalisation, and 46% in transport.[2]

As the pandemic adds to existing challenges, it also offers the opportunity to rebuild better. To accompany the recovery, member states' Stability and Convergence Programmes and the EU's Recovery and Resilience Facility emphasise public investment. The slogan is to "rebuild better" with investments that support digitalisation and more sustainable production. If well-managed, such an emphasis on public investment would be a welcome novelty. It benefits from the monetary policy environment, in which central banks lowered refinancing costs by setting ultra-low interest rates and by purchasing large amounts of government bonds and other financial assets. However, history tells us that such a window of opportunity, created by the need and ability to spend, might close fast. Hence the urgency to make best use of the available resources to strengthen economic growth sustainably.

To be successful, investment programmes need to be properly operationalised, monitored, and evaluated. In the current environment, access to finance to fund

---

1   See EC (2020) and EIB (2021), Chapter 4.
2   See EIB (2021), Chapter 9.

                https://doi.org/10.11647/OBP.0280.01

public investments is not an issue for most member states. The challenge lies in operationalising investment plans and in executing, monitoring, and evaluating them. Public investment should be catalytic, crowding in private investment. As such, any investment program needs to be well-coordinated and should be complemented by structural reforms that lower barriers to private sector investment.

1.1 Government Investment Since the Global Financial Crisis

Despite a recent uptick, government investment in the European Union has been subdued since the Global Financial Crisis (GFC). EU government investment had fallen to 2.8% of GDP in 2016, the lowest level in twenty-five years. This trend was reversed only very recently: relative to GDP, government investment recovered to 3.3% of GDP in 2020 (Figure 1).[3,4]

Southern Europe is in the spotlight. Following the GFC, investment fell in all countries that had experienced some sort of investment boom in the previous decade but especially in Southern Europe following the European sovereign debt crisis. As markets questioned countries' ability to roll over debt, their borrowing costs rose. Government investment rates in Southern Europe fell 1.2 pp of GDP in the years following the sovereign debt crisis relative to the average before GFC, a 34% decline. While the recent uptick in Southern Europe by 0.4 pp of GDP is magnified by the sharp decline in GDP due to the pandemic, real government investment in Southern Europe in 2020 rose 6.7% relative to 2019.

During the fiscal consolidations following the sovereign debt crisis, government investment accounted for the lion's share of the cut in government expenditures in the EU, even though it only comprised 5% of total expenditures. In 2016, six years after the start of the fiscal consolidation, the share of capital expenditures in total expenditures was about 5 pp lower than the average share over 2000–07 in Southern Europe (Figure 2). By 2020, it reached -2 pp below the pre-GFC average. This decline occurred despite falling interest expenditures. The mirror image of these declines is the increase in total primary expenditures, which remained more than 5 pp above their pre-GFC average. While not as large, this expenditure shift was present in most of the other EU member states.

Government gross fixed capital formation fell more where fiscal consolidations were larger. In western and northern countries, despite fiscal consolidation efforts, gross fixed capital formation of the government remained broadly stable, as a share of GDP. In Central and Eastern Europe, the fiscal consolidation started later, lasted for a

---

3   We use the ratio of investment to GDP and the investment rate interchangeably here. The same is true for investment and gross fixed capital formation. Unless stated explicitly, government investment refers to gross fixed capital formation of the general government, where general government includes all levels of government within a country—local, regional, and central.

4   This increase in the investment rate was only partially due to the large decline in GDP in 2020, because EU real government investment in 2020 increased by 2.9% relative to 2019.

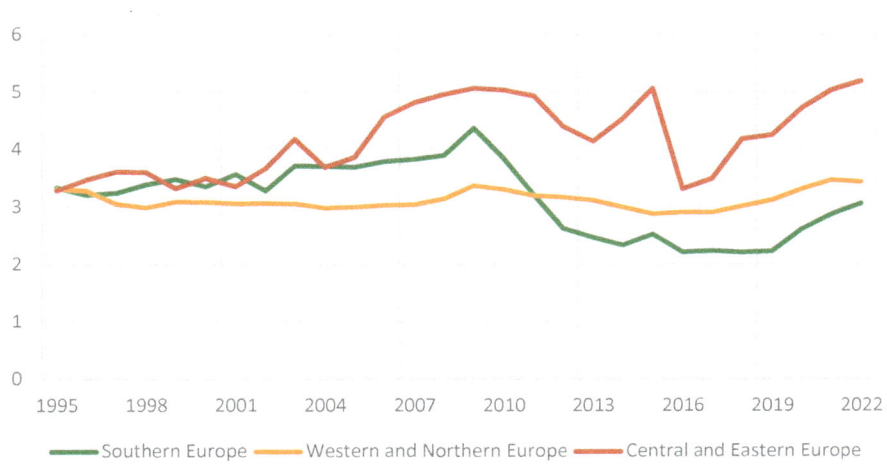

Fig. 1 Gross Fixed Capital Formation (GFCF) of the General Government, % GDP.[5]

Source of data: EC Macroeconomic Database (AMECO), and authors' calculations.

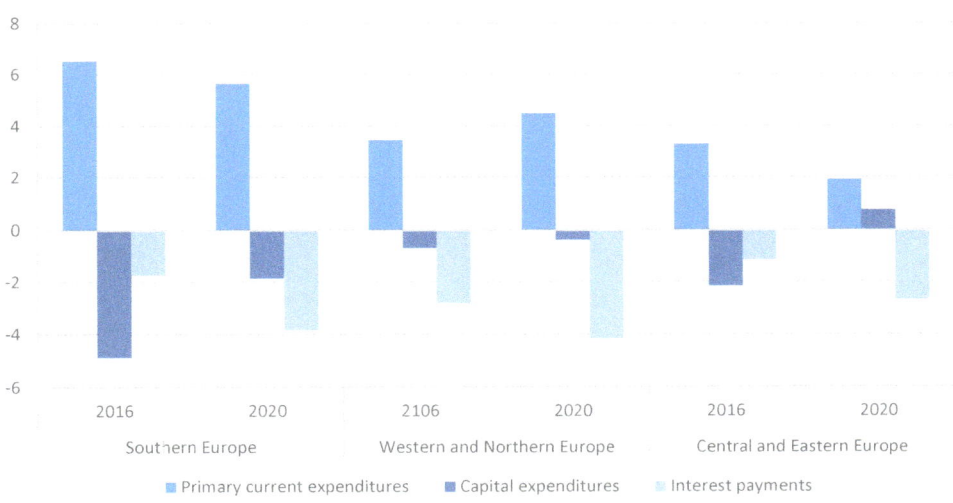

Fig. 2 Change in the Composition of Total Expenditures of the General Government Relative to the Average, 2000–07.

Source of data: EC Macroeconomic Database (AMECO), and authors' calculations.

---

5   We group countries as follows: Southern Europe comprises Cyprus, Greece, Italy, Malta, Portugal, and Spain. Western and Northern Europe consists of Austria, Belgium, Denmark, Germany, Finland, France, Ireland, Luxembourg, the Netherlands, and Sweden. The group of Central and Eastern Europe comprises the remaining EU member states—Bulgaria, Croatia, Czechia, Estonia, Hungary, Latvia, Lithuania, Poland, Romania, Slovakia, and Slovenia.

shorter time, and was much more abrupt: government investment fell by 14% in just two years (2012–13). In the two years that followed, however, it rebounded, increasing by 12%. These large swings can be mostly explained by the importance of European Structural and Investment Funds for government investment in this group of countries. Southern Europe, in turn, experienced the largest decline in real government GFCF in the EU: in the six years between 2010 and 2016, it fell by 46%.

Investment of subnational governments fell disproportionately more after the GFC. Averaging over member states with a centralised and a federal institutional structure, local government investment accounts for about half the investment of the general government in the EU. State government investment, which comprises the remaining subnational investment, accounts for about 11%. The remaining 42% is for central governments. In the years following the GFC, investment of subnational governments fell disproportionately more. In the EU, the decline of subnational government investment accounted for about 77% of the decline of the investment of the general government (Figure 3).

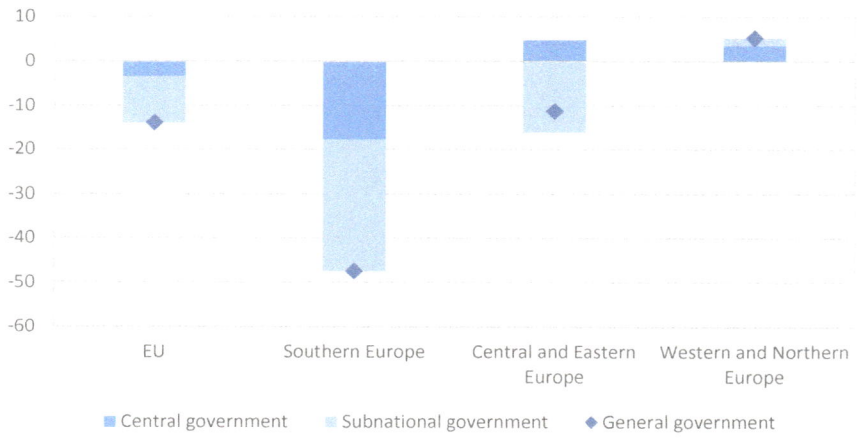

Fig. 3 Total Change in GFCF of the General Government and Contributions by Levels of Government, 2009–16, %.

Source of data: Eurostat Government finance statistics and authors' calculations.

The quality of infrastructure suffered. Infrastructure investment fell in lockstep with government investment across the EU (Figure 4a), driven by the decline in subnational investment spending. The deterioration and lower availability of infrastructure services led, in turn, to dissatisfaction with infrastructure provision (Figure 4b). Declining government investment reinforced the negative effect on the economy exerted by private sector deleveraging after the GFC.

Such declines in government investment during fiscal consolidations are common. Governments are pressed to reduce deficits typically in periods of economic hardship or immediately after such periods, when unemployment levels are high and many

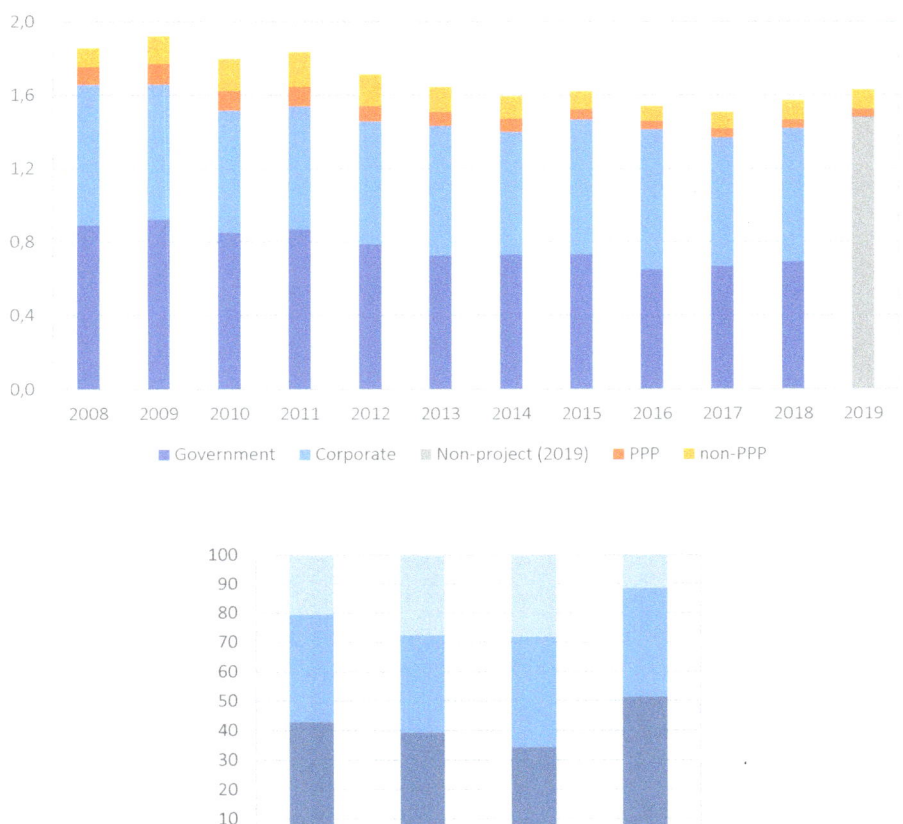

Fig. 4 Infrastructure Investment in the EU, % GDP (Panel a) and Adequacy of Infrastructure Stock of Transport Infrastructure (Panel b).

Source of data: Eurostat, European PPP Expertise Centre (EPEC), IJ Global, and EIB staff calculations (Panel a); EIB Municipality Survey 2020 (Panel b).

people still feel the negative consequences. In such periods, reducing investment expenditures instead of entitlements and social expenditures remains the politically easier choice despite the negative future consequences of reduced investment.

These declines are typically large and protracted. We estimate the effects of fiscal consolidations on the government investment rate using local projection methods (Jordà, 2005). To identify fiscal consolidations, we use a narrative approach based on over 3500 fiscal measures for sixteen OECD countries following Alesina et al. (2017). Our analysis shows that fiscal consolidations result in large and persistent declines in the ratio of government investment to GDP (Figure 5). Results illustrate the substantial and persistent effects of fiscal consolidation on government investment. Seven years after the start of a fiscal consolidation, government investment remains 0.5 pp of GDP lower, which represents a 14% decline from an average government investment of 3.6% of GDP.

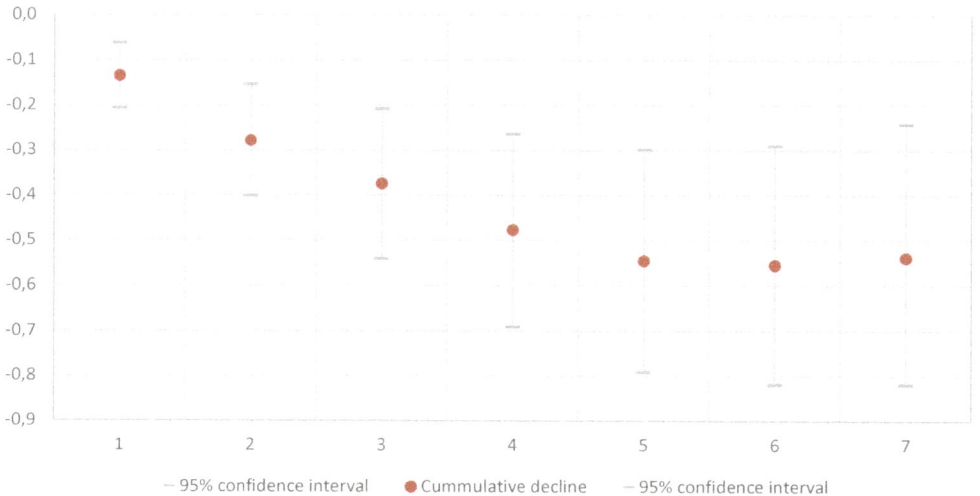

Fig. 5 Response of Government Investment Following a Fiscal Consolidation, Cumulative pp of GDP.

Source of data: Authors' calculations.

Years of underinvestment and increasingly ambitious climate targets created wide investment gaps. According to the EU Commission, about €350 bn of additional investment is needed annually during 2021–30 relative to the previous decade if 2030 climate and energy targets are to be met. At the same time, most EU municipalities report investment gaps in the EIB's Municipality Survey. Two thirds see gaps in climate change mitigation and adaptation, 47% in digitalisation, and 46% in transport.

1.2 Rebuilding Better: The Response to the Pandemic and the Outlook for Public Investment

EU fiscal policy responded to the pandemic in two phases: dealing with the emergency and laying the foundation for a sustainable recovery. During the emergency phase, starting in March 2020, member states increased fiscal spending and postponed revenues. The resulting deficits were financed by debt issuance. The EU backed their actions by suspending state aid rules and borrowing limits.[6] In the following weeks, various EU institutions complemented member states' policies by offering their own

---

6   https://ec.europa.eu/commission/presscorner/detail/en/ip_20_496.

support schemes. The ESM extended a safety net for sovereign borrowers via the Pandemic Support Scheme. The European Commission created a support scheme for workers in its SURE programme, while the EIB provided liquidity support for SMEs by creating a €25 bn Pan-European Guarantee Fund (EGF).

Having dealt with the emergency, the EU Commission presented its proposal for a recovery plan, Next Generation EU (NGEU), at the end of May 2020. This plan became the core of the EU's fiscal strategy during the recovery phase.[7] The centrepiece of NGEU is the Recovery and Resilience Facility (RRF), under which member states have access to grants and loans worth about €672.5 bn. The RRF is funded through the issuance of debt by the European Commission. Member states with lower per capita GDP and higher pandemic-related economic damages will receive a larger share of the funds.

The aim of the recovery plan is to "rebuild better". The idea was to stimulate aggregate demand with measures targeted at increasing the economy's supply capacity—to "rebuild better"—by fostering digital and other infrastructure and by tackling climate change. While the Commission set out the themes for this recovery package, including minimum investment thresholds for climate (37%) and digital (20%) investments, it was up to member states to set out how they intended to spend the funds in their Recovery and Resilience Plans. The European Commission's role also included approving the plans and monitoring their implementation. Finally, the European Commission tried to ensure that the various EU member states' fiscal policies were coordinated. It required that RRF-funded spending should not replace but add to existing public investment, and that it should be accompanied by the reforms proposed as part of the European Semester.

As a result of national and EU-wide fiscal policy measures, public investment is forecast to rise, in particular during 2021–23. Relative to GDP, the intended level of spending—around 3.5% of GDP in 2021–2023—is about €80 bn larger than the 2.9% average for 2016–19 (Figure 6). The countercyclical nature of the RRF is visible in the concentration of GFCF spending during the first three years of the RRF's life span. As allocations under the RRF are tilted towards member states that have a lower per capita GDP, and suffered more from the crisis, the increase in spending is more pronounced in Southern and Eastern Europe. In Southern European countries, GFCF is expected to rise from an average 2.2% in 2016–19 to 3.0–3.1% of GDP in 2021–23. In Central and Eastern European countries, the increase in GFCF could be as large as 1.9 pp, from 3.8% to 5.7% of GDP.

As part of public investment, capital transfers are set to rise. Capital transfers include recapitalisations and incentive schemes for investments in the private sector. National governments tend to require co-financing for investment incentives by the private sector, enabling RRF funds to generate investment in excess of the support provided. A preliminary analysis of member states' Recovery and Resilience Plans (RRPs) suggests

---

7   Europe's moment: Repair and prepare for the next generation (europa.eu).

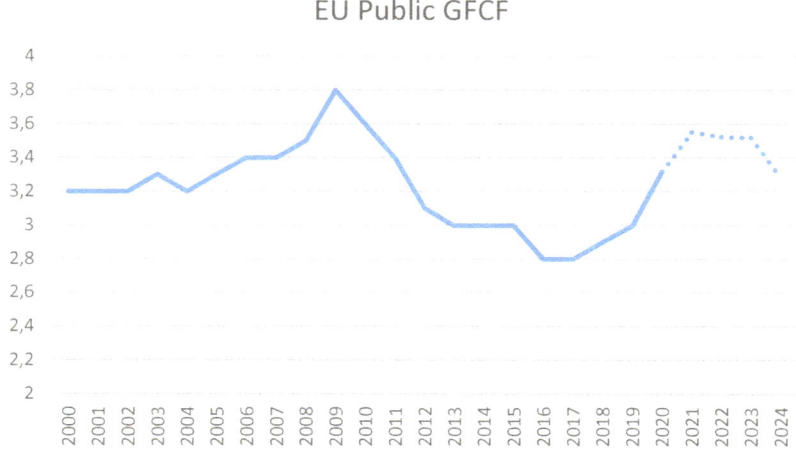

Fig. 6 EU Public GFCF, % GDP.

Source of data: EU Member States' Stability and Convergence Plans (April 2021) and authors' calculations.

that RRF-financed capital transfers are set to be largest relative to GDP in Southern Europe (Table 1). Most of these capital transfers are investment incentives. As a result, capital transfers are projected to increase, close to the levels hit in the aftermath of the Global Financial Crisis and the subsequent European sovereign debt crisis (Figure 7). In those years, the increase was mainly linked to the public acquisition of domestic ailing banks (the lion's share of the increase was in fact due to Ireland and Germany in 2010, and to Greece, Spain, Cyprus, and Portugal in 2012–14). Just as public GFCF, capital transfers are set to rise over the next couple of years to 1.6% of GDP in 2022. On average over 2021–23, capital transfers are expected to be 1.4% of GDP, around €60 bn per year more than the 2016–19 average.

Table 1 RRF-Funded Public Investments and Expenditures (% of 2020 GDP)

Region	GFCF	Capital transfers: Investment incentives	Capital transfers: Recapitalisations	Current expenditure
EU	1.9	1.2	0.1	1.0
North and West	0.4	0.4	0.0	0.2
East	5.4	2.0		0.9
South	3.9	2.6	0.8	2.9

Source of data: EIB preliminary evaluation of EU member states' RRPs as of end of June 2021.

Fig. 7 EU Capital Transfers, % GDP.

Source of data: EU member states' Stability and Convergence Plans (April 2021) and authors' calculations.

A large share of RRF spending will be directed towards climate mitigation and digitalisation. RRPs generally describe investment projects in much detail and place them into the context of European and national policy. Three aspects stand out. The first is the priority of spending on climate mitigation and digitalisation. Member states plan to exceed the Commission's targets: 41% of spending will help mitigate climate change, while 28% is related to digitalisation (Figure 8). In particular, Northern and

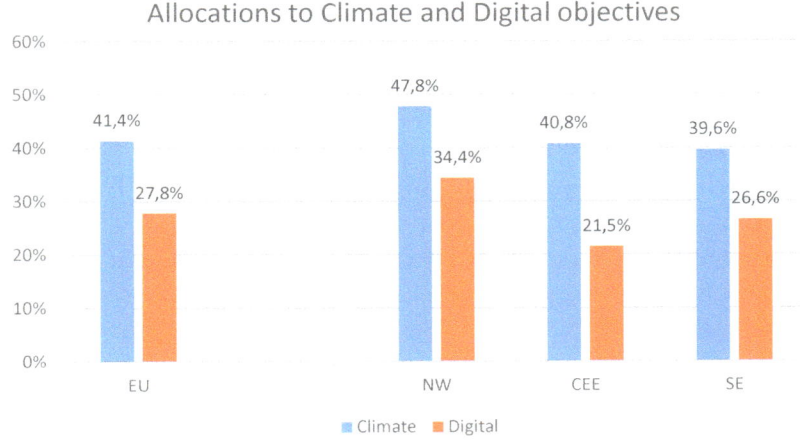

Fig. 8 Actual Climate and Digital-Related Share of Funds.

Source of data: EU member states' Recovery and Resilience Plans and authors' calculations.

Western European countries allocate a large share of their RRF funds to climate mitigation (Luxemburg, Denmark, Belgium, Finland, and France are at or above 50% of the resources). Southern countries, hit more severely by the pandemic, allocate somewhat more to other areas.

Support for R&D will also be larger than in the past. Public R&D spending is set to increase, particularly in Southern and Eastern European countries. As a share of GDP, total resources from RRP allocated to public R&D are particularly large in Southern Europe (0.4% of GDP in total over six years). On an annual basis, this is about a sixth of Southern Europe's public R&D spending in 2019 (Table 2).

Table 2 Public and Private R&D Spending (% of 2020 GDP)

Region	RRF spending on public, higher education, and private non-profit R&D	Public, higher education, and private non-profit R&D (2019)	RRF intended spending on private business R&D	Private business R&D (2019)
EU	0.1	0.7	0.1	1.5
North and West	0.0	0.9	0.2	1.9
East	0.2	0.5	0.1	0.8
South	0.4	0.5	0.1	0.8

Source of data: Eurostat; EIB preliminary evaluation of EU member states' RRPs as of end of June 2021.

Capital transfers to promote private-sector R&D are relatively less important in Southern and Eastern European countries, and more important in the North and West. Capital transfers can generate a larger amount of investment by requiring the private sector to co-finance some of the investments. In the Recovery Plans, these capital transfers typically target green technologies (research related to green hydrogen being a clear example with explicit allocations in Italy, France, and Finland), strategic sectors (aeronautic sector), or the innovative capacity of SMEs. The types of subsidies vary across countries and programmes: they include tax allowances (for example, in Denmark for R&D), procurement by public-private partnerships (Ireland, France), and setting up investment funds that aim to co-finance investments in certain areas, such as tourism (Cyprus, Greece, Belgium, and Italy).

1.3 The Implementation of Public Investment Plans Determines Their Success

To be successful, large public investment programmes need to be properly operationalised, monitored, and evaluated. A commitment to spending is not sufficient. Plans need to be well-designed. They need to identify barriers to investment and market failures to justify the public intervention. They then need to be operationalised by defining concrete projects that should be financed and that would not have been realised without public support.

Despite differences in design, the European Fund for Strategic Investments (EFSI) provides some lessons. Just like the RRF, EFSI has been set up in the wake of a crisis to tackle its consequences. EFSI's objective was to stimulate investment in the aftermath of the 2008–09 financial crisis. Similar to the RRF, EFSI targets a range of areas: infrastructure, environment, human capital, and improving SMEs' access to finance. Both programmes require that the supported projects address market failures and that they could not have been carried out under existing EU programmes ("additionality"). In contrast to the RRF, however, EFSI did not offer grants but shares project risks with its beneficiaries. EFSI funds are used to provide loans, loan guarantees, credit enhancements, and equity-type products, including investments into private investment funds. Its institutional deployment is also different: while the RRF enables the European Commission to provide grants and loans directly to member states, EFSI uses a loss-sharing agreement between the European Commission and the EIB to allow the EIB Group to support riskier projects and borrowers. EFSI closed for new projects in 2020.

EFSI offers lessons about the importance of investment advisory, private co-financing, additionality of investments, and transparency. First, barriers to investment do not only stem from access to finance. The capacity to identify concrete projects and implement them is equally important. For EFSI, the EIB not only provided loans but also advisory services. The European Investment Advisory Hub offered technical assistance, support and training for preparation, management, monitoring, evaluation, audit, and control of projects, and a platform for cooperation with partner institutions. Similar services should be made available when implementing RRF funds.

Second, public sector investment should be catalytic. Member states could amplify the impact of RRF funds by involving the private sector and national and supranational development banks in the funding of the projects. As of the end of 2020, EFSI supported 732 investments in infrastructure and innovation, totalling €69.6 bn, and 816 operations to improve access to finance for SMEs,[8] totalling €33.0 bn. The combined size of these operations was far smaller than those envisaged by the RRF. However, because EFSI support also attracted funds from other investors, including from the private

---

8   Here, firms with fewer than 500 employees.

sector, these operations mobilised considerably more investment. The EIB estimates that EFSI mobilised over €545.3 bn of investment. To facilitate the co-financing of private investors, the European Investment Project Portal was set up, allowing project promoters to advertise their projects and investors to search for opportunities. Even though much of the support from the RRF comes in the form of grants without any co-financing requirements, member states can choose to require their RRF-supported projects to be co-financed. Indeed, many plan to do so, in particular when providing investment subsidies to the private sector.

Third, given the large size and short deadlines of RRF funds, particular care needs to be taken to ensure that RRF funds generate additional investments rather than replace existing financing sources. Experience from EFSI suggests that the larger the supply of funds relative to the amount of projects waiting to be financed, the greater the risk that public funding only replaces other funding instead of generating additional investment. For the part of EFSI targeted at improving access to financing for SMEs, ECA (2019) found no evidence of replacement of other funds: according to interviews with experts, SMEs' demand for funds substantially exceeded supply. The EIB's own evaluation finds that EFSI operations provided financial and non-financial benefits which the market could not have provided, or not to the same extent, nor within the same time frame. ECA (2019) argued that about two thirds of EFSI-financed projects might not have been realised without EFSI support.

Whether all RRF support leads to additional investment remains to be seen. RRF-funded projects need to be additional to projects that take money from other EU sources. There is no corresponding requirement for projects without EU funding. In many countries, RRF funds may not be large relative to investment gaps but they are large relative to what the private and public sectors normally invest. In addition, implementation deadlines are relatively short, providing member states with an incentive to tag projects for RRF funding that were ready to be implemented anyway. Member states themselves, however, expect RRF funds to lead to additional investments. Based on forecasts of investments that some member states provided in their Stability and Convergence Programmes, capital spending funded by the RRF is about as large as the difference in average investment from 2021–24 to 2016–19 (Figure 9).[9]

Fourth, transparency, at a minimum, helps the perception of the investment programme and does not lead to significantly higher costs. While the key benefit of transparency is to help ensure that financial support is used for its intended purpose, it can also help the public perception of the investment programme. In response to criticisms by the European Parliament and Civil Society Organisations, EFSI's transparency was strengthened. The EIB published the rationale for decisions over EFSI funding and a scoreboard used by the EIB to assess EFSI operations while protecting commercially sensitive operations. As a result, the perception of EFSI improved.

---

9   e.g., Belgium, France, and Italy.

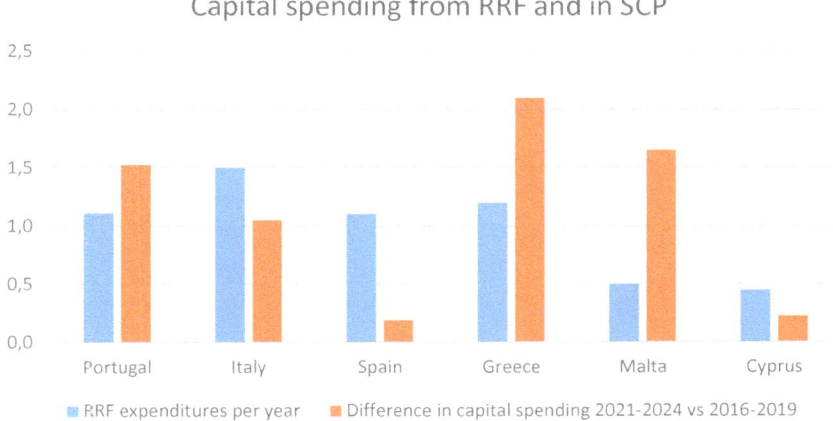

Fig. 9 RRF-Funded Capital Spending, % GDP.

Source of data: EU member states' Stability Plans (April 2021) and authors' calculations.

Finally, investment plans should also be complemented by structural reforms. Public investments offset investment gaps that arise because market failures or investment barriers thwart private investment. Structural reforms can eliminate some investment barriers and raise GDP substantially. This was recognised in 2014 when structural reform recommendations complemented the creation of EFSI. It remains very relevant today. Consider the example of Italy, which plans RRF-funded investments of almost 12% of 2020 GDP over the next six years. A staff working document by the European Commission estimated that these investments will lift Italy's GDP permanently.[10] By 2040, Italian GDP could still be 1.1% higher relative to the case in which the investments were not implemented. Implementing structural reforms, even if these only halved the distance to the best performers, are thought to be able to raise GDP by 17% by 2040.

1.4 Will This Time Be Different?

Governments have learnt their lesson about the effects of precipitated fiscal consolidations. Many EU governments addressed the economic downturn in 2008–09 with fiscal stimulus programmes. These programmes were, however, quickly reversed in 2010–11 as some governments were forced by markets to reduce borrowing and hence expenditure. Others, despite lack of market pressure, decided that it was prudent to consolidate budgets. Ten years later, things look different. Government expenditures rose substantially in 2020 to address the health crisis and its economic fallout. Investment increased in lockstep. Moreover, governments plan to increase investment even further in the next three years.

---

10   European Commission (2021).

Current conditions are exceptionally benign with very low borrowing rates and little market pressure due to the ECB government-bonds buying programmes. Despite high indebtedness of some EU member states (Figure 10), borrowing rates remain low, also owing to large-scale government bond-buying programmes of the ECB. In his presidential address to the American Economic Association in 2019, Olivier Blanchard (Blanchard 2019) argues that when nominal growth of GDP exceeds the nominal interest rate, governments can afford moderate deficits and yet keep stable or even decreasing debt to GDP ratios.[11] Moreover, he argues that, at least in the US, nominal growth is more often than not higher than the nominal interest rate.

The ongoing recovery creates a window of opportunity in which governments can act by investing. With borrowing rates close to zero and the continuing economic upswing, governments can focus on implementing structural policies and sustaining higher expenditures to address long-term issues like digitalisation, climate change, and social cohesion.

Governments should also understand that the current benign conditions might change quickly. Blanchard made very clear in his lecture that he was calling for a "richer discussion" on the topic rather than to return policymaking to the thinking of the 1960s, when the mainstream IS-LM model demonstrated that expansionary fiscal policy is essentially free, while ignoring the government budget constraint. Rather, policymakers should take the current situation as a lucky confluence of favourable conditions, which may deteriorate suddenly at any point in the future. Thus, policymakers should take advantage and address the pressing longer-term challenges to their countries, but remain mindful that fiscal stimulus has not become perpetually free.

An early return to the provisions of the Stability and Growth Pact in 2023 carries risks for public investment.[12] Government expenditure rose sharply in 2020 and revenues declined, resulting in large increases in government debt in the EU (Figure 10). The size of the debt increase was higher for countries with higher pre-pandemic debt and sharper declines in economic activity in 2020. While European policymakers remain committed to supportive policies to strengthen the recovery, the decision to reintegrate the EU fiscal rules in 2023 could require large fiscal consolidations in some countries, creating risks for public investment. If fiscal rules were reimposed without any changes, highly indebted countries may once again opt for cutting public investment to make ends meet.

Policymakers face a difficult trade-off between letting the economy recover for longer by postponing fiscal consolidation and the risk that their borrowing costs rise

---

11 This claim is seen as controversial by many. See, for instance, the dedicated section in the AEA Papers and Proceedings: https://www.aeaweb.org/issues/592. Blanchard himself said that this proposition was to stimulate debate rather than to assert fact.

12 See the European Commission's Economic Governance Review for a discussion of how governance frameworks can support economic growth and sustainable government finances.

before they have countered the increase in debt-to-GDP ratios. Currently, even highly indebted countries are able to borrow and roll over debts due to large-scale bond buying programmes of the ECB. This, however, cannot be taken for granted if inflation picks up significantly, for instance. After all, current debt levels and increases largely exceed those in the period of the European sovereign debt crisis that precipitated the large fiscal corrections in Southern Europe. That said, the RRF constitutes the first European example of a common, joint fiscal policy action that it is based on risk-sharing and on the issuance of a common debt. The RRF explicitly increases EU cohesion and solidarity. This precedent may make it less likely that financial markets will succeed in testing the strength of member states' commitment to the currency union than in 2011–12.

Fig. 10 Change in General Government Debt and Debt Levels in 2019, % GDP.

Source of data: EC Macroeconomic Database (AMECO), and authors' calculations.

Note: The size of the bubbles reflects the size of the decline of GDP in 2020.

1.5 Conclusion

Following the COVID-19 crisis, the new mantra is to "rebuild better". A strong commitment to supporting investment has emerged and been reflected, *inter alia*, in the EU's Recovery and Resilience Facility. This is welcome news, as Europe had only just started to recover from a twenty-five-year low in public investment intensity. Investment gaps are large, in particular in the context of the structural changes required to put the economy on an environmentally more sustainable path.

Is this time different? The current fiscal programmes appear to avoid the cut to public investment that has typically followed recessions in the past. Refinancing conditions are, for the moment, exceptionally benign, creating a window of opportunity in which governments can act by investing and gradually putting their debts onto sustainable paths. These conditions might worsen quickly, however. Hence the urgent need to make best use of the funds to strengthen economic growth. In order to be successful, public investment programmes need to be properly operationalised, monitored, and evaluated, and should be should be complemented by structural reforms boosting private investment.

References

Alberto, A., O. Barbiero, C. Favero, F. Giavazzi and M. Paradisi (2017) "The Effects of Fiscal Consolidations: Theory and Evidence", Working Paper 23385, *Working Paper Series*, National Bureau of Economic Research.

Blanchard, O. (2019) "Public Debt and Low Interest Rates". *American Economic Review* 109(4): 1197–229.

European Investment Bank (2021) *Chapter 4: Tackling Climate Change: Investment Trends and Policy Challenges*. Investment Report 2020–2021. EIB: Luxembourg.

European Commission (2020) *Stepping up Europe's 2030 Climate Ambition: Investing in a Climate-Neutral Future for the Benefit of Our People*. SWD (2021) 176 Final, September.

European Commission (2021) *Analysis of the Recovery and Resilience Plan of Italy*. SWD (2021) 165, April.

European Court of Auditors (2019) *European Fund for Strategic Investments: Action Needed to Make EFSI a Full Success*. Special Report no. 3.

European Investment Bank (2018) *Investment Report 2018/2019: Retooling Europe's Economy*. EIB: Luxembourg.

Jordà, Ò. (2005) "Estimation and Inference of Impulse Responses by Local Projections", *American Economic Review* 95(1): 161–82.

2. From Fiscal Consolidation to the *Plan de relance*

Investment Trends in France

Mathieu Plane and Francesco Saraceno

Introduction

This chapter traces the trends of public investment and public capital in France from the 1970s. Compared to other OECD countries, both the level of public capital and the quality of infrastructures in France are high. But the trend over at least the last ten years is not favourable. Gross public investment has been on a declining trend for years, and net public investment has shown an even greater drop, becoming negative. The depreciation of public capital today is not compensated by new investment. The net worth of public administrations is still positive but has suffered a significant fall and reached a worrying low point. Indeed, since 2005 public debt has grown faster than public capital. The first part of the chapter will summarise and actualise the analysis of Plane and Saraceno (2020) on the dynamics of the public capital stock in France. The second part will initially look at the French response to the COVID-19 crisis and then describe the €100 bn *Plan de relance (Plan de relance)* that was presented in September 2020.

2.1 Trends in Public Investment before the Pandemic

How did public capital in France evolve from the late 1970s? What are its main characteristics and how is it measured? Which public institutions hold this capital? How did investment flows and depreciation shape it? What is the net position of public administrations today? This section will address these questions.

What is referred to as public capital covers a wide variety of assets, such as land, residential buildings, ports, dams, roads, but also intellectual property rights. It is necessary to break down the "wealth of the state" into these different components to understand its dynamics considering, as we will show below, that price (most notably

https://doi.org/10.11647/OBP.0280.02

land prices) and volume effects may play a significant role in explaining the evolution
of the different components, and of aggregate figures.

The data we use are from the INSEE national accounts, which are public; our analysis
covers the period 1978–2020 for the decomposition of net wealth and 1949–2020 for
investment. INSEE reports the consolidated level (general government, GG) and its
components, distinguishing between the central government (CG), local governments
(LG), social security administrations (SSA), and other government agencies (OGA).

Public investment in France has seen contrasting trends in recent decades. While it
was rather dynamic until the late 2000s, at the turn of 2010 the fiscal stance changed, and
a substantial part of fiscal consolidation was achieved by reducing capital expenditure.
Indeed, the reduction of public investment has contributed to almost a third of fiscal
consolidation even though investment only represented 6% of public expenditure. The
share of public investment on GDP, which had largely been above 4% since the 1960s
(Figure 1), fell below that level in 2011 and, during the period 2015–18, reached its
lowest level since 1952. Spurred on by the new rules of local communities' management
and the effect of the electoral cycle linked to municipal elections, the investment rate
has improved in 2019–2020 but has not, however, returned to its average level of the
2000s. In 2020, due to health restrictions, public investment contracted by 4.4% but
held up rather well in the face of the decline in GDP (-7.9%). Nevertheless, the drop in
investment fatally impacted the stock of public capital.

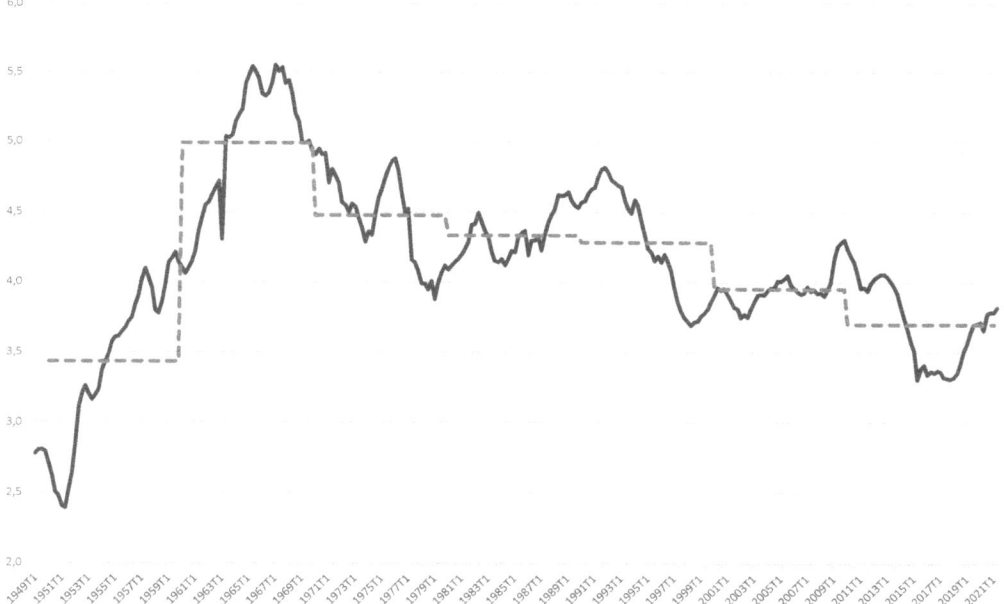

Fig. 1 General Government Investment Rate (as a % of GDP).

Source of data: Insee. Figure created by the authors.

In 2020, the consolidated public sector had a positive net wealth in spite of the negative impact of the COVID-19 crisis (Table 1). Total assets held represented 172% of GDP, of which 103% was for non-financial assets. Financial liabilities totalled 164% of GDP. The net worth in 2020 was therefore 8.2% of GDP, around €2800 per capita.

Table 1 Decomposition of General Government Net Wealth

	As a % of GDP			In euros per head
	1978	*2007*	*2020*	*2020*
Non-financial assets	60.8	90.4	102.8	35210
Financial assets	27.6	52.6	69.0	23620
Financial liabilities	33.7	84.9	163.5	56020
Net worth	**54.7**	**58.1**	**8.2**	**2810**

Source of data: INSEE and authors' calculations.

While positive, the consolidated net wealth is at its lowest level since 1978. Indeed, after reaching a record level in 2007 (58% of GDP), it has lost fifty points of GDP in the space of thirteen years. The reasons for this sharp drop are to be found on the net financial liabilities (debt) side that increased substantially while non-financial assets increased slightly.

This net worth is unevenly distributed among different levels of government. Indeed, it is very positive for local administrations (70% of GDP in 2020), very negative for the state (-80% of GDP in 2020), and slightly positive for social security administrations and other government agencies (8% and 10% respectively). Broadly speaking, the central government—which runs recurrent public deficits—has accumulated public debt; low-debt local governments hold non-financial assets, be it land, buildings, or civil engineering works. With the economic and financial crisis, from 2008 on, the central government net worth deteriorated considerably, as public deficits and debt increased. On the other hand, the net worth of local governments remained high and relatively stable over the same period due to a stable value of non-financial assets and of their debt.

In 2020, non-financial assets (NFAs) of the general government represented 60% of total assets and accounted for 103% of GDP. These figures can be further divided into fixed capital (produced NFAs), which is the result of past public investments, and land (non-produced NFAs).

Fixed assets account for 55% of GDP, mostly civil engineering works and non-residential buildings (47% of GDP), with 8% being public housing, machinery and equipment, weapon systems, and intellectual property rights. Non-produced NFAs represent 47% of GDP, most of which (98%) constitutes land owned by the general government. Unlike fixed assets, non-produced NFAs do not depreciate, and their

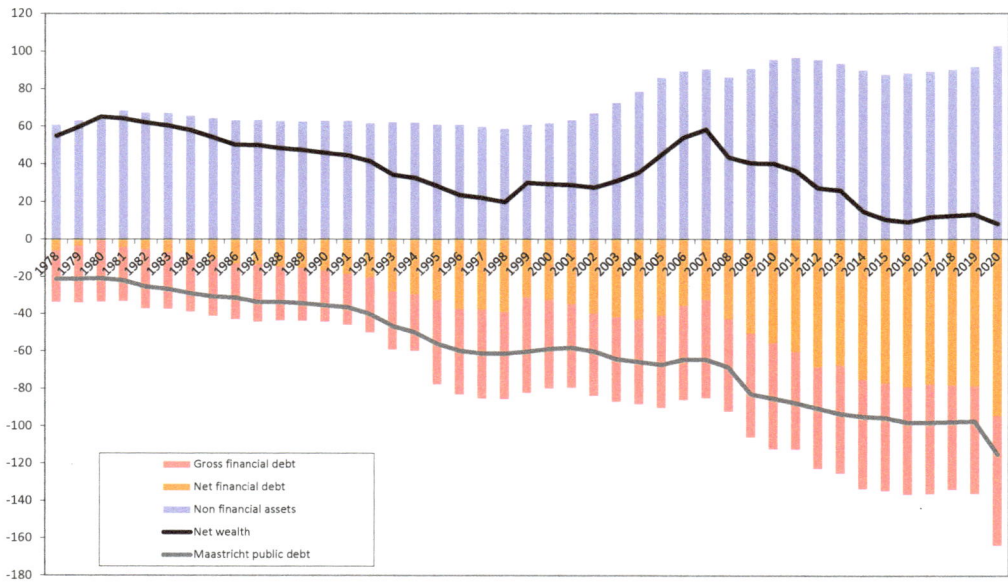

Fig. 2 Evolution of General Government Net Wealth as a % of GDP.

Source of data: Insee. Figure created by the authors.

evolution depends mainly on land prices. These prices have been the main cause of change since the 1970s (details on the decomposition by type of assets and by level of government can be found in Plane and Saraceno 2020).

Fixed capital is given by calculating the past accumulation of realised investments net of depreciation. Between the end of the 1970s and 2020, the value of fixed assets held by the general government ranged from 47% to 55% of GDP, showing significantly lower volatility than the value of non-produced NFAs. This is because fixed assets experience much smaller price changes than land.

Since 1978—but also since 2007—it has been the non-residential buildings, and to a lesser extent the intellectual property rights, which have seen the larger increase of their share in fixed assets.

The analysis of gross investment needs to be complemented by the net flow of fixed assets (net investment), to assess the dynamics of the capital stock (abstracting from the effects of revaluation of the existing stock). Thus, if gross investment is greater (lower) than the depreciation of capital (consumption of fixed capital, CFC, in national accounts' nomenclature), then net investment increases (decreases) and the stock of capital increases (decreases). Unlike fixed assets, non-produced NFAs (land) and inventories may experience changes in value but are not subject to consumption of fixed capital. CFC only applies to fixed assets.

Over the period from the late 1970s to the first half of the 1990s, general government net investment was strong, averaging more than 1% of GDP per year (Figure 3). It even experienced a strong boom over the period 1987–92, averaging above 1.4% of GDP per year. From 1993 to 1998 however, general government net investment declined sharply, reaching 0.5% of GDP in 1998, a decrease of 1% of GDP in the space of six years. Like in other European countries, this is mostly due to the effort to meet the Maastricht criteria in the run-up to adopting the euro: the cyclically adjusted deficit for France decreased from 4.6% of GDP in 1993 to 1.8% in 1998. Past this phase, net investment recovered, then fluctuated between 0.7 and 0.9% of GDP over the 2000–10 period, without ever returning to the level observed during the 1980s and the first half of the 1990s. But it is mainly from 2011, following the Global Financial Crisis, that net investment has experienced a break. Since then, it has been at its the lowest level since the late 1970s, when the wealth accounts were introduced.

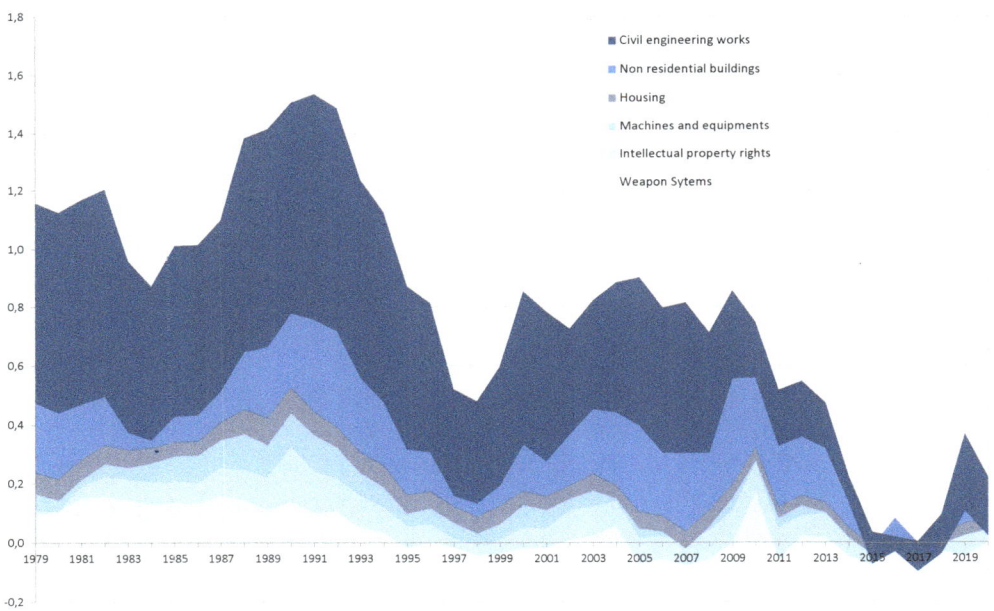

Fig. 3 Net General Government Investment by Component as a % of GDP.

Source of data: Insee. Figure created by the authors.

Thus, during the period 2014–18, France has spent about 0.7% of GDP (about €17 bn by year in constant 2020 euros) less on net investment than it did during the period 2000–10, and 1.4% (approximately €34 bn by year in constant 2020 euros) less than during the period 1990–92.

While the central government contributed positively, albeit weakly, to net investment until the early years of the 2000s, since 2005 central government net investment has moved into negative territory. It is, in fact, local governments which have historically been the main contributors to net government investment. However, since 2007—on the one hand, with the Global Financial Crisis that reduced own resources levied by local governments, and, on the other hand, with the reduction of endowments to local governments that followed fiscal consolidation—net investment by local governments has collapsed from 0.8% of GDP in 2007 to 0% in 2016. Since then, it has recovered slightly, to a level that barely offsets the destruction of capital by the central government and by social security administrations.

The picture that emerges from the analysis of stocks and flows is rather consistent and gives two main messages: the first is that public investment and the stock of capital have been largely affected by the macroeconomic cycle. In the two significant phases of fiscal consolidation—the run-up to adopting the euro in the 1990s and the aftermath of the sovereign debt crisis—investment was strongly reduced. Especially in the latter case, net investment turned negative of zero for all levels of government, thus reducing the stock of capital that, before the pandemic, was at an all-time low. The second message, that emerges in particular from the analysis of stocks, is that in spite of these trends in investment, the capital stock in France is still significant (and larger than in other countries, as can be seen by looking at the other chapters of this outlook). One might ask then if the effort of consolidation, and the disproportionate burden that it has laid on public investment, at least led to more sustainable public finances.

If we compare the evolution over the last twenty years of non-financial assets' net flows in relation to the primary net financial flow (financial assets—financial liabilities—interest expenses), which we consider here as a proxy of the net worth, two sub-periods emerge clearly. The first, which runs from 1996 to 2008, is a period in which the additional public net financial debt (excluding interest expense) was more than offset by the net accumulation of non-financial assets, leading to a positive net value on this period, which means that the general government stock of wealth has increased in value over this period, even abstracting from price effects. The second period, which runs from 2009 to 2020, shows a new pattern in which the net debt increase is no longer offset by an increase in public non-financial capital, generating a sharp deterioration in government net worth. The economic and financial and economic crisis has led to a sharp increase in public debt. Fiscal consolidation started being implemented in 2011: while on one hand it has partly reduced new financial commitments, on the other hand this has been more than offset by a reduction in the net accumulation of non-financial assets. This is further proof of the fact that the burden of fiscal consolidation was disproportionately laid on the shoulders of public investment. The sharp reduction in net worth therefore casts doubt on the effectiveness of fiscal consolidation in strengthening the public finances outlook for France.

2.2 Public Investment during the Pandemic

A recovery in public investment began in the two years before the COVID-19 crisis, with an increase of nearly 14% between the end of 2017 and the end of 2019. This movement was linked to the electoral cycle of municipal elections and the government's desire to preserve investment within the framework of the targeted budget contract with local communities. While a partial reversal in public investment was expected after the municipal elections, the drop observed in the first half of 2020 is out of proportion to that observed in previous electoral cycles (Figure 4).

Indeed, the COVID-19 crisis led to a drop of 11% in public investment during the first half of 2020 compared to the second half of 2019 (with a fall to 16% during the second quarter of 2020). By way of comparison, the three strongest half-yearly decreases observed for the previous seventy years were between 5% and 6%. The fall in public investment during the first half of 2020 was therefore twice as strong as the most severe reversals since 1950.

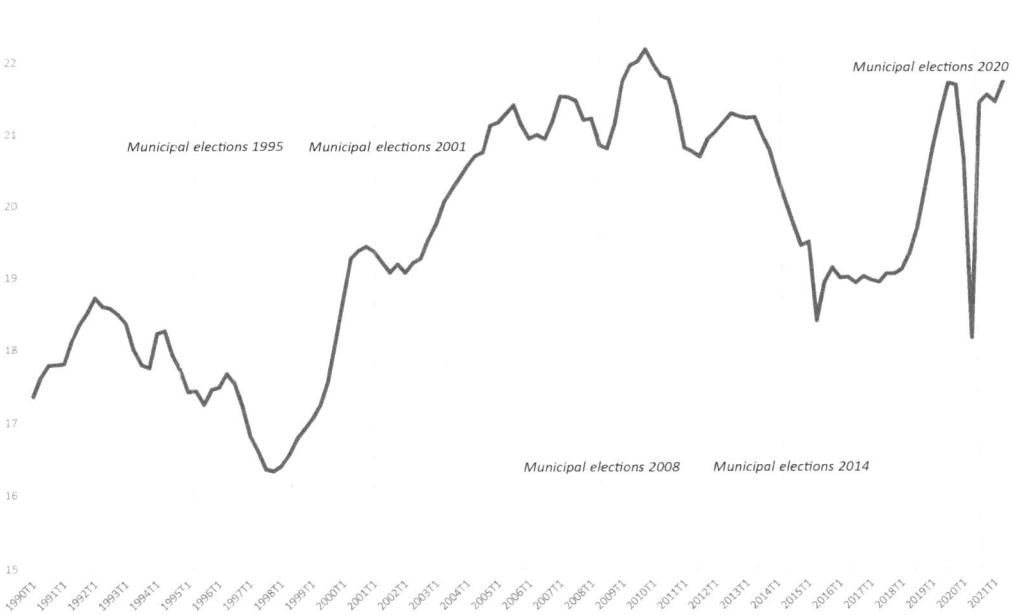

Fig. 4 General Government Investment—Constant Prices, in Billion Euros.

Source of data: Insee and authors' calculations.

The reason for the drop can be traced to the virtual halt of the economy. The first lockdown, from 17 March to 11 May 2020, was characterised by very strong health restrictions and a historic drop in GDP of more than 30% during the period. The restrictive measures of that lockdown impacted most sectors of the economy, including construction, with the almost total shutdown of most construction sites. The construction sector lost more than 60% of its added value in April 2020 (compared to a pre-COVID situation), leading to a historic fall in public investment.

However, from the third quarter of 2020, public investment returned close to its pre-COVID level despite two other lockdowns (in November-December 2020 and March-April 2021). This is because the two subsequent lockdowns were less restrictive: activities related to construction were no longer stopped, and non-teleworking activities were, in general, less restricted. In addition, the government voted in September 2020 for a €100 bn *Plan de relance*, which includes a section on public infrastructure, with particular emphasis on the thermal renovation of public buildings and increased planned investment from the start of the year 2021 (see Section 3.4).

Overall, public investment contracted by 4.4% in 2020. This is a relatively modest drop, especially when compared to the fall in the level of activity, the highest on record. It is not the most important contraction in recent times; in 2014 and 2015, public investment fell more than 4%, despite positive growth rates, because of fiscal austerity and the reduction of local governments' endowments. The pandemic overall had a lesser negative impact on public investment than fiscal consolidation. The resilience of public investment in 2020 has helped to slow down the fall in activity and contributes to the ongoing and future recovery of the French economy. However, taking into account the depreciation of public productive capital, net investment only increased to 0.2% of GDP in 2020. It is 0.2 points % of GDP less than in 2019. The investment gap to be filled, stemming from the drastic drop of the first semester, is of almost €5 bn.

2.3 The *Plan de Relance* of September 2020

There are several reasons that lead us to believe that, as of today, the multiplier of public investment for France would be quite significant, in the upper range of estimates (Creel et al. 2011; Le Garrec and Touzé 2020). First, the French government finances its ten-year debt at a historically low nominal rate (around 0.2% in June 2021), which means that the real rate is almost zero and is becoming negative with the desirable return of an inflation rate close to 2%. Second, in spite of recent spikes in inflation, the medium-term forecast for inflation remains subdued, so that interest rates will remain low for quite some time; this will limit crowding out of private investment (see Chapter 7 of this volume). Finally, the output gap and (more importantly) the slack in the labour market leads us to believe that, in the short run, the multiplier will also be quite large.

It is in this context that the French government unveiled, in September 2020, the contents of the *Plan de relance* worth €100 bn over two years, part of which (€40 bn) is financed with funds from the Recovery and Resilience Facility, the flagship item of the Next Generation EU programme. Like all other major EU countries (except for Italy), France made the choice of only using the grants of the Recovery Facility. Of the €100 bn, around €36.7 bn will be dedicated to public investment (see Table 2).

Table 2 The Investment Component of the *Plan de relance* (in Billion Euros)

Ecological transition		18	Competitiveness		3.6
Energy renovation	Thermal renovation of public buildings	4		Support for the space sector and funding of dual space research	0.515
	Energy renovation and heavy rehabilitation of social housing	0.5		Digital upgrading of the state: digital identity, digitization of public services (schools, justice, culture)	1.5
	Energy renovation of VSEs/SMEs	0.2	Culture	Support for sectors, heritage renovations	1.6
Biodiversity, the fight against artificialisation	Densification and urban renewal (wasteland rehabilitation, support for mayors for the densification of housing)	0.65	**COHESION**		15.1
	Biodiversity in the territories, risk prevention and strengthening resilience	0.3	Health Segur / Addiction	public investment	6
	Water networks and modernisation of sewerage stations, including overseas	0.3	Territorial cohesion	Digital development throughout the country (very high speed, digital inclusion)	0.5
Circular economy and short circuits	Investment in recycling and re-use (including support for the plastic sector)	0.226		Support for local and regional authorities: revenue guarantees and direct support for local investment	5.2
	Modernisation of waste sorting/recycling centres and recovery	0.274		*Plan de relance* of the Banque des territoires (construction of social housing, land for small businesses)	3
more	Greening ports	0.2		Modernization of the national road network and strengthening of bridges	0.35
Green infrastructure and mobility	Building the resilience of electricity grids	0.05			
	Developing everyday mobility	1.2			
	Rail (SNCF Network aid, rail freight, small lines,	4.7			

The *Plan de relance* is focused on three components, each weighing a third of the total: an "ecological transaction" component, for around a third of the plan (€30 bn); a "competitiveness" component (€34 bn), aimed at supporting businesses (especially small and medium enterprises) with aid and tax cuts; and a "cohesion" section (€36 bn), for the most part dedicated to supporting local communities. If we look at the public investment components of the plan (the €36.7 bn detailed in Table 2), ecological transition has the lion's share, with €18 bn (50% of total investment), followed by cohesion (€15.1 bn or 40% of public investment). Only 10% of the public investment component of the plan will go to competitiveness.

If we look into the details of the ecological transition component, €4.5 bn will be allocated to the thermal renovation of public buildings, and to the energy renovation and major rehabilitation of social housing. Investment in transport (daily mobility, rail networks, and other transport infrastructure) will absorb €6.5 bn. With regard to competitiveness, the public investment effort will be concentrated on the digital upgrading of the central and local governments, in particular the digitisation of public services (€1.5 bn) and support for heritage renovations in the domain of culture. With regard to the cohesion component, public investment will mainly be allocated to health (€6 bn), support for investment by local authorities (up to €5.2 bn), and the *Plan de relance* of the *Banque des Territoires* (construction of social housing and land for small businesses), for €3 bn.

Like for other countries, the challenge for France is the deployment of the *Plan de relance* according to the timeline presented to the Commission. The disbursement of funding will be conditional to the attainment of milestones and results detailed in the plan. The second issue is a territorialisation of the *Plan de relance*, especially for its investment component. We saw that local authorities account for a large part of public investment. Capacity building and coordination among local governments and the central government will be central to the success of the plan.

On top of the €6 bn devoted in 2020 to measures to promote youth employment, green technologies, and infrastructure, the *Plan de relance* should, based on our estimates,[1] mobilise €34 bn in 2021 (1.4% of GDP) and €28 bn in 2022 (1.1% of GDP). A reasonable assessment of the impact of these expenditures requires a detailed and disaggregated analyisis, as sectoral and functional multipliers may be quite different (for details, see Ducoudre et al. 2020). A significant percentage of the *Plan de relance* rolled out in 2021 (38%) focused on non-targeted support for businesses, in particular through a cut in production taxes. In a time of high uncertainty, these measures will not be particularly effective in revitalising investment in the short-term and will have a low multiplier the first year (estimated at 0.3). While the *Plan de relance* is betting on

---

1   Our evaluation is focused only on the *Plan de relance* and doesn't consider the emergency measures for 2020–21 which represent 7.2% of GDP. The main objectives of these short-term measures are to maintain revenues of households and firms, limit job destruction, and fund emergency health expenditures.

public investment, only 30% of the plan for 2021 is used to fund public investment. Even though the public investment multipliers are high (close to one), the slow speed of project implementation explains the expected modest improvement in growth in 2021 induced by public investment. In 2022, the share of the *Plan de relance* earmarked for public investment is expected to increase to 39%.

In contrast, job retention schemes, measures to promote employment and strengthen equity capital, sector-based subsidies, and assistance for the poorest households are supporting employees' income and the financial position of companies coping with the long-term impact of the health restrictions and changes in consumer behaviour. These measures, which represent 43% of the plan for 2021, will yield a strong multiplier effect in the short term (Figure 5). The *Plan de relance* is projected to boost GDP by 1.3% in 2021 (after an impact of 0.3% of GDP in 2020), which corresponds to a multiplier of 0.9. In 2022, the *Plan de relance* measures are expected to amount to €28 bn euros (1.1% of GDP) and to have an impact on growth of 0.8% of GDP. The fiscal multiplier in 2022 (0.7) would be slightly below that of 2021, mainly because of the increasing share of non-targeted measures (39%); in contrast, the weight of targeted measures declines sharply between 2021 and 2022 (from 43% to 20%). In total, the *Plan de relance* would result in a cumulative gain in economic activity of 2.4% of GDP over the period 2020–22, for a cumulative fiscal impulse of 2.8% of GDP, which corresponds to a multiplier

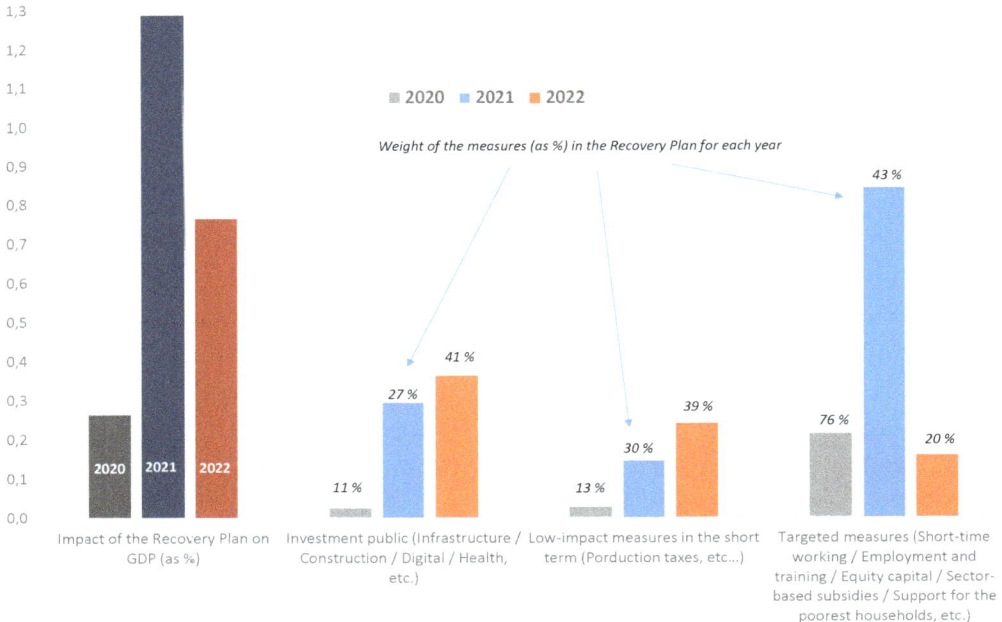

Fig. 5 Impact of the *Plan de relance* on French GDP and Breakdown by Three Categories of Measures, % of GDP.

Source of data: Draft budget for 2021, French *Plan de relance* Digest, Stability Programm 2021–27, and OFCE forecasts.

of 0.85. Over the same period, the public investment component would boost GDP by 0.7%, representing 30% of the total impact of the *Plan de relance*.

On 11 July 2021, President Macron announced a new investment plan to follow the €100 bn *Plan de relance* and "build the France of 2030". While the 2020 stimulus plan was composed of very disparate measures, the new one would only target investment for strategic sectors, such as hydrogen, semiconductors, or electric batteries. The resources devoted to these future investments in the 2020s will be unveiled on the occasion of the budget project for 2022, presented in the fall of 2021. The plan will hopefully significantly increase public investment, and eventually strengthen the potential growth rate of the French economy.

2.4 Conclusion

In the run-up to the COVID-19 crisis, France followed the trend of all the European countries, who in the past decade have seen public investment decrease quite substantially and capital stock deplete. It is true that, thanks to the sustained investment dynamics of previous decades, France ranks highly in both the quantity of public capital and the quality of its infrastructures; but in terms of flows, it is today near an all-time low. The reversal started at the time of the Global Financial Crisis of 2008. Despite the rhetoric of the time, national account data show that it was not countered with a public investment push: the sharp increase of debt between 2007 and 2017 did not correspond to an accumulation of public capital. On the contrary, investment paid the heaviest toll in the subsequent consolidation phase, when both expenditure reduction by the central government and cuts to transfers to local administrations (the largest owner of non-financial assets) resulted in a significant loss of public capital. Thus, in the space of a decade, the French general government saw its net investment drop to very low levels, and its net worth decrease by fifty points of GDP, to an all-time low in 2018. An even greater source of concern is that the previous increase of the net worth, in the 2000s, is mostly attributed to a price effect of non-produced non-financial assets (land and real estate; see Plane and Saraceno 2020, for details).

In 2018 and 2019, thanks—amongst other things—to the electoral cycle associated with the municipal elections, public investments seemed to recover slightly. But with the pandemic and the harsh lockdown of spring 2020, it dropped brutally in the second quarter of the year. Despite the subsequent rebound, its overall level for 2020 marks yet another drop.

The European Commission, led by Ursula von der Leyen, that took office in late 2019 has put public investment, most notably in ecological transition and digitalisation, at the centre of its agenda. These priorities were carried into the massive effort for the recovery that the Commission has launched with the Next Generation EU programme, more specifically with the Recovery and Resilience Facility. France has decided to embed the Facility grants financing in its *Plan de relance* that, over two years, will devote

€100 bn to recovery (of which €36.7 bn will go to public investment), so that the effects of the pandemic will definitively be left behind. The *Plan de relance* allocates the funds along the guidelines given by the Commission, with particular emphasis (compared to other countries) on the green component.

This effort is quite considerable, but it is certainly not going to be enough for the task of completing the modernisation and the greening of the French economy. There will certainly be the need for further long-term investment plans. This is why, past the pandemic, the emphasis will go back to national fiscal policies. Most of the essays contained in the previous volume of the *European Public Investment Outlook* (Cerniglia and Saraceno 2020), including our chapter on France, called for a preferential treatment for investment (a "golden rule"). The consultation process on the reform of the Stability Pact, slowed down by the pandemic, is now in its final stages, and the Commission will formulate a reform proposal in the coming months. A golden rule, even if limited to some categories of spending such as digitalisation and ecological transition, would be particularly important for a large economy like France, in which domestic demand and sustained investment (both public and private) are necessary to ensure long-term growth.

The explosion of public debt during the pandemic might nevertheless force us to be cautious of the capacity to carry on the necessary public investment efforts. In other words, it is legitimate to ask whether the fiscal space exists for the massive investment in key sectors such as ecological transition. Global public debt has reached a level that is unprecedented, exceeding the peak reached during World War II (IMF 2021). This is not the case for France's public debt, which could nevertheless reach a high level of 116% of GDP in 2021, according to the most recent figures, i.e., eighteen points of GDP more than in 2019, and nearly sixty points more than in 2007. Nevertheless, this unprecedented rise of public debt emerges in a context of historically low levels of interest rates (Ragot 2021), that are at or close to zero for maturities of up to ten years. It should be remembered that the French State raised, at the beginning of 2021, a record amount of seven billion fifty-year at a fixed rate of 0.59%, attracting in the process orders for seventy-five billion. The peculiarity of this period, therefore, is that despite historically high debt levels, interest payments for France have never been so low in the past forty years. Since 2007, the effective cost of debt has been decreasing because of falling effective interest rates. This tendency towards subdued interest rates is likely to persist, in a situation of structural excess savings. This, in turn, will keep central bank policy rates close to the current zero or negative rates over the medium run.

The widespread increase of public debt is, of course, the unintentional result of the 2008 and COVID-19 crisis. But it is also the result of a political choice, made possible in an environment of low interest rates, in order to stabilise aggregate demand and avoid a sharp rise in unemployment. The near-zero interest rates on long maturities offers France a real opportunity to invest in projects with high economic, social, and environmental returns and to enhance its potential growth. This long-term investment policy, with returns larger than costs, would be a wise economic choice. Markets and the ECB are handing to France the opportunity to strengthen its economy and improve competitiveness, as well as the wellbeing and standard of living of its population, while at the same time improving sustainability, thanks to better long-term growth prospects. It would be a shame to let this opportunity slip. The new investment plan to "build the France of 2030", presented in October by President Macron, goes in this direction, and this is a good thing for the French economy.

References

Cerniglia, F. and F. Saraceno (eds) (2020) *A European Public Investment Outlook*. Cambridge: Open Book Publishers, https://doi.org/10.11647/obp.0222.

Creel, J., E. Heyer and M. Plane (2011) "Petit Précis de Politique Budgétaire Par Tous Les Temps: Les Multiplicateurs Budgétaires Au Cours Du Cycle", *Revue de l'OFCE* 116: 61–88, https://doi.org/10.3917/reof.116.0061.

Ducoudré, B., M. Plane, R. Sampognaro and X. Timbeau (2020) "The French Recovery Strategy—Setting the Course for a Climate-Neutral and Digital Future?", *Europa, Friedrich-Ebert-Stiftung*, December.

Le Garrec, G. and V. Touzé (2020) "Le Multiplicateur d'investissement Public: Une Revue de Littérature", *OFCE Working Papers*, December.

IMF (2021) *IMF Fiscal Monitor: A Fair Shot*, April, https://www.imf.org/en/Publications/FM/Issues/2021/03/29/fiscal-monitor-april-2021.

Plane, M. and F. Saraceno (2020) "Public Investment and Capital in France", in F. Cerniglia and F. Saraceno (eds), *A European Public Investment Outlook*. Cambridge: Open Book Publishers, pp. 33–48, https://doi.org/10.11647/obp.0222.02.

Ragot, X. (2021) "More or Less Public Debt in France?", *OFCE Policy Brief* 86, 9 March.

3. Public Investment in Germany

Much More Needs to Be Done

Katja Rietzler and Andrew Watt

Introduction

The analysis of the German situation in last year's issue of the *European Public Investment Outlook* described public investment and the public capital stock since the German reunification. It contrasted the development of German infrastructure with economic and population growth, and showed that public investment had been insufficient for more than a decade. The country needed massive public investment in a number of fields to modernise its infrastructure as well as ensure that Germany meets its own climate policy goals (Dullien et al. 2020c). This year's chapter looks at the most recent developments. It begins with an overall analysis of public investment across policy fields and the activities of different levels of government. The next section focuses on the massive stimulus package, which the German government launched in summer 2020—the so-called "Konjunktur- und Zukunftspaket" (stimulus and future package). We analyse the investment content of the package and the progress of its implementation. The third section focuses on the German Recovery and Resilience Plan (Deutscher Aufbau und Resilienzplan, DARP) as part of the EU's NextGeneration programme, noting the very substantial overlap with the domestic stimulus plan. The fourth section presents recent simulations by the Macroeconomic Policy Institute (IMK) with the National Institute's Global Economic Model (NIGEM), which show that under the current financial conditions a substantial credit-financed public investment initiative is compatible with a reduction of the debt-to-GDP ratio (Dullien et al. 2021). The concluding section sums up the resulting policy recommendations.

3.1 Public Construction Investment Softened in the Pandemic, Equipment Massively Increased

Since the early 2000s, Germany has recorded a substantial investment backlog, which has become more and more prominent in the economic policy debate in the wake of a

 https://doi.org/10.11647/OBP.0280.03

report by the DIW Berlin in 2013 (Bach et al. 2013). As already shown in the previous *European Public Investment Outlook* (Dullien et al. 2020c), net public investment was negative during much of the last two decades. Stimulus packages following the financial crisis of 2008–09 caused a temporary increase in public investment. However, when they were phased out in 2012, real gross fixed capital formation of the government sector in Germany was only slightly above the level of the year 2000.

A sustained upward trend started only in 2015 (Figure 1).[1] It was driven by two main factors: firstly, Germany's population rose sharply due to the migration of hundreds of thousands of refugees, creating an urgent need for additional infrastructure; secondly, the fiscal situation improved rapidly with the strong recovery after the Global Financial Crisis. From 2014 onwards, both the federal government and the states (taken together) recorded rising fiscal surpluses, which made it easier to finance new investment projects. The increase was particularly pronounced in construction as well as machinery and equipment,[2] whereas other investment[3] had already been on a steady upward trend since the 1990s.

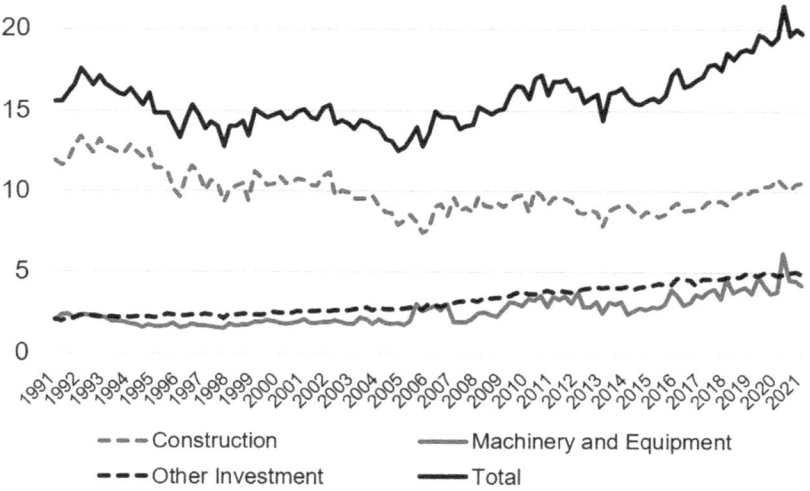

Fig. 1 Quarterly Real Gross Fixed Capital Formation of the Government Sector (in Billion Euros, Prices from 2015).

Source of data: Destatis, Quarterly National Accounts, seasonally adjusted, 1991 Q1 until 2021 Q1.

The public investment backlog is most pronounced in construction, where net investment has been negative since 2003. In 2015 the negative public construction investment trend was reversed, but depreciation still exceeded new construction

---

1   Data as of early August 2021.
2   Since the introduction of the ESA 2010 in 2014, public investment in machinery and equipment includes military spending on weapons.
3   Other investment consists mostly of investment in research and development.

investment in 2020. Insufficient infrastructure investment is largely a problem of the local government level, which is responsible—amongst other things—for schools, childcare facilities, and municipal roads, and accounts for about 60% of construction investment. Local government investment increased steeply after 2017, in parallel to rising investment grants both from the states and from federal programmes. However, after years of stagnating investment, the municipalities face serious bottlenecks. They have insufficient staff in their planning departments after years of job cuts and are confronted with capacity constraints in a booming construction industry (Scheller et al. 2021). Nevertheless, municipal investment, 85% of which is construction investment, rose by 33.3% in real terms (Figure 2). The national data conceal considerable regional disparities.

Developments since the first quarter of 2020 have been dominated by the COVID-19 pandemic and other one-off factors. Government construction investment declined two quarters in a row last summer, and is now slightly below the pre-crisis level and slightly below the level of twenty years earlier. In the second quarter of 2020, investment in machinery and equipment surged and declined again in subsequent quarters. According to Destatis, this temporary increase was due to a large defence project as well as regional spending on the railways. Overall, public gross fixed capital formation has lost some momentum in recent quarters.

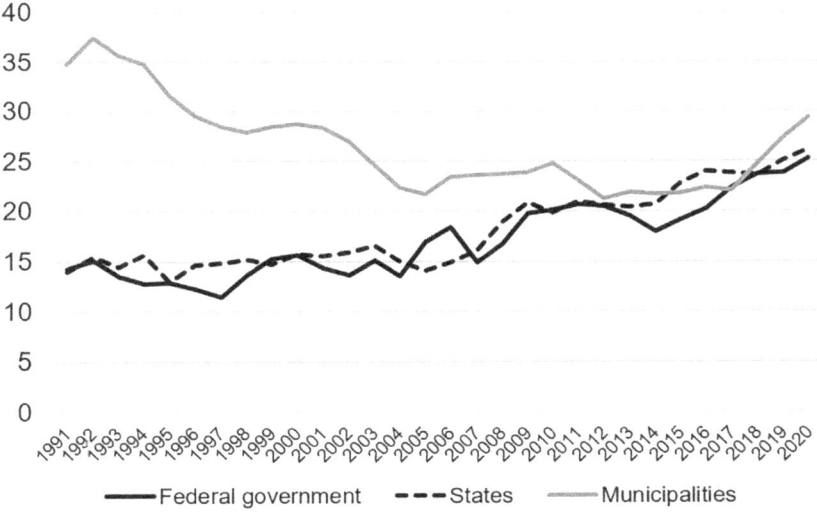

Fig. 2 Annual Real Gross Capital Formation of Government Subsectors (in Billion Euros, Reference Year 2015).

Source of data: Destatis, Annual National Accounts, price adjustment by IMK using weighted deflators for government subsectors. Investment of social security is not presented, as it is negligible.

3.2 Investment Projects under the Stimulus and Future Investment Package: Limited Scope and Slow Progress

On 3 June 2020, the German government published its "stimulus and future package". Its focus was on stabilising incomes and consumption, as well as businesses, in the COVID-19 crisis. Key elements were a temporary lowering of the VAT rate in the second half of 2020, a reduction of the renewable energy levy in 2021, and generous subsidies to support businesses adversely affected by the anti-COVID measures. In addition to the usual criteria of being timely, targeted, and temporary (Elmendorf and Furman 2008), the package also aimed to be transformative. This is why it is split into two parts: a stimulus package ("Konjunkturpaket") and the future package ("Zukunftspaket"), a medium-term programme consisting largely of investment in key areas such as decarbonisation and climate-friendly mobility, digitalisation and the modernisation of the health sector. The total volume of quantified measures in both packages adds up to €171.6 bn, of which roughly €130 bn was supposed be effective in 2020–21 (BMF 2020; Dullien et al. 2020a).

As several measures were not quantified— e.g., the extension of the short-time work scheme beyond 2020—and subsidies to business as well as spending to contain the pandemic have repeatedly been upgraded, the overall volume of the package could be even higher. The measures of the Zukunftspaket amount to €57.9 bn, of which €43.9 bn is either direct public investment or investment grants.[4] At the same time, the stimulus package includes investment totalling €13.9 bn. Overall investment in the stimulus and future investment package thus amounts to €57.8 bn, or roughly one third of the total quantified amount (Table 1).

At first sight, this looks impressive. However, in some cases, the planned implementation stretches beyond 2025, translating into an annual allocation in the single-digit billions of euros. Total investment in the stimulus and future investment package thus covers only about 12% of the requirements identified by the IMK and IW Köln in their joint report, which was endorsed by both the German Trade Union Confederation and the Federation of German Industries (Bardt et al. 2019). The order of magnitude of the institutes' estimate, a total of €457 bn over ten years, was classified as "not implausible" by the Board of Academic Advisors at the Federal Ministry of Economic Affairs and Energy (BMWi 2020).

Furthermore, not all of the investment is additional. €10 bn of the package refers to planned investments of the federal government that were to be brought forward. If one looks at the statistics of the past year, there has not been much additional investment. According to the national accounts, gross capital formation of the federal government at current prices increased by just €1.9 bn in 2020.

---

4   The future investment package also includes measure such as additional staff in the health sector (€4 bn), humanitarian aid in the pandemic (€3 bn), or an equity increase for Deutsche Bahn (€5 bn), which mostly covers losses of the German rail company during the crisis.

Moreover, implementation is lagging in some areas. An example is the national hydrogen strategy, the largest individual item of the future investment package, with a total scope of €7 bn.[5] Of this amount, less than €0.6 bn is to be disbursed until the end of 2021. As the package was only launched in mid-2020, it was clear that not too much could be achieved that year, but, at less than €0.4 bn, the plan for 2021 is also quite unambitious, after being scaled down from €1.7 bn in the original draft budget. This is all the more problematic if one takes into account that the government's hydrogen strategy is far too small in dimension, compared to what would be needed. A recent working paper by Tom Krebs of the University of Mannheim, one of Germany's leading experts on investment, calls for a much more ambitious hydrogen strategy combining massive infrastructure investment (both in Germany and across Europe) and industrial policies. With an overall budget of €100 bn until 2030, it would be more than eight times the size of the current plans. More importantly, it envisages a much more active role of the government and substantial hydrogen production within Germany, which is seen as a prerequisite for sustaining Germany's technological leadership position (Krebs 2021).

When assessing the impact of the stimulus measures on investment, it is insufficient to look only at direct investment expenditures in the packages, as some measures have a beneficial indirect effect. As the municipalities play a central role in German infrastructure investment, their financial situation is vital. Depending strongly on the highly cyclical trade tax (Gewerbesteuer), the municipalities would have had to cut spending, investment in particular, if the federal and state governments had not reimbursed the revenue losses of the trade tax fully in 2020.[6] In addition, the federal government raised its reimbursements of municipalities' expenditure on accommodation and heating for long-term unemployed people substantially and permanently. This enabled the municipalities to continue investing strongly, albeit at a slightly slower pace than in the two preceding years, most probably also because of restrictions in the pandemic. As revenue losses continue in 2021, with federal and state governments not planning to compensate the municipalities for their revenue losses again, it remains to be seen whether the municipalities can sustain their dynamic investment activity.

3.3 German Recovery and Resilience Plan: Substantial Overlap with Stimulus and Future Package

In a major step forward for European integration, in late 2020, after fraught negotiations, the member states agreed to set up a Recovery and Resilience Facility

---

5   With an additional €2 bn earmarked for international cooperation on hydrogen and €3 bn from European sources, the total hydrogen budget adds up to €12 bn (Krebs 2021).

6   Federal and state governments each bore half of the trade tax revenue losses. The Federal Ministry of Finance reported the federal share as €6.1 bn (BMF 2021).

(Watzka and Watt 2020). Under the scheme, the European Commission is empowered to borrow, on behalf of the EU, hundreds of billions of euros on financial markets. Up to €672.5 bn is to be made available to member states, roughly half as grants, and the other half as loans. The money is to be spent on agreed priorities. The mechanism, in a nutshell, is for member states to submit national plans which are approved first by the Commission, then the Council. Funds are then disbursed, providing member states achieve agreed milestones. Disbursement and programme expenditures are foreseen to run until 2026. The member states have committed to servicing these debts over the long term (until 2058) via the EU budget—if agreement can be reached by means of new "own resources".

Germany submitted a first draft of its national plan at the end of 2020, and the final version—Deutscher Aufbau- und Resilienzplan (DARP)—on 27 April 2021. It runs to 1250 pages. Germany is seeking funding only under the grants pillar of the RRF: it is not applying for RRF loans, as the servicing costs of such loans are not lower than Germany can currently obtain on financial markets. The discussion here focuses on aspects that can be considered, in a broad sense, as public investment;[7] planned reforms are not discussed.

3.3.1 Overview of the DARP

For Germany, the volume for grants available under the RRF is small. It is estimated to be €23.6 bn in 2018 prices and €25.6 bn in current prices; this is less than 0.8% of annual GDP (2020) and will be spread over a period of six years (2021–26). In macroeconomic terms, the RRF is of limited direct importance for Germany, much less than the domestic stimulus and recovery package. This reflects both the fact that the RRF is strongly redistributive in favour of low-income member states and those hardest hit by the pandemic (Watzka and Watt 2020) and also Germany's decision to forgo the loans component. The country also benefits indirectly, however, via the boost the RRF gives to its close trading partners.

The German government puts a value of just under €28 bn on the forty measures brought together in the DARP, for which it is seeking EU funding. These are divided into six priorities which are structured a little differently, but overall are congruent with the six policy areas set out in the RFF. They are:

1. Climate and energy

2. Digitalisation of the economy and infrastructure

3. Digitalisation of education

---

7   In its analysis of the DARP (DARP, p. 1110), the DIW classifies around 61% of spending as either public investment or an investment subsidy. But a substantial proportion of what is termed government consumption in the naitonal accounts (just under 21% of DARP spending) can be considered investment in a broader sense (e.g., salaries of additional educational or healthcare staff).

4. Strengthening social inclusion

5. Strengthening the health system, especially related to pandemics

6. Modern administration/removing investment barriers

An overview of the division of planned expenditures between these six priorities (and some of the most important subcategories) is given in Table 1—which also shows spending plans in the national "stimulus and future package"—and in Figure 3.

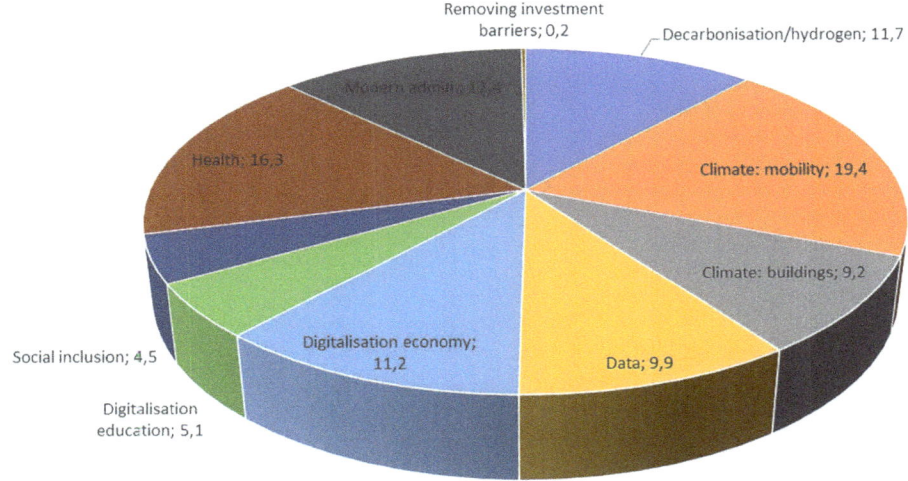

Fig. 3 Contribution of Main DARP Sections to Total Expenditure, in %.

Source of data: DARP, p. 10.

EU rules stipulate that at least 37% of expenditure of the RRF should be on climate-protection projects; 20% is to be devoted to digitalisation. According to the German government, more than 40% of DARP-spending is concentrated in the first priority, climate/energy. Regarding digitalisation, Germany has made this goal explicit in pillars two and three of the DARP, which total more than 25%. Because digitalisation has been "mainstreamed" across other thematic areas, Germany claims that as much as 50% of spending under the DARP will contribute to the digitalisation goal.

There is considerable scope for applying false labels—"greenwashing"—and double-counting in such claims. With this in mind, we take a closer look at the main proposed projects. To simplify the exposition, Chapters 2 and 3, and 5 and 6 are considered together.

Table 1 Comparison of German RRF and Domestic Stimulus Plan.

Components of Resilience Plan	Euro bn	Measures of stimulus and future package ("Konjunktur- und Zukunftspaket")	Euro bn
Decarbonisation based on renewable hydrogen	3.3	National hydrogen strategy	7.0
Hydrogen-based mobility	0.5		
Other climate-friendly mobility	6.2	Charging station infrastructure, modernisation of buses and trucks, subsidy for electric vehicles ("Innovationsprämie")	5.9
Climate-friendly construction and modernisation of buildings	2.6	Modernisation of buildings to reduce greenhouse gas emissions	2.0
Data as resource of the future	2.8	Communication technologies for the future	2.0
Digitalisation of the economy	3.1	Investment subsidies for vehicle producers and their suppliers, Centre for Digitalisation and Technology Research	2.5
Digitalisation of the education system	1.4	-	
Strengthening social inclusion	1.4	Expansion of childcare services, stabilisation of social contribution rates 2021, federal programme to protect apprenticeships	8.5
Strengthening a resilient health system	4.6	Package for the public health service and future programme for hospitals, Subsidies for CEPI and German vaccine development	7.8
Modern public administration	3.5	Online access bill and modernisation of public registers	3.3
Total German Reconstruction and Resilience Plan	29.3	Total of comparable items	39.0
		Total stimulus and future package of which: investments (excluding equity increase of the German public railway company)	171.6 57.8

Source of data: German Reconstruction and Resilience Plan (Deutscher Aufbau und Resilienzplan, DARP), Written Statement of the German Council of Economic Experts on DARP, Table 7 of Annex, simplified and aggregated presentation of IMK, German Federal Government (2020).

3.3.2 Climate and Energy

The climate and energy pillar consists of three packages of measures: decarbonisation with a focus on renewable (green) hydrogen, efforts to promote climate-friendly mobility, and construction/housing. Representing 40.3% of the total, it is, by a considerable margin, the most important section of the DARP.

A total of €3.26 bn is allocated to decarbonisation. Notable is the cooperation with, in particular, France on developing electrolysis capacity to produce green hydrogen and distribute it to end-users. (By contrast, the DARP does not offer support for other mature renewable power sources such as wind and solar power.) But even with the addition of hydrogen-related research and innovation funding, only €2.2 bn is set aside to develop a technology that is still in its infancy. While the priority given to this area is appropriate, funding appears derisory (as already noted above for the national stimulus and future package). Similarly, the offer of carbon contracts for difference, in which the government subsidises firms undertaking long-term carbon-reducing investments that are not currently profitable at present carbon prices, is a promising approach. Against the background of political barriers to an adequate carbon price and the lack of a border-adjustment mechanism, it has a direct impact in carbon-intensive industries, and also substantial indirect effects, as it aids the breakthrough of new technologies. However, it is set up as a pilot scheme and has a budget of only a little over half a billion euros. For context: one study suggests that decarbonising part of the German steel industry alone (shifting the so-called primary route to hydrogen-based reduction) would require, in addition to a massive expansion of renewable energy supply, some €30 bn euros of investment by the steel companies themselves (Berger 2020).

What is striking about the section on climate-friendly mobility is the almost complete focus on road transport. Only €227 m of the €5.4 bn envisaged to promote climate-friendly mobility is dedicated to improving rail transport. And even that is focused narrowly on engine technology: there is no place for a more general expansion of the rail network or train services.[8] Local public transport is included only via a subsidy program, albeit a sizable one (€1 bn), to purchase electric buses. Overwhelmingly, the aim of the policies in this section of the DARP is to promote the electrification of private motorised transport. Almost half (€2.5 bn) of the total is foreseen as an "innovation premium" of €9000 for new purchases of electrical vehicles (plug-in hybrids up to €6750). Not a single euro is foreseen to promote cycling—for instance, by improving inner-city cycling infrastructure or increasing the use of bikes for commuting.

While it is a valid policy goal, for economic and social reasons, to manage the transition of the German car industry from internal combustion engines, the almost complete focus on it at the expense of other interests is regrettable. A study by the Forum Ökologische Marktwirtschaft (2021) notes that the DARP represents an improvement on the original version of the plan which, notably, contained more than €1 bn in subsidies to upgrade heavy goods vehicles to lower-emission diesel engines. This expensive subsidy to fossil-fuel road transport was removed, primarily because it was thought likely to be rejected due to the "do no significant (environmental) harm" injunction applying to all RRF-funded measures (DARP, p. 1071). While the promotion of electrical vehicles is an important element in achieving climate goals—assuming a parallel move to decarbonise electricity generation[9]—the subsidisation of the acquisition of new vehicles and the expansion of the charging network primarily benefits upper-income households and firms providing company cars.

The section on climate-friendly construction/renovation is dominated by a €2.5 bn subsidy for renovation of buildings to reduce their energy use through insulation, and allow for the modernisation of heating systems, etc. This is to be used to expand an existing national scheme, permitting an estimated 40,000 additional housing units to benefit.

---

8   But see also the section on digitalisation.
9   Plug-in hybrid vehicles are also eligible for support although their ecological impact is, to say the least, disputed.

3.3.3 Digitalisation of the Economy and Infrastructure, and of Education

These two chapters of the DARP represent around €5.9 bn and €1.4 bn respectively, together more than a quarter of the DARP. German political discourse, accentuated by the experience during the pandemic, has been seized by the view that Germany lags behind its peers in terms of digitalisation. Germany is attempting via an IPCEI initiative[10] to develop its (and Europe's) potential in the areas of microelectronics (started in 2018) and, more recently, cloud infrastructure, to gain a foothold in these areas.

The most striking feature of the digitalisation of the economy section, however, is the quantitative predominance—at almost €1.9 bn—of support for a very specific sector, the automobile industry, which as shown above is also a prime beneficiary of projects under the climate pillar. Policymakers justify this focus (DARP, p. 455) with reference to the huge challenges facing the sector to shift to electric vehicles and to cope with cost competition, particularly among part-supplying SMEs. It is difficult, though, to see why this is really support for "digitalisation" rather than sectoral investment support, focused on a strategically important sector. On the other hand, this part of the DARP does contain an investment in rail infrastructure (identified above as missing from the mobility section) in the form of digitalisation of rail signalling and communication systems (€500 m).

The experience of the pandemic, with pupils forced to learn at home for extended periods, and local authorities and even individual schools forced to seek individual workarounds, has certainly revealed the need for a "digital education offensive". The programme is of very modest size, however. Alongside the purchase of equipment for teachers and investment in their skills development (€500 m), it contains elements whose priority is not immediately obvious, such as support for the educational institutions of the German army (€100 m). The largest single project (€630 m) is to set up a "meta-platform" to systematise and improve access to digital educational content. The focus on the "meta" level—and the associated nebulous description of what this measure can achieve in practice—reflects the fact that, in Germany, education is the prerogative of the federal states.

3.3.4 Social Inclusion

The foreseen measures are small in volume, with a strong focus on children and young people, an explicit goal of the EU-level RRF. The two quantitatively most important schemes are to improve childcare (€500 m) and ensure an adequate supply of apprenticeships/dual training courses, particularly for disadvantaged groups. A goal is to increase labour market participation, and indirectly also to contribute to undergirding the pension system, one of Germany's country-specific

---

10   Important Project of Common European Interest.

recommendations. In the case of childcare, the funds will enable investment needs that have become more acute due to the pandemic to be met. The apprenticeship promotion programme offers financial support to companies who, despite the impact of the pandemic, take on additional trainees (including, for example, those who have lost their trainee placement in another company as a result of the crisis).

In short, these are sensible programmes that respond to real needs rendered more pressing by the pandemic; however, the quantitative dimensions are very limited.

3.3.5 Strengthening the Health System and Modernising Public Administration

It goes without saying that the COVID-19 pandemic threw down huge challenges to national health systems. Just over 16% of DARP is allocated for health-related measures. Specifically in the case of Germany, problems with inadequate digitalisation became apparent, leading to delays in processing tests and patchy reporting on the progress of the pandemic, and a lack of coordination between local health authorities. In view of this, more than €800 m is foreseen to be invested in this area.

Germany—the home of BioNTech, whose vaccine (produced in cooperation with Pfizer) has been the mainstay of the European vaccination campaign—plans to invest an additional €750 m in COVID-vaccine research and development under the DARP. By a substantial margin the largest programme in this area, at €3 bn, it is a "future programme" for hospitals. The program is to be "frontloaded", with spending concentrated in 2021; the corresponding legislation was already passed last year. Here, the main aim is to improve the digitalisation of hospitals. They will be able to claim financial support for the necessary physical and human-capital investment. This is arguably one programme where a specific need, occasioned by the recent crisis, has been identified, and a commensurately substantial sum set aside to address the issue; this programme alone represents around 10% of the entire DARP.

The considerations detailed in the specific case of the public health system apply more generally to the German public administration; the problems of a reticent adoption of digital hardware and processes are the same. Similarly, therefore, a programme has been launched to address these problems through investment in physical and human capital. Here, too, the main element is a €3 bn support programme for investment in digitalisation, to make it user-friendly for citizens while dealing with the complexities of Germany's three-layered federal administrative system. Additionally, two specific initiatives have been launched, whose aim is to enable citizens to identify themselves in online communication with the administration, while avoiding data-protection pitfalls and abuse by criminals, and permitting interoperability between different parts and levels of the administration; a first crucial step is to have a single identification number for each citizen.

As in other areas, this section of the DARP is doubtless focused on an important reform area, one also identified as part of the European Semester in the country-specific recommendations. However, the specific contribution (and additionality) of the DARP is questionable. The legislative processes have been underway for many years in some cases. The corresponding investments are now being, to some extent, booked under the DARP, but they would have proceeded under purely national financing in the absence of the RFF.

3.3.6 Overall Assessment

The DARP (p. 1103) contains a study undertaken by the DIW research institute, according to which long-run GDP is expected to be almost 2% higher than in the absence of the programme. The counterfactual here, though, is that the measures enumerated under the DARP are otherwise not implemented (full additionality). The overlap between the national stimulus and future programme and the DARP measures is very substantial, however. For Germany, the RRF has very largely not been perceived as an opportunity to take on additional tasks or increase the ambition of planned projects. Already planned projects, which would otherwise have been funded by domestic borrowing, are now to draw on RRF funding.

As regards prioritisation, in broad-brush terms the DARF is in accordance with the required focus on climate change and digitialisation. Indeed, the latter is like a red thread running through much of the programme. This is in accordance with recent country-specific recommendations issued to Germany by the EU, and reflects perceived weaknesses revealed by the pandemic.

A more granular look, however, reveals some issues of concern. Striking is the focus, under the "green" and "digital" labels, on the automobile sector. While there are economic and social justifications supporting what is clearly a far-reaching adjustment in a strategically important sector, the neglect of other modes of transport stands out. Some measures, such as subsidisation of plug-in hybrid cars, are arguably inimical to environmental goals. An admittedly speculative interpretation is that this represents, in part, an attempt to show that "Europe" is supporting the German car industry against the background of criticism that EU-imposed fleet emission requirements have placed a heavy burden on German automobile production. In other areas (such as the hydrogen economy and support for industrial decarbonisation) envisaged measures are appropriate, but the scale of funding is very limited.

3.4 Substantially Higher Credit-Financed Public Investment Does Not Threaten Debt Sustainability

Some insight into the likely effects of additional public investment, whether under the purely domestic budget or as part of the German recovery plan, can be gained from a recent simulation of a credit-financed investment programme conducted by the IMK (Dullien et al. 2021).

Based on conservative estimates of unmet infrastructural needs (Bardt et al. 2019), the authors simulate a public investment programme totaling €460 bn (in 2019 prices, equal to around 13% of 2019 GDP) over ten years. At the end of the period, the public capital stock is about 25% higher than without the programme. The simulation is conducted using the macroeconomic model NiGEM. The investment is credit-financed. No monetary policy reaction is assumed during the first two years. The simulation runs for thirty years.

The simulations use three different assumptions. The first is with the standard version of NiGEM: here, the public and private capital stocks act as substitutes. The larger public capital stock depresses the marginal productivity of the entire capital stock. As this is neither theoretically not empirically plausible, two illustrative alternative simulations were undertaken. In a technological-improvement scenario, the rate of technical progress is assumed to be boosted by the higher public investment (for instance, due to the provision of a better broadband network). Secondly, in a more far-reaching intervention, the output-elasticity of the public capital stock is set at 0.3, in line with empirical evidence in the literature.

In the basic scenario, in which the short-run fiscal multiplier is only around 0.8%, substantially below most estimates in the current low-interest-rate environment, GDP is around 1.7% higher at the end of the programme compared to baseline. In the longer run, the multiplier is higher—around 2%, in line with much of the recent literature—and the GDP effect is substantial at 3–4%. Private investment is crowded in, the total capital stock is some 4% above baseline, and potential output is about 3% higher. The additional credit-financed investment means that initially the debt-to-GDP ratio is some 10 pp higher than without a programme. But this one-off cost is matched by permanently higher potential output. Because of this, the debt-to-GDP ratio is the same as without the programme at the end of the thirty-year simulation period. Even with low multipliers, the impact is positive: output is higher while the debt-to-GDP ratio is the same as without the investment offensive.

The positive impacts on output and potential growth are substantially higher in the two alternative simulations. Accordingly, the period after which the programme is self-financing (in the sense of a debt-to-GDP ratio no higher than baseline) is substantially shorter. While there is clearly considerable uncertainty about the real-world size of the multiplier, which in practice would depend, not least, on exactly which sorts of public investment received additional impetus, the two alternative simulations are considered more plausible and the quantitative effects given above are likely at the bottom of the plausible range.

The implications of this simulation are clear. Germany has substantial scope to increase credit-financed public investment with positive economic impacts and no longer-run negative effects on debt-to-GDP ratios. This could be done purely domestically or, if the financial terms become favourable, by taking up the loans available under the RFF.

3.5 What Germany Needs after the COVID-19 Crisis: Reform of Fiscal Rules and Stabilisation of Investment at a High Level

In parallel to the European Union's upgrade of its climate goals, the German government also raised its ambitions, aiming to reach climate neutrality by 2045. On top of already considerable investment needs, this requires even more capital spending much earlier. The investment projects of the stimulus and future package cover only a fraction of Germany's massive investment requirements. The Recovery and Resilience Plan is even smaller in size and overlaps substantially with the national stimulus and future investment package; it therefore provides only limited additional investment. This is not a problem in itself: it is right that the EU RRF has a strongly redistributive function and supports states hit hardest by the COVID-19 crisis. Germany has the means to do much more on its own.

From early on in the COVID-19 crisis, both the European fiscal rules and the German debt brake were suspended, which allowed both federal and state governments to incur substantial additional debt to fight the crisis. While nobody knows when the pandemic will finally be over, the debate about fiscal consolidation after the crisis is already in full swing and was a key issue in the autumn general election. There is a high probability that there will be neither substantial reforms of the debt brake nor tax increases to finance the massive additional investment requirements. Current discussions of financing options focus on a variety of measures ranging from making use of public companies to cutting ecologically harmful subsidies. This are unlikely to be enough, however.

Germany and the whole of the EU needs a sustained investment strategy. In Germany, public investment, which has recently been determined much more by the availability of current revenues than an assessment of longer-run needs, must be stabilised at a satisfactory level in the medium- to long-term. This is particularly important for the municipalities, which play a vital role for infrastructure investment. They will only employ the additional staff needed to implement investment projects if they receive sufficient funds on a permanent basis instead of having to rely on successive small-scale federal programmes. This would also provide the planning certainty that the construction industry needs to increase its capacities. As the municipalities receive substantial investment grants from the states, they are also affected indirectly by the debt brake, which prevents federal states taking on any new debt in normal times.

The federal level has slightly more fiscal space, being allowed to incur structural debt of 0.35% of GDP per year. This is only about a quarter of the additional requirements. Furthermore, the current cyclical adjustment method tends to underestimate cyclical effects and thus has a procyclical bias (Heimberger 2020; Heimberger and Truger 2020).

At EU level, the current economic governance review should be used to modernise the fiscal rules. A viable option would be an expenditure rule combined with a "golden rule" for investment as proposed by Dullien et al. (2020b). At the same time, the debt limit of 60% of GDP should be defined more flexibly, taking account of the macroeconomic environment (especially negative real interest rates). This would also be a good opportunity to reform the German debt brake, which in many respects is not fully consistent with the European rules (Dullien et al. 2021, pp. 18–19).

References

Bach, S., G. Baldi, K. Bernoth, B. Bremer, B. Farkas, F. Fichtner, M. Fratzscher and M. Gornig (2013) *Wege zu einem höheren Wachstumspfad,* DIW Wochenbericht 26: 617.

Bardt, H., S. Dullien, M. Hüther and K. Rietzler (2019) *For a Sound Fiscal Policy: Enabling Public Investment,* IMK Report 152e, November. Düsseldorf.

Berger, R. (2020) "The Future of Steelmaking: How the European Steel Industry Can Achieve Carbon Neutrality", *Roland Berger Focus,* 05/2020, https://www.rolandberger.com/publications/publication_pdf/rroland_berger_future_of_steelmaking.pdf.

BMWi (2020) *Öffentliche Infrastruktur in Deutschland: Probleme und Reformbedarf Gutachten des Wissenschaftlichen Beirats,* Bundesministerium für Wirtschaft und Energie, Berlin.

Bundesministerium der Finanzen, BMF (2021) *Vorläufiger Abschluss des Bundeshaushalts 2020,* BMF-Monatsbericht, January.

Bundesministerium der Finanzen, BMF (2020) *Corona-Folgen bekämpfen, Wohlstand sichern, Zukunftsfähigkeit stärken,* Ergebnis des Koalitionsaus-schusses vom 3. Juni 2020, Berlin.

Dullien, S., K. Rietzler and S. Tober (2021) *Ein Transformationsfonds für Deutschland,* IMK Study 71, January.

Dullien, S., E. Jürgens, C. Paetz and S. Watzka (2021) *Makroökonomische Auswirkungen eines kreditfinanzierten Investitionsprogramms in Deutschland.* IMK Report 168.

Dullien, S., S. Tober and A. Truger (2020a) "Wege aus der Wirtschaftskrise: Der Spagat zwischen Wachstumsstabilisierung und sozial-ökologischer Transformation", *WSI Mitteilungen,* 73, June 2020.

Dullien, S., C. Paetz, A. Watt and S. Watzka (2020b) *Proposals for a Reform of the EU's Fiscal Rules and Economic Governance,* IMK Report 159e, Düsseldorf.

Dullien, S., E. Jürgens and S. Watzka (2020c) "Public Investment in Germany: The Need for a Big Push". In F. Cerniglia and F. Saraceno (eds) *A European Public Investment Outlook.* Cambridge: Open Book Publishers, pp. 49–62, https://doi.org/10.11647/obp.0222.03.

Deutscher Bundestag (2020) *Beschlussempfehlung des Haushaltsaus-schusses (8. Ausschuss) zu dem Entwurf eines Gesetzes über die Feststellung des Bundeshaushaltsplans für das Haushaltsjahr 2021 (Haushaltsgesetz 2021)—Drucksache 19/22600—Einzelplan 60.* Bundestagsdrucksache 19/23323. Berlin.

Elmendorf, D.W. and J. Furman (2008) "If, When, How: A Primer on Fiscal Stimulus", *The Hamilton Project Strategy Paper,* Brookings Institution: Washington, DC.

Forum Ökologische Marktwirtschaft (2021) *Deutscher Aufbau- und Resilienzplan: Verpasste Chance für eine klimafreundliche und soziale Mobilität,* Policy Brief, aktualisierte Version 28.04.21.

Heimberger, P. (2020) "Potential Output, EU Fiscal Surveillance and the COVID-19 Shock", *Intereconomics* 55(3): 167–74, https://doi.org/10.1007/s10272-020-0895-z.

Heimberger, P. and A. Truger (2020) *Der Outputlücken-Nonsense gefährdet Deutschlands Erholung von der Corona-Krise*, https://makronom.de/der-outputluecken-nonsense-gefaehrdet-deutschlands-erholung-von-der-corona-krise-36125.

Scheller, H., K. Rietzler, C. Raffer and K. Kühl (2021) "Baustelle zukunftsfähige Infrastruktur: Ansätze zum Abbau nichtmonetärer Investitionshemmnisse bei öffentlichen Infrastrukturvorhaben", *Friedrich Ebert Stiftung*, Wiso-Diskurs 12/2021.

Watzka, S. and A. Watt (2020) *The Macroeconomic Effects of the EU Recovery and Resilience Facility*, IMK Policy Brief 98, October 2020, Düsseldorf, https://www.imk-boeckler.de/de/faust-detail.htm?sync_id=9110.

4. Relaunching Public Investment in Italy

Giovanni Barbieri and Floriana Cerniglia

Introduction

The official outbreak of COVID-19 in Italy in March 2020 dealt a considerable blow to the national economy. Out of all the EU countries, Italy has suffered the most from the pandemic, and has experienced the worst contraction of its GDP since WWII. The economy has been further stressed by a reduction in consumption and a drop in tax revenues; furthermore, the health crisis has put the national healthcare system under severe strain. All of this has and will continue to contribute in the future to the redefinition of its budgetary policy.

However, 2020 was also a turning point for public investments in Italy, thanks to the widespread conviction that a robust socioeconomic structure, capable of resisting exogenous shocks such as those caused by the COVID-19 pandemic, can be obtained only by a thorough and consistent policy of tangible and intangible public investments. There are encouraging signs pointing in this direction. The new Italian government has not only planned an increase in public capital investments, but it has also committed to redefining the regulatory framework in many areas. These general policy objectives are strongly thought to be capable of jump-starting public investments in Italy, and overcoming the slow, cumbersome, and ineffective processes that have systemically affected Italy for more than two decades. At the European level, the COVID-19 pandemic has highlighted the limits of a rigorous conception of budgetary policy based solely on complying with the Stability and Growth Pact rules and with fiscal "austerity" rules. This is the foundation on which Next Generation EU (NGEU) has been developed and adopted. It is a programme which aims to relaunch the European economy through a massive plan of public investments in sectors that are considered strategic both for the survival of the economies of EU member countries and for the EU as a whole.

This chapter will provide an update of the data on public investments in Italy, which was presented and discussed in a previous work (Cerniglia and Rossi 2020). We

https://doi.org/10.11647/OBP.0280.04

will also address the measures taken by the Italian government to tackle the economic fallout caused by the pandemic, and consider the impact of NGEU funding on public investments in Italy in the coming years.

4.1 Public Investments in Italy

Public investments, which had declined from 3.7% to 2.1% from 2009 to 2018, gained new momentum in 2019 and 2020. In 2019, they went up to 2.3% of GDP. The increase in 2019 was in large part attributable to the measures adopted by previous governments that made it possible to overcome both the limits imposed by the Internal Stability Pact at different levels of government (regions and municipalities) and the freeze on spending surpluses. These two circumstances allowed the sublevels of government to release funds, thereby increasing their share of capital expenditure for infrastructure investments by an additional 20%.

In 2020, notwithstanding the slowdown due to the pandemic in the first half of the year, public investments increased from €41.4 bn to €44.2 bn. Due to a contraction in GDP, the investments-to-GDP ratio climbed to 2.7% (OCPI, 2021).[1]

The state intends to continue its steady flow of public investments over the coming years, also with the help of the NGEU funds. The target for public investments in 2021 is €55.6 bn (3.2% of GDP). The DEF 2021 forecasts an increase to €62.9 bn by 2024 (3.2% of GDP). This level is higher than the average pre-pandemic level (3% for the period 1995 to 2009) and previous forecasts (NADEF 2019), as shown in Figure 1.

More disaggregated data will be used to update the trends assessed in the previous work (Cerniglia and Rossi 2020). In this section, we will use the Conti Pubblici Territoriali dataset (hereafter CPT) released by the Italian Agency for Territorial Cohesion. We present data on capital expenditure by the Italian Public Administration (PA) and by the Enlarged Public Administration (Enlarged PA). The PA includes the central government as well as local and regional governments. EPA includes the PA and national and local public companies and utilities.[2] The data cover 2017–18. The CPT data enable us to obtain a clear-cut picture of the share of capital expenditure in North-Central Italy and in the "Mezzogiorno". Public capital expenditure consists of three components: 1) public investments (expenditure for infrastructure, machinery, and equipment) 2) money transfers, for example to private companies, public institutions, etc.; 3) shareholding and the provision of loans. The following tables and figures refer to capital expenditure without shareholding and loans.

---

1   If the public investment-to-GDP ratio is calculated assuming that the nominal GDP growth in 2020 is equal to that of 2019 (i.e., excluding the effects of the crisis), Italy's ratio would still have grown from 2.3% to 2.4%. This is a remarkable performance, even if it is not possible to assess to what extent the increase in expenditure is due to a rise in the price of investments, rather than to an actual increase in the volume of investments.

2   Further details on this data source can be found in Cerniglia and Rossi (2020).

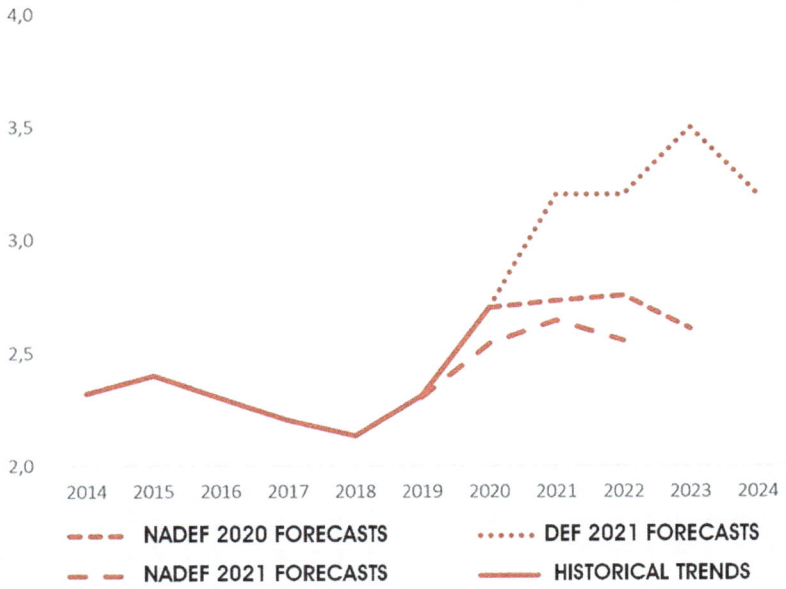

Fig. 1 Programmed Public Investments.

Source of data: OCPI (2021) on NADEF 2019, NADEF 2020, and DEF 2021 data.

The capital expenditure in Italy of the Enlarged PA in 2018 amounted to €67.4 bn, a +2.7% increase from the previous year. In terms of macro areas, the figure can be broken down into €46.1 bn for the north-central area and €21.3 bn for the south, as shown in Figure 2.

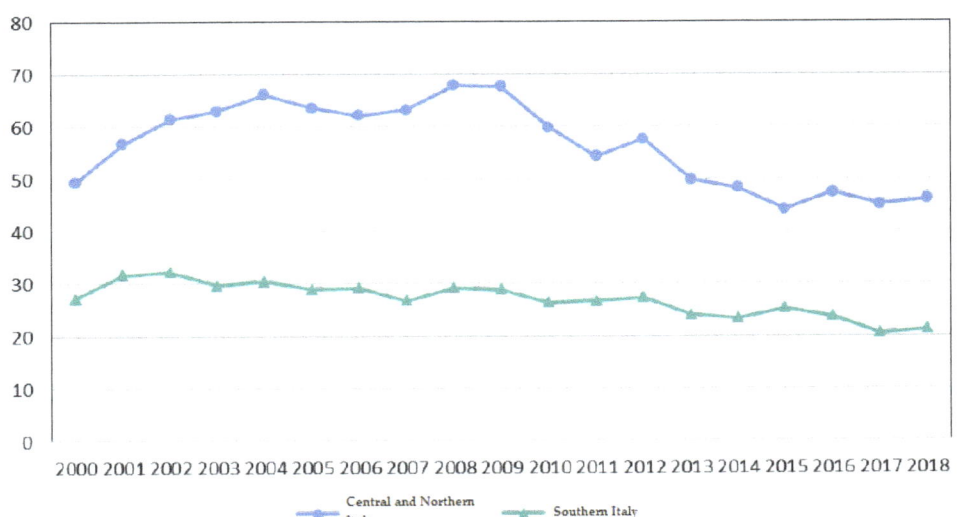

Fig. 2 Capital Expenditure (billion euros at Constant 2015 Prices).

Source of data: CPT (2020).

Looking at the per capita data, we see an increase in capital expenditure in both macro areas. In the north-central area there was an increase from €16,263 per capita in 2017 to €16,612 in 2018, with a real variation of +2.1%, while in the south it went from €12,403 per capita to €12.706 (+2.4%). Notice that the increase in capital expenditure follows an increase in GDP in both macro areas. In the "Mezzogiorno", the capital-expenditure-to-GDP ratio was +5.4% in 2017 and +5.6% in 2018, as shown in Figure 3.

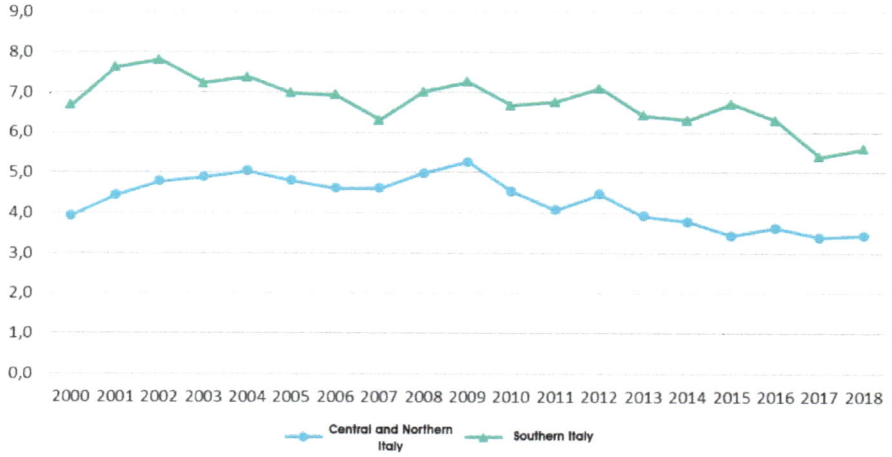

Fig. 3 Capital Expenditure (% GDP).

Source of data: CPT (2020).

Figure 4 provides a snapshot of only public investments.

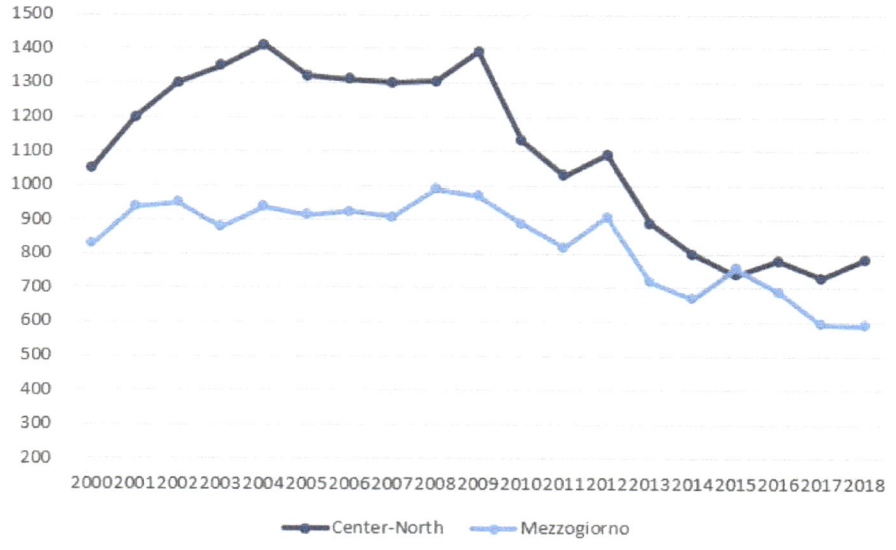

Fig. 4 Investments.

Source of data: CPT (2020).

In 2018, there was a +5% increase in investments in the Enlarged PA, bringing per capita expenditure back to €768. The largest increase in spending occurred in the energy sector (Eni, Enel).

In the "Mezzogiorno", on the other hand, per capita investment expenditure remained stagnant at €583. This is mainly due to a decrease in investments by Anas, Poste Italiane, and local public utilities.

In the following graphs we now consider only the PA.

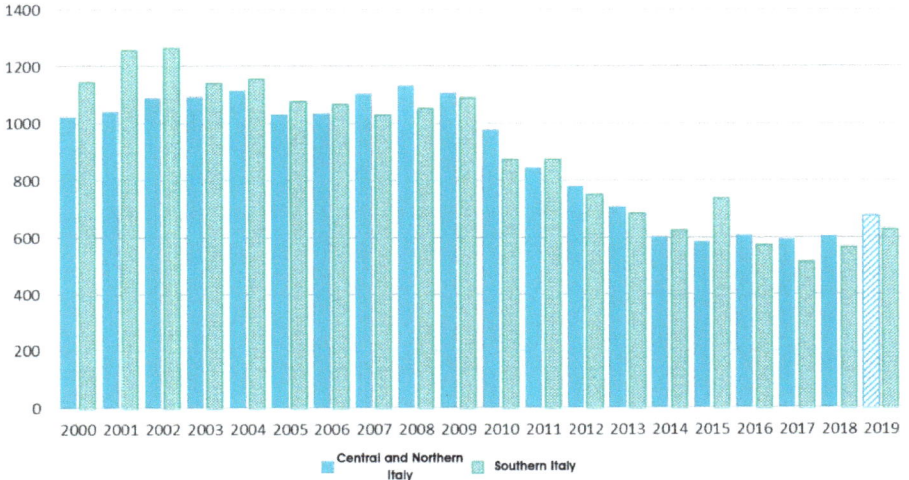

Fig. 5 Capital Expenditure by Macro Area.

Source of data: CPT (2020).

Note that at the territorial level (CPT 2020), the "Mezzogiorno" saw an increase of 23% in central government expenditure, but not much growth in expenditure by regional and local governments. The north-central area, on the other hand, registered an increase in expenditure by the central government (+11%) as well as by the regional and other sublevels of government (+14%).

Figure 6 shows the expenditure trend when considering only investments. In the north-central area in 2018, there was an +8.8% increase in investments compared to the previous year, mainly due to positive actions by regional and local governments. The "Mezzogiorno" stabilised, after its economic collapse in 2017, but with lower levels of investments by national and local public companies and utilities (CPT 2019).

Last, Figure 7 shows the variations in investments and transfers for 2017 and 2018 across the macro areas and levels of government.

The increase in expenditure by the central government in the "Mezzogiorno" was limited for investment (+4.4%), but significant for transfers to households and businesses (+29.7%).

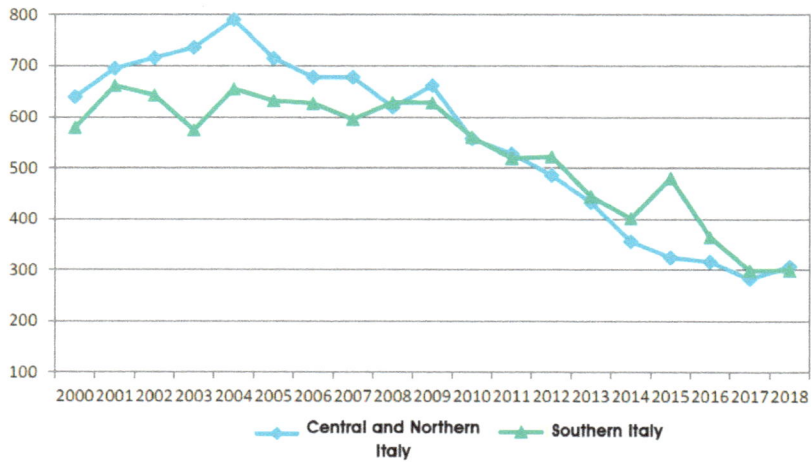

Fig. 6 Capital Expenditure for Investments by Macro Area (Net of Financial Items).

Source of data: CPT (2020).

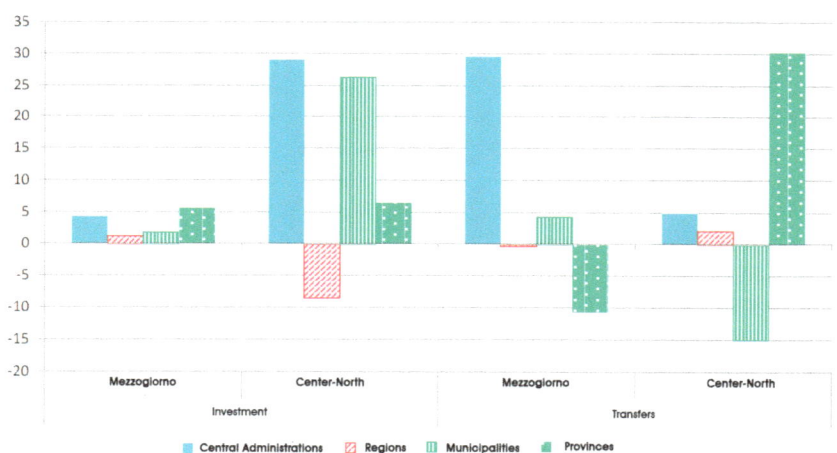

Fig. 7 Variations in Expenditure in 2017 and 2018 for Investments and Transfers in the Main PA Compartments by Macro Area (Calculations Based on Constant 2015 Prices).

Source of data: CPT (2020).

In the north-central area, the positive trend of the central government's expenditure in investment and transfers was inverse to that of the south: investment expenditure grew by +29% while transfers increased by +5%. When considering the sublevels of government, there was considerable stability in both investment and transfer expenditures in the south (+1.3% and -0.3%, respectively), while the north-central area saw a contraction in investment expenditure (-8.4%) and limited growth in transfers (+2.1%).

Municipal expenditure was positive, though limited, in the south for both investment and transfers (+1.9% and +4.4%, respectively). In the north-central area the trend was positive for investment (+26.4%), but negative for transfers (-14.9%). Expenditure by province increased for the "Mezzogiorno" in terms of investment (+5.7%), but decreased for transfers (-10.6%). In the north-central area, the trend was positive for both items, but it was considerably more significant for transfers (+30.3%) than for investment (+6.6%).

4.2 The National Recovery and Resilience Plan: Financial Resources for Public Investment[3]

In 2020, the Italian gross domestic product (GDP) decreased by -8.9% in real terms compared to 2019. Final consumption decreased by -7.8% and gross fixed capital formation by -9.1%. At the same time, the deficit-to-GDP ratio was -9.5% compared to -1.6% in 2019 (DEF 2021).[4] The general government debt-to-GDP ratio rose to 155.6%, growing by 20.8 points compared to 2019 (134.8%) (ISTAT 2021a).

The deterioration in tax revenues contributed to the worsening of the Public Administration's net borrowing indicators. In 2020, tax revenues decreased by €25,183 bn compared to 2019 (-5.3%). The change was also determined by legislative measures[5] implemented to defer tax and social security contributions for businesses, the fine arts, and other professional activities. In order to address the economic damage caused by the pandemic, in 2020 the Italian government adopted fiscal stimulus measures amounting to approximately €130 bn through a series of decrees.[6] The "relaunch" decree, the largest economic measure in Italy's recent history, is a set of measures worth a total of €55 bn in net borrowing, primarily aimed at alleviating the strain caused by the lockdown measures on the Italian healthcare system, and the affected productive sectors and workers who, as a consequence, lost their jobs. All these measures led to an increase in 2020 in the general government deficit of approximately €108.1 bn (-6.5%/GDP). The deficit is expected to increase by €31.4 bn in 2021 (-1.8%/GDP), €35.3 bn in 2022 (-1.9%/GDP), €41.4 bn in 2023 (-2.2%/GDP), and €41.3 bn in 2024 (-2.1%/GDP).[7]

---

3   Most of the data in this section are taken from "Il Piano Nazionale Di Ripresa E Resilienza—schede di lettura n.06 and n.219", and were compiled by the Servizio Studi di Camera e Senato, 27 May 2021 http://documenti.camera.it/leg18/dossier/pdf/DFP28.pdf.

4   The DEF ("documento di economia e finanza") is the government's medium term budgetary framework and is presented to parliament every April. It is a substantial document that describes the government's financial objectives and the pertaining reforms in compliance with the constraints of the Stability and Growth Pact. The Nadef (nota di aggiornamento al DEF) is an update of the DEF in relation to the new data and information on trends within the macroeconomic and public finance framework; this update is presented to parliament every September.

5   Legislative Decree DL8 April 2020, n.23.

6   Cura Italia (D.L. n.18 /2020), Liquidity (D.L. n.23/2020), Relaunch (D.L. n.34/2020), August (D.L. n.104/2020), Ristori (D.L. n.137/2020), Ristori-bis (D.L. n.149/2020), Ristori-ter (D.L. n.154/2020), Ristori-quater (D.L. n.157/2020).

7   Among the largest expenditures are those provisions benefiting businesses (€56.1 bn in 2020), institutions providing ordinary and exceptional wage subsidies, COVID-19 subsidies, ordinary and

As for GDP growth, the government forecast (DEF 2021) is of a substantially flat trend for the first half of 2021, followed by a robust rebound in Q3, and a continued notably positive shift in the latter part of the year. At the time of writing, both the Bank of Italy (2021) and the European Commission (2021) had estimated an annual growth rate of approximately 5% for GDP in 2021.[8] A return to pre-crisis levels of economic activity is expected to occur in the last quarter of 2022, according to the DEF (2021). As for the rate of unemployment, in 2018 it was 10.6%, in 2019 it was 10%, and in 2020 it was 9.2%.[9]

The EU has put in place substantial stimulus measures to counteract the economic crises caused by the pandemic. Italy presented its National Recovery and Resilience Plan (PNRR) to Brussels at the end of April 2021. It is an ambitious plan, 266 pages long. Italy is among the main beneficiaries of the NGEU, i.e., of more than €200 bn. It is also the second country, after Spain, which will benefit from the highest share of grants, a circumstance that could prove favourable for implementing short-term investments and stimulating economic recovery.

The Italian PNRR has six main missions, which follow the six-pillar structure defined by Regulation 2021/241 of the European Parliament and the European Council.[10] The six missions are: 1. Digitisation, innovation, competitiveness, culture and tourism; 2. Green revolution and ecological transition; 3. Infrastructure for sustainable mobility; 4. Education and research; 5. Social inclusion and cohesion; 6. Health. These missions are in turn further broken down into sixteen components covering a variety of fields of action.[11] The six missions and sixteen components translate into 133 different types of investment and 49 economic-institutional sectoral reforms worth a total of €235.12 bn, of which €191 bn is financed by the Recovery and Resilience Facility (RRF), €13 bn by REACT-EU for 2021–23, and a further €30.6 bn by the Complementary Fund[12] through

---

emergency solidarity funds, and the NASPI and DIS-COLL unemployment subsidies. A one-off benefit totalling €9.2 bn in 2020 has also been established for self-employed workers, employees in the tourism sector, agricultural workers meeting specific requirements, VAT-registered professionals, workers enrolled in the entertainment pension fund, and domestic workers.

8   The real GDP growth rates were +0.9% in 2018, +0.3% in 2019, and -8.9% in 2020 (Source: Ameco).

9   As this work goes to print, employment in Italy has not yet returned to pre-pandemic (February 2020) levels. There are still at least 260,000 more people unemployed, the rates of employment and unemployment remain lower than before, and the rate of inactivity has increased by +0.7. A territorial analysis has highlighted a similar employment trend in the two macro areas for the fourth quarters of 2019 and 2020: an overall decrease by -2% in the "Mezzogiorno" and -1.9 in the north-central area. Women and young workers have been impacted the worst: female employment has decreased more in the "Mezzogiorno" (-3.0%) than the north-central area (-2.4%). The same is true for young workers under 35: -6.9% in the "Mezzogiorno" vs -4.4% in the north-central area. See https://www.istat.it/it/files//2021/09/CS_Occupati-e-disoccupati_LUGLIO_2021.pdf and Svimez/Enbic 2021.

10 https://eur-lex.europa.eu/legal-content/EN/TXT/?uri=CELEX%3A32021R0241.

11 The sixteen components are listed in Table 1. For example, the first mission has three components indicated as M1C1, M1C2, and M1C3.

12 The Complementary Fund, established by D.L. No. 59 on 6 May 2021, is an instrument provided by the PNRR with a total endowment of €30.6 bn for the period from 2021 to 2026. The Italian government has expressed its willingness to set up this fund to finance specific actions that complement and supplement the PNRR. These spending commitments comply with the provisions in EU Regulation

the budget changes approved by the Italian Council of Ministers on 22 April 2021. These capital expenditure commitments have been allocated for the period 2021–26 by D.L. no. 59 of 6 May 2021. On 22 June 2021, the Italian PNRR was officially approved by the European Commission, which described it as the most substantial, innovative, and courageous European transition and recovery plan.

Figure 8 below shows the subdivision of the RRF's funding (€191 bn) for the six missions, and Table 1 shows the complete and detailed breakdown of PNRR expenditure by source of financing.

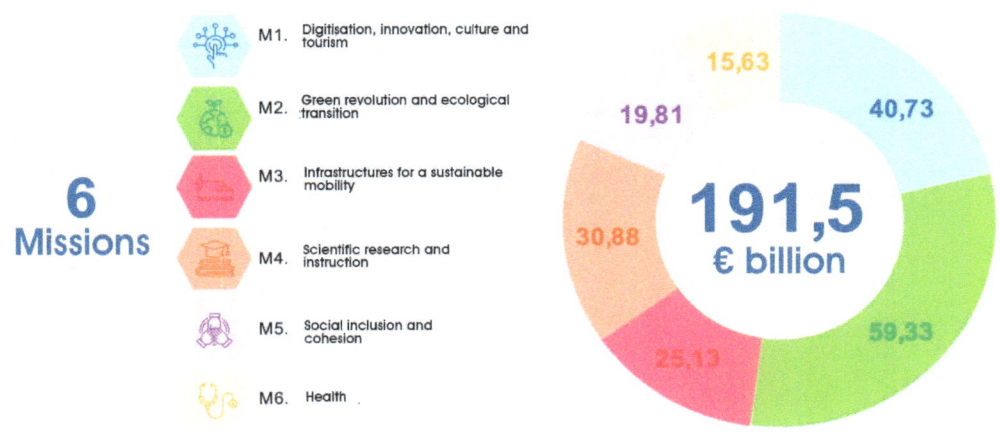

Fig. 8 RRF's Allocation of Resources by Mission.

Source of data: Italian PNRR plan.

The PNRR stipulates that at least 37% of its resources must be allocated to green transition and 20% to digital transition across missions. The component of the PNRR which, in absolute terms, has received the largest share of resources is "Digitisation, innovation, and competitiveness in the production system", with an allocation of €30.57 bn (M1C2).

As already stated, the plan foresees 133 different types of investment and 49 economic-institutional sectoral reforms (public administration, the justice system, streamlining rules and procedures, public procurement, the tax system, and strengthening social protection schemes).

Italy must now address both the consequences of the pandemic and its long-standing system frailties. In fact, the potential for real growth over the next years will not only depend on the considerable resources available, but also on the significant reforms foreseen by the PNRR. The government expects the transversal reforms to provide the required structural innovations for improving fairness, efficiency, and competitiveness, and consequently to boost the general state of the economy.

2021/241: https://www.gazzettaufficiale.it/atto/serie_generale/caricaDettaglioAtto/originario?atto. dataPubblicazioneGazzetta=2021-05-07&atto.codiceRedazionale=21G00070&elenco30giorni=true.

Table 1 PNRR Expenditure by Source of Financing (in billion euros)

M1: Digitisation, innovation, competition, culture and tourism	PNRR (a)	REACT-EU (b)	Complementary Fund (c)	Total (d= a+b+c)
M1C1 – Digitisation, innovation and security in the Public Administration	9.75	0	1.40	11.15
M1C2 - Digitisation, innovation and competitiveness in the productive system	23.89	0	5.88	30.57
M1C3 – Tourism and culture 4.0	6.68	0	1.46	8.13
Mission 1 Total	40.32	0.80	8.74	49.86
M2: Green revolution and ecological transition				
M2C1 – Sustainable agriculture and the circular economy	5.27	0.50	1.20	6.97
M2C2 – Energy transition and smart mobility	23.78	0.18	1.40	25.36
M2C3 – Energy efficiency and upgrading buildings	15.36	0.32	6.56	22.24
M2C4 - Protection of land and water resources	15.06	0.31	0	15.37
Mission 2 Total	59.47	1.31	9.16	69.64
M3: Infrastructures for sustainable mobility				
M3C1 – HS/HC railways and safe roads	24.77	0	3.20	27.97
M3C2 – Intermodal transport and integrated logistics	0.63	0	2.86	3.49
Mission 3 Total	25.40	0	6.06	31.46
M4: Education and research				
M4C1 - Boosting educational services: from kindergartens to universities	19.44	1.45	0	20.89
M4C2 – From research to firms	11.44	0.48	1.00	12.92
Mission 4 Total	30.88	1.93	1.00	33.81
M5: Social Inclusion and cohesion				
M5C1 – Employment policies	6.66	5.97	0	12.63

Source of data: Authors' own elaboration on PNRR data.

In short, the resources and reforms are necessary for unclogging three bottlenecks that have plagued Italy for decades. The PNRR has thoroughly identified them and stated that the cross-sector reforms aim to bridge the generational, territorial, and gender divides. These objectives are somewhat intertwined given that the employment issue for women and the youth in Southern Italy is decidedly worse. In fact, Daniele Franco, Minister of Economy and Finance, when presenting the Plan on 28 April 2021, clearly stated that: "only if we close the gender, generational and regional gaps can we obtain robust and sustainable growth in the medium term".

Unemployment among young people in Italy is quite high.[13] Furthermore, the employment gender gap in Italy, which was already pronounced before the pandemic, has now worsened further. Prior to the pandemic, one out of two women in Italy did not work. The employment rate was much worse in the south (33.2%) than in the north-central area (60.4%). In 2019, the male employment rate was 68%, while the female rate was 50.1%. The pandemic has affected economic sectors where higher rates of females are employed (food and beverage, tourism, etc.). In 2020, the rate of unemployment dropped to 49% for women and 67.2% for men.[14] The PNRR tackles the gender gap issue by dedicating resources to social infrastructure (building more child daycare facilities, increasing full-time school classes, etc.), and incentives for women-owned businesses and more women entering STEM fields.[15]

The final, or fourth part, of the PNRR provides an assessment of the macroeconomic impact of the measures included in the Plan. As can be seen from Table 2, when considering the best possible scenario, in 2026 (thanks to the effect of the investment multiplier), Italy's GDP should increase by 3.6 pp with respect to the baseline scenario.

Table 2 GDP Impact of the PNRR: Different Investment Efficiency Hypotheses (% Deviation with Respect to the Baseline Scenario)

	2021	2022	2023	2024	2025	2026
GDP—Best scenario	0,5	1,2	1,9	2,4	3,1	3,6
GDP—Medium scenario	0,5	1,1	1,6	2,0	2,4	2,7
GDP—Baseline scenario	0,5	0,9	1,4	1,5	1,7	1,8

Source of data: PNRR Table 4.3, p. 249.

13 Italy has the third worst level of youth unemployment in Europe, with high peaks especially in the south. In 2019, the two regions worst off were Sicily and Campania—both had a youth unemployment rate of 53.6%.
14 While the initial impact of the pandemic was decidedly harsher on women, it now seems that, as in other advanced economies, it is more balanced. There have been some signs of positive and more balanced changes in female labour force participation in Q1 of 2021.
15 From the outset of the pandemic, the gender gap issue was immediately addressed by Elena Bonetti, Minister for Families and Equal Opportunities; see: "Women for a New Renaissance" (2020) and "The National Strategy for Gender Equality" (2021): http://www.pariopportunita.gov.it/news/pari-opportunita-bonetti-presentata-la-strategia-nazionale-per-la-parita-di-genere-2021-2026/.

4.3 Conclusion

The year 2020 marked a turning point in terms of infrastructure investment in Italy. Foremost, notwithstanding the pandemic, investment has not decreased thanks to measures adopted during the previous two years. Furthermore, the conviction (in Italy and Europe) that investment is needed for promoting growth and as a tool for maintaining the essential resilience needed to face other fundamental challenges (the environment, for example) has been strengthened as a consequence of the pandemic. Therefore, the growing investment trend set in motion in the first months of 2020, before the COVID-19 outbreak, was also the result of measures taken since 2018. From a qualitative and quantitative stance, 2020 marked a break from the previous "austerity-led" decade. The national programming agenda went from a policy approach focused on current spending and the compression of capital expenditure to a strategy based on growth-oriented infrastructure investment, geared toward the newly established objectives of energy and digital transition. The pandemic, with its recessionary effects on the economic system, stimulated this trend, and led to the current PNRR where investment is explicitly oriented towards a green and digital transition.

The PNRR also contains a seminal strategy for "restoring" the Italian economy and a specific focus on economic convergence and territorial cohesion for the south and the rest of the country. As already stated, inverting the tendency toward increasing the north-south divide is one of the primary objectives of the PNRR: the gap has existed since 1861, when Italy became a nation state, but it has gotten worse in recent years, especially since the economic and financial crisis of 2008–09.[16] The average per capita investment in infrastructure in the "Mezzogiorno" over the past decade was around €780, which is 17% less than the €940 per capita average in the north-central area.[17] The absence of impactful growth-oriented policies has thrust this part of the country down the path of economic stagnation and constant deindustrialisation. It is no coincidence that Southern Italy is one of the most economically depressed areas in the European Union (Senato della Repubblica 2018). Even before the outbreak of the pandemic in 2019, the Conte II government, aware of the problem, formulated an *ad hoc* plan aimed

---

16   For further details on the north-south divide, see the data provided by Svimez (http://lnx.svimez. info/svimez/), a research centre established in 1946 for the purpose of studying the economy of the "Mezzogiorno". It publishes annual reports and other studies on the north-south divide.

17   See a recent study by the Bank of Italy (Bucci et al. 2021) based on CPT 2020 data. This study is also a seminal analysis of the infrastructure endowment by region: from infrastructure for transport (road and rail) to infrastructure for telecommunications, from the quality and types of services provided for water and energy to essential public services like healthcare and waste management. Reducing the north-south infrastructure gap was one of the declared objectives of delegation law n.42 in 2009 on fiscal federalism. It is an objective that exists only on paper, since nothing has been done in all these years to bridge the infrastructure gaps, albeit this is partially due to budget cuts and a lack of explicit measures and data on the infrastructural gaps. The PNRR could finally be the means through which to enact a specific strategy.

at countering and addressing the critical issues afflicting the south.[18] The sustained effort to redirect Italy's economic trajectory, characterised by low growth and increasing inequalities, is particularly evident in the PNRR's allocation of funds for the south. In fact, around 40% of the PNRR's resources (approximately €82 bn) will go to the eight regions that make up the "Mezzogiorno". According to the PNRR, this funding is pivotal to the south's economic development—in fact, its share of GDP is forecasted to increase to 23.4% in 2026. This is a significant objective given that, currently, the south accounts for 34% of the overall population, but it contributes to only 22% of Italy's GDP. Moreover, in addition to the funds allocated by the PNRR, another €58 bn will be provided by the Development and Cohesion Fund (DCF), €54 bn by the 2021–27 Structural Funds, €8.4 bn by React-EU, and another €9.4 bn by the planned investment in the Salerno-Reggio Calabria railway line. Despite the flow of funds, there are also many risks that the convergence objectives will not be achieved. To begin with, the Plan lacks a precise breakdown of investment by territory for each mission and component.[19] In addition, there are no clear criteria for allocating the resources, which creates the tangible risk that funds could be diverted, including for the south, to projects and networks that already exist and need to be completed, rather than to areas in which investment (especially social investment) needs to be created from scratch in order to generate the inclusion and development necessary for lasting and generative growth. It is also important to note a further risk that many of the resources will be allocated through incentive mechanisms for firms; however, the existing firms who are in a position to benefit from them prevail in the richest regions of the country. Another risk is the fact that many of the resources will be allocated through public procurement. It is not unreasonable to hypothesise that in the weaker areas, like the "Mezzogiorno", the local administrations will not be sufficiently equipped for these projects and could remain outside the allocation of the resources mechanism. The PNRR's impact on the "Mezzogiorno" will depend on its implementation. On this, the Minister for the South, Mara Carfagna, has stated on numerous occasions that every effort will be made to guarantee that Southern Italy receives at least 40% of the PNRR's resources.[20]

---

18   The plan, drawn up by Giuseppe Provenzano, Minister for the south, is called PianoSud2030 (Plan for the South 2030); it envisages a strategic investment programme of €21 bn over a three-year period, from 2021 to 2023, through national budgetary funds and the recovery of the last round of financing from the Development and Cohesion Fund and the European Structural Funds. The Plan also counts on new funds from the EU Programming for 2021–27 of approximately €123 bn for Southern Italy through the same instruments. The mission of PianoSud2030 has been partially absorbed by the National Recovery and Resilience Plan. https://www.governo.it/sites/new.governo.it/files/PianoSUD2030.pdf.

19   A precise and binding allocation of resources at the territorial level for the "Mezzogiorno" exists only in 33 of the 133 different types of investment and in 5 from the Complementary Fund. According to certain estimates, it amounts to approximately €23 bn, a bit more than one fourth of the overall resources (€82 bn) allocated for the "Mezzogiorno". See Crf Viesti (2021a; 2021b).

20   In July 2021, an article was hinged to the "simplification" decree (D.L of 31 May 2021, no. 77) guaranteeing Southern Italy 40% of the total funds to be allocated through the PNRR.

In a nutshell, the actual implementation of the PNRR will depend on the governance mechanism and on the decision-making process that a multilevel government, as is the case for Italy, must undertake in defining public policies through consultation and coordination between the State, regions, and municipalities. Part 3 of the PNRR is dedicated to implementation and monitoring, and refers to a series of dispositions that must be adopted on governance. As we write this chapter, some of the measures have just been approved or are in the process of being defined.

The "simplification" decree (D.L. of 31 May 2021 no. 77, adopted into law in July 2021) first of all contains a series of measures that should simplify the planning phase, allocation of resources, implementation of projects, and definition of the Plan's governance. More specifically, a steering committee acting as a "control room" has been established, chaired by the President of the Italian Council of Ministers, in which the relevant ministers and undersecretaries participate depending on the issues being discussed. It is essentially a variable-geometry mechanism. Others can be invited to join the meetings, such as the President of the Conference of Regions and/or of the Municipalities. Even more important is the provision whereby the President of the Council is substituted in the case of delays or non-compliance by other organs or institutions of the public administration. The decree also includes simplification measures that affect some of the sectors covered by the National Reform Programme (including ecological transition, public works, and digitalisation), in order to facilitate their complete implementation.

To conclude, for Italy, the main challenge will be to utilise PNRR funds effectively and break free from a past characterised by poor performance in managing public infrastructural investment. Italy, as one of the main beneficiaries of the NGEU, has an important role in ensuring its success. If the resources provided effectively boost investment and promote convergence and growth in Italy, the NGEU will have been a success and it will have provided a significant contribution to European integration.

References

Agenzia per la Coesione Territoriale (2019) *Nucleo di Verifica e Controllo, Area 3 Monitoraggio dell'attuazione della politica di coesione e Sistema Conti Pubblici Territoriali, Relazione Annuale CPT 2019*, Politiche nazionali e politiche di sviluppo a livello territoriale, CPT Temi, Roma, https://www.agenziacoesione.gov.it/wp-content/uploads/2019/11/Temi_11_Rap portoCPT_2019.pdf.

Agenzia per la Coesione Territoriale (2020) *Nucleo di Verifica e Controllo, Area 3 Monitoraggio dell'attuazione della politica di coesione e Sistema Conti Pubblici Territoriali, Relazione Annuale CPT 2020*, Politiche nazionali e politiche di sviluppo a livello territoriale, CPT Temi, Roma, https://www.agenziacoesione.gov.it/wp-content/uploads/2020/12/Relazione_annuale_ CPT_2020_Politiche_naz_svil.pdf.

Banca d'Italia (2021), *Proiezioni Macroeconomiche Per L'economia Italiana*, June 11, https://www.bancaditalia.it/pubblicazioni/proiezioni-macroeconomiche/2021/Proiezioni-Macroeconomiche-Italia-giugno-2021.pdf.

Bucci, M., E. Gennari, G. Ivaldi, G. Messina and R. Moller (2021) *I divari infrastrutturali in Italia: una misurazione caso per caso*, Questioni di Economia e Finanza (Occasional Papers) n. 635, Banca d'Italia, https://www.bancaditalia.it/pubblicazioni/qef/2021-0635/QEF_635_21.pdf.

Camera dei Deputati e Senato della Repubblica (2021) *Il Piano Nazionale di Ripresa e Resilienza— Schede di lettura NN. 06, N. 219*, Servizio studi, 27 maggio 2021, http://documenti.camera.it/leg18/dossier/pdf/DFP28.pdf.

Cerniglia, F. and F. Rossi (2020), "Public Investment Trends across Levels of Government in Italy". In F. Cerniglia and F. Saraceno (eds) *A European Public Investment Outlook*. Cambridge: Open Book Publishers, pp. 63–81, https://doi.org/10.11647/obp.0222.04.

European Commission (2021) *Summer 2021 Economic Forecast: Reopening Fuels Recovery*, European Economy, Institutional Paper 156, https://ec.europa.eu/info/sites/default/files/economy-finance/ip156_en.pdf

Franco, D. (2021) *Dichiarazione del ministro Franco sul PNRR con i colleghi di Francia, Germania e Spagna*, Ministero dell'Economia e delle finanze, Roma, 28 aprile, www.mef.gov.it.

ISTAT (2020) *Livelli di istruzione e ritorni occupazionali. Anno 2019*, Istituto Nazionale di Statistica, Roma, https://www.istat.it/it/files//2020/07/Livelli-di-istruzione-e-ritorni-occupazionali.pdf.

ISTAT (2021a) *Conto trimestrale delle Amministrazioni Pubbliche, reddito e risparmio delle famiglie e profitti delle società*, Istituto Nazionale di Statistica, Roma, https://www.istat.it/it/files//2021/04/comunicato-QSA-2020Q4.pdf.

ISTAT (2021b) *Rapporto Annuale 2021. La situazione del paese*, Istituto Nazionale di Statistica, Roma, https://www.istat.it/storage/rapporto-annuale/2021/Rapporto_Annuale_2021.pdf.

ISTAT (2021c) *Indicatori territoriali per le politiche di sviluppo*, Statistiche sez. indice, indicatori e dati Lavoro, Istituto Nazionale di Statistica, Roma, https://www.istat.it/storage/politiche-sviluppo/Lavoro.xls.

MEF (2020) *Nota di Aggiornamento al Documento di Economia e Finanza*, http://www.dt.mef.gov.it/modules/documenti_it/analisi_progammazione/documenti_programmatici/nadef_2020/NADEF_2020_Pub.pdf.

MEF (2021) *Documento di Economia e Finanza, Sezione 1—Programma di Stabilità*, http://www.dt.mef.gov.it/modules/documenti_it/analisi_progammazione/documenti_programmatici/def_2021/DEF_2021_PdS_15_04.pdf.

MEF (2021) *Le diseguaglianze di genere in Italia e il potenziale contributo del PNRR per ridurle*, July 9, https://www.mef.gov.it/focus/Le-diseguaglianze-di-genere-in-Italia-e-il-potenziale-contributo-del-PNRR-per-ridurle/.

OCPI (2021) *La ripresa degli investimenti pubblici*, Osservatorio sui Conti Pubblici Italiani, June, https://osservatoriocpi.unicatt.it/ocpi-pubblicazioni-la-ripresa-degli-investimenti-pubblici.

Presidenza del Consiglio dei Ministri (2021) *Piano Nazionale di Ripresa e Resilienza*, aprile 2021, https://www.governo.it/sites/governo.it/files/PNRR.pdf.

Senato della Repubblica (2018) *The Impact of Cohesion Policies in Europe and Italy*, Research Paper no. 11, Impact Assessment Office, https://www.senato.it/service/PDF/PDFServer/BGT/01083823.pdf.

SVIMEZ/ENBIC (2021) *Il lavoro nella pandemia: impatti e prospettive per persone, settori e territori*, Report 2021, http://lnx.svimez.info/svimez/wp-content/uploads/2021/06/REPORT-SVIMEZ-ENBIC.pdf.

Viesti, G. (2021a) *Il PNRR determinerà una ripresa dello sviluppo?*, Rivista il Mulino, giugno 2021, https://www.rivistailmulino.it/a/il-PNRR-determiner-una-ripresa-dello-sviluppo.

Viesti G. (2021b) *Gli investimenti del PNRR e del Fondo Complementare nel Mezzogiorno*, https://www.forumdisuguaglianzediversita.org/gli-investimenti-del-pnrr-e-del-fondo-complementare-nel-mezzogiorno/.

5. Public Investment in Poland

Adam Czerniak and Sebastian Płóciennik

Introduction

Nearly three decades of constant and relatively high economic growth has made it possible for Poland to initiate a catch-up with the most developed European economies. In 2000, GDP per capita amounted to less than €6500, representing only 29% of the average. Two decades later, in 2019, it reached €12,700, 48% of the average (Eurostat 2021a).

To continue this positive trend, Poland must fulfil several requirements—from a stable demographic situation, higher-level innovation, and efficient infrastructure to a better supply of public goods, like healthcare. One can hardly imagine a success in these areas without the government being ready to participate as a generous investor.

The purpose of this study is to analyse prospects for increasing the scale of public investment in Poland after the pandemic. It will indicate the most promising areas of the state's activity and the priorities of the current government in investment. Further, it will offer an overview of the conditions required for rising public investment, including growth prospects and macroeconomic environments, as well as fiscal capacities, labour market features, and effectiveness of governance. A special place will be devoted to a new opportunity for a significant increase in public investment, which is Next Generation EU (NGEU)—the European Union's programme aimed at combatting the long-term effects of the pandemic and the economic crisis.

The first part of the text is devoted to a short look at Poland's experience in the field of public investment, both in terms of past policies and in more recent quantitative developments. The second part of the text focuses on the conditions required for a boost in public investment. The third part covers the analysis of the National Recovery Plan (Krajowy Plan Odbudowy, KPO)—the Polish vision of how the funds offered under the NGEU should be utilised in the national economy.

5.1 Historical Background

The topic of public investment in Poland is not free from political associations and ideological debates. Historical experiences play a significant role here.

 https://doi.org/10.11647/OBP.0280.05

On the one hand, there is a strong collective memory of the role of the government's economic activity in recreating Polish statehood after the First World War. The challenge of sewing together the regions previously divided by borders required investment in transport infrastructure, of which the highlight was the seaport in Gdynia. Further achievements included the Central Industrial District (COP) in the south-east of the country, which aimed to create the economic backbone of the Second Republic (Grata 2019). The outbreak of the Second World War wiped out this promising effort.

The period after 1945—with the command economy and the communist state—is also a background for today's discussions on public investment, albeit mostly in a negative sense. One of the crucial experiences of this time was the attempt to accelerate the growth of state investment financed by foreign loans in the 1970s. This did not lead to the expected increase in productivity, but rather a huge foreign debt, which also contributed to the collapse of the economy (Komornicka 2020). A both overwhelming and ineffective state, the domination of a "dirty" heavy industry and low-quality public infrastructure of the communist era largely explains the support that Poles gave in the late 1980s to the shock transformation aimed at a rapid shift to a free market.

5.2 Turning Points

In the 1990s, the Polish economy entered a period of disinflation and budget constraints—conditions which are hardly favourable to public investment. The priorities of the post-communist transformation were the restructuring of the general governance sector and the acceleration of privatisation processes in areas previously treated as the sole domain of the state. The situation began to change in the second half of the 1990s, when economic growth significantly accelerated. Moreover, a far-reaching administrative reform was carried out and increased the role of local, self-government authorities in the economy. Across the last decades, the enlarged voivodeships and relatively autonomous districts and communes have undertaken around half of public investment (Figure 1). The reform was undoubtedly a turning point for public investment in post-communist Poland.

The next breakthrough came with the accession to the European Union in 2004. Poland gained access to huge community funds. This allowed for a systematic increase in the level of public investment, which was especially visible in the first Multiannual Financial Framework (6% in 2011—see Figure 2). The funds, combined with the means of central and local government, were allocated, e.g. to the development of previously neglected transport infrastructure. The inflow of capital through this channel has massively contributed to GDP growth and improved the competitiveness of Polish business. However, some experts have criticised the allocation key as being oriented too much towards the demand side in less developed regions, instead of boosting the growth potential of Poland (Gorzelak 2014).

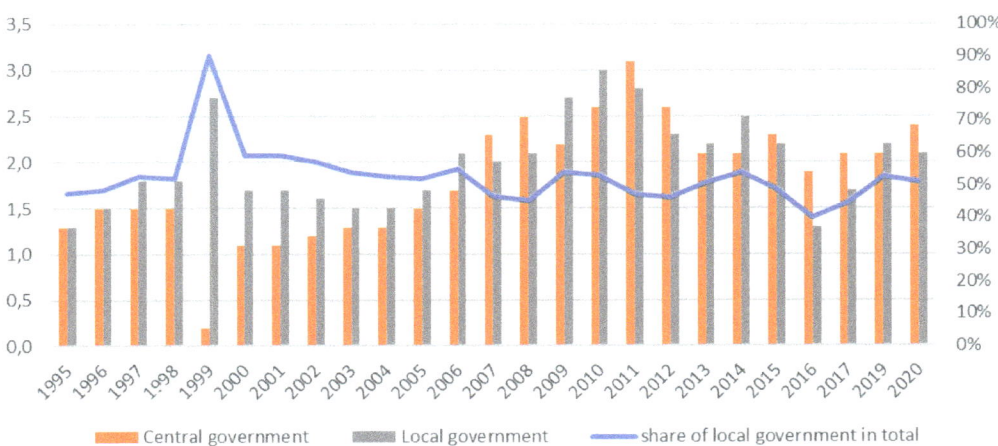

Fig. 1 Gross Fixed Capital Formation: Central Government and Local Government Expenditures as % of GDP, 1995–2020.

Source of data: Eurostat.

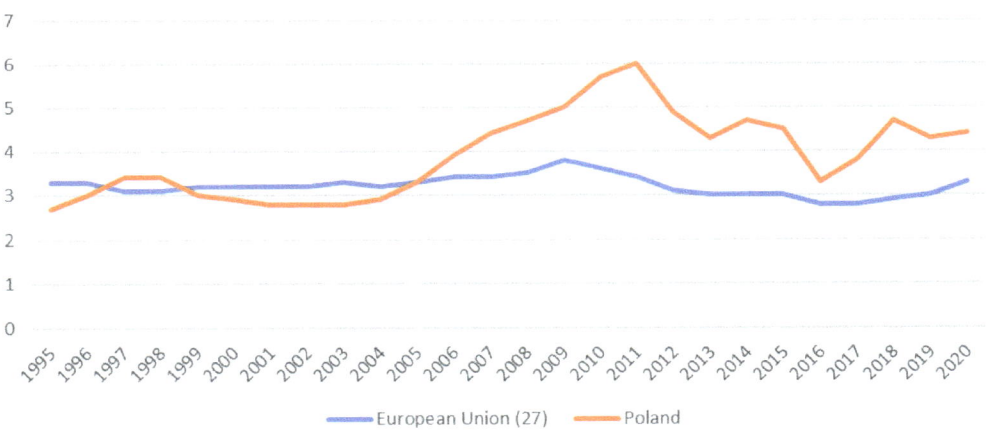

Fig. 2 Gross Fixed Capital Formation: General Government Expenditure in Poland and the European Union (27 Member States) as % of GDP, 1995–2020.

Source of data: Eurostat.

The third important moment for the public investment sphere in Poland was the financial and economic crisis, which began in 2008 and weakened the neoliberal bias dominating after 1989. Political elites began to the see the state's activity—more regulations, and involvement in the fight against the crisis—as a necessary precondition for a stable economic order. Thus, the government of the Civic Platform decided at that time in favour of a large fiscal stimulus. As part of this, large public projects emerged, like express inter-regional roads and the liquid-gas terminal in Świnoujście on the Baltic Sea. Afterwards, the crisis discussion about the rise of public investment continued. In the background stood the question of how to escape from the "dependent market economy" (Nölke and Vliegenthart 2009) to a more innovation-friendly system.

This line of thinking became mainstream when the United Right (Zjednoczona Prawica) came to power in 2015. One of the main goals of the new government was to accelerate the modernisation of the economy through large centrally-led projects. The Strategy for Responsible Development (Strategia na Rzecz Odpowiedzialnego Rozwoju, SOR; KPRM 2017), designed by the then-Minister of Finance Mateusz Morawiecki, has become the flagship declarative document. The government's plans included spectacular ideas that had not been seen since the 1970s: for the construction of a state-owned electric car factory (Izera), the dredging of the Vistula Spit—which is to allow the development of the port of Elbląg—and the construction of the Central Airport (CPK), a transport hub located near Warsaw.

The last important turning point for the sphere of public investment in Poland was the outbreak of the pandemic and the economic crisis in 2020. It strengthened the belief that in the face of an external shock and a massive fiscal expansion is necessary. The government did not hesitate to boost deficit spending to 7% of GDP in 2020 (according to Eurostat)—mainly in the form of protective programmes for enterprises and employees. However, the government also declared new public investment plans. Their determinants, size, and content will be presented below.

5.3 Determinants for Public Investment Increases

5.3.1 Investment Needs

Poland is still one of the poorest countries in the European Union. Despite rapid economic growth and substantial real convergence over the last quarter of a century, in 2020, GDP per capita in Poland was equal to €13,640—the fourth lowest level among the twenty-seven EU member states, and only 46% of the EU27 average. Many factors contributed to this outcome, of which path dependence (i.e., a very low starting point at the beginning of the transformation period) is most likely the dominant one. Putting aside the discussion on the past, it is best to focus on future possibilities and investment needs, since achieving high capital intensity and the capacity to innovate is the only way to sustain the process of real convergence in times of an ageing society. This, however, seems to be a problem for Poland, as the total investment rate has been decreasing steadily in recent years (MFiPR 2020), reaching an all-time low of 16.7% of GDP in 2020 (see Figure 3). Such a process happened despite the government goal to increase the total investment rate (private and public combined) above 20% of GDP, as explicitly expressed in the Strategy for Responsible Growth in 2017.

The decrease in propensity to invest was mostly seen among private entrepreneurs, who hoarded a record amount of savings and restrained from engaging in long-term and large-scale investment activity. Moreover, their willingness to invest in R&D endeavours aimed at increasing their future efficiency was also relatively low-standing,

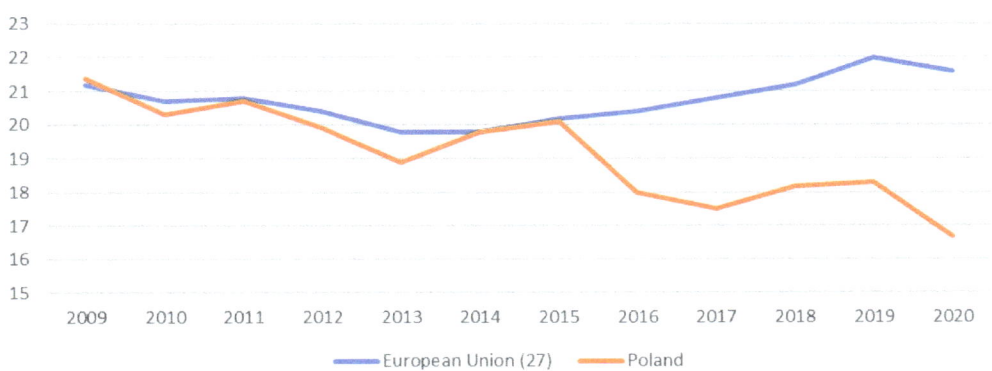

Fig. 3 Gross Fixed Capital Formation in Poland and the European Union as % of GDP, 2009–2020.
Source of data: Eurostat.

at 0.83% of GDP in 2019 as compared to 1.46% on average in the EU27. However, no consensus has emerged on the reasons for this outcome. Some economists point out the relatively high margins and low labour costs of Polish companies, which decrease the incentives to invest in more efficient and capital-intensive technologies. Others focus on rising business uncertainty after the Global Financial Crisis, amplified by the increasing labour shortages in Poland—which are connected to low labour activity, low retirement age, and an ageing society—discouraging entrepreneurs from large-scale investment in increasing output capacity. Another group of experts focuses more on aspects of the political economy after the change of government in 2015. They argue that a more redistributive model of social policy—along with higher uncertainty relating to fiscal burdens and the deterioration of the rule of law—deemed high investment activity as too risky for entrepreneurs, who must be prepared for an unexpected increase in the tax wedge, nationalisation attempts, and higher demand volatility. Some analyses also indicate that a lower investment rate is a natural side effect of the economic transformation, away from capital-intensive heavy industry towards a service-oriented economy dominated by small and medium enterprises. In our opinion, the truth lies somewhere in the middle, as each factor exhibits its impact on different groups of entrepreneurs, leading to a substantial decline in private investment activity that calls for urgent government action. Without action, there is a serious threat that the convergence process in Poland will come to a halt, as economic growth led solely by consumption will eventually generate excessive inflation and push Poland in the direction of economic turmoil.

The most urgent public investment needs are clearly pointed out in recently-published government documents—Strategy for Responsible Growth in 2017, Poland's Energy Policy adopted in 2021, the forthcoming healthcare strategy for 2021–27, and almost all of the National Recovery Plan and the Polish Deal (Polski Ład), drafted and presented by the governing party PIS (Law and Justice) in mid-May of 2021. After studying these documents, a clear-cut picture emerges. The most important issues that need to be addressed are the transformation of the energy sector, digitilisation of the economy, society and public administration, housing affordability, improvement of the quality and availability of the healthcare system, and modernisation of transport infrastructure, both through building new motorways and investing in railways. Solving these issues requires a coherent plan with multi-source financing, as the joint costs of all these ventures can be estimated at a mind-blowing amount of over one trillion PLN—to be spent over this decade. If these plans succeed and the government can satisfy its financing needs at a low interest, then the fulfilment of this changeover strategy will bring long-term benefits to the economy and society. However, there are plenty of pitfalls that need to be avoided in the process, especially connected to large-scale government projects, such as the plan to build a central airport hub in the crop fields of Central Poland.

5.3.2 Macroeconomic and Institutional Environment

The pandemic disrupted a long period of fast economic growth in Poland. The recessions triggered by lockdowns caused GDP to decline by 2.7% in 2020—relatively little compared to most EU countries. The mild course of the crisis is owed to the structure of the economy, of which key sectors are industrial branches and business-oriented services. The most vulnerable branches, like tourism, play a lesser role than in the southern EU member states.

The outlook for the post-pandemic rebound is very positive. According to the Spring Forecast of the European Commission, GDP growth is expected to accelerate to 4% in 2021 and 5.4% in 2022. High levels of savings, consumer confidence, and the expected rise of investment in the private sector create a solid base for recovery. An additional factor driving growth will be external demand, boosted by the also rebounding euro area economy (European Commission 2021a, p. 110).

Under these circumstances, inflation—already high before the pandemic—may pose a difficult challenge. In 2020, the HICP index increased by 3.7%. The European Commission predicted in the Spring Forecast that the indicator will reach 3.5% in 2021 and start falling slowly to 2.9% in 2022—more than twice what it is in the euro area (European Commission 2021a). There is a lively debate in Poland on how much this development is caused by temporary and external factors, and when the central bank should react by exiting from its ultra-expansionary monetary policy. Concerns about overheating the economy are on the rise and it may provoke questions if additional boosts in spending within the area of public investment make the problem worse.

The next determinant is the fiscal situation. The pandemic forced the Polish government to increase public spending. As a result, in 2020, the general government deficit amounted to 7% of GDP. In 2021, the situation should improve due to an increase in tax revenues and lower expenditure on "shields" for enterprises. In 2022, the indicator should already have dropped below 3%. Despite a clear deterioration of the fiscal situation, Poland still meets the public debt criterion. In 2020, the debt level increased to 57.5%, but by 2022 it should drop to 55%. There is not so much spending space left to reach the warning thresholds written in the law, which foresees austere measures against further rise of debt. In the context of higher public investment, there is a lively debate about a possible revision of the legal framework for the fiscal policy in Poland towards more permissive rules.

The labour market situation also constitutes a potential limit for the boost of public investment. Poland has spectacularly low unemployment levels— with a level of 3.2% in 2020, it belongs to best performing countries in the EU. Even considering the near completion of aid programmes launched during the pandemic, unemployment levels should not, according to the European Commission, exceed 3.5% in the next two years. However, a potential emerging problem may be a deficit in workforce and the fast rise of wages, which could further boost the already high inflation levels. Political constraints on immigration, as well as a quickly deteriorating demographic situation (with an expected two-million drop in population by 2040; Eurostat 2021b), combined with the low retirement age, will not make the situation easier. Under these circumstances, public investment plans may face the problem of quickly rising labour costs or even a lack of sufficient workforce to achieve its goals.

Finally, the factor which should be taken into account when increasing public investment is the effectiveness of the administration in preparing projects, organising tenders, and controlling the spending of funds. A good point of reference for the assessment of this criteria is the ability to absorb EU funds. Luckily, Poland does not look substandard in comparison with other member states. According to the Multiannual Financial Framework 2007–16, it performed slightly better than the EU average, and the rate of absorption was higher than in neighbouring countries (the Czech Republic, Hungary, Slovakia, and Germany; Darvas 2020).

5.4 The National Recovery Plan

5.4.1 General Information

The National Recovery Plan (Krajowy Plan Odbudowy—KPO) is the Polish agenda for disbursing EU funds from the Recovery and Resilience Facility (RFF). Poland's allocation from the RFF is €34.6 bn, out of which €23.9 bn comes in the form of subsidies and €10.8 bn in the form of loans granted within the RFF to Poland. This translates into ca. 156 bn PLN of funds (6.7% of GDP per year from 2020) that should be disbursed until 2026. According to the KPO, the majority will be used to increase public investment (87.1 bn PLN) and the rest to stimulate private gross fixed capital formation (68.9 bn PLN). As shown in Figure 4, the government wants to start injecting the EU funds into the Polish economy as early as 2021, and expects the expenses to peak between

2023–25. In our opinion, this process will be delayed, as at the time of writing (August 2021), the KPO has not yet been accepted by the European Commission, minimising the probability that money will reach the real economy before early 2022.

Table 1 National Recovery Plan Funds by Purpose and Expected Year of Disbursement, 2020–26, in bn PLN.

	2020	**2021**	**2022**	**2023**	**2024**	**2025**	**2026**	**2020–2026**
Public investment	0.0	1.9	12.9	20.7	19.3	20.9	11.4	87.1
Private investment	0.7	2.3	9.8	14.6	14.7	13.4	13.4	68.9
TOTAL	**0.7**	**4.2**	**22.7**	**35.3**	**34**	**34.3**	**24.8**	**156**

Source of data: Ministry of Finance, 2021.

The start date of the disbursement of EU funds is additionally uncertain due to several inconsistencies between the KPO and the European Commission's policy agenda, including the European Semester. There are also some doubts whether the disbursement of the funds properly addresses the requirement to spend at least 37% of the funds on Green New Deal projects and at least 20% on acceleration of the digitilisation process.

These incoherencies can be traced back to the eclectic mode of preparation. The Polish government began to write the KPO in July 2020 (Klub Jagielloński 2021). In theory, the process was coordinated by the Ministry of Funds and Regional Policy, which is responsible for spending EU funds in Poland, but in practice it became a process of multilateral struggles between various ministries to get the biggest chunk of the funds, with the Minister of Economic Development being in the leader's seat. Eventually, the Prime Minister's Chancellery took over the coordination of the process and decided case-by-case which projects to include in the KPO.

This process transformed the KPO into a collection of bottom-drawer legislatives, i.e., various ideas from ministries, state agencies, state-owned companies, and local governments that had been put aside due to lack of funding. Many of them were of poor quality or based on unrealistic assumptions. It was only at the final stage that they were combined into larger sets of initiatives, but still requiring better coherence and a stronger link to the RFF agenda.

Eventually, in the autumn of 2020, the Prime Minister's Chancellery arranged the KPO agenda into a plan matrix and, after a period of internal consultations, it will open the discussion to social partners and the general public at the end of February 2021. After some minor amendments, the National Recovery Plan was approved by parliament in May 2021. The final version of the KPO consists of five main parts (or components): (A) resilience and economic competitiveness (B) green energy and lower energy consumption (C) digital transformation (D) efficiency, availability, and quality of the healthcare system, and (E) green and smart mobility.

5.4.2 Five Components of the National Recovery Plan

Resilience and economic competitiveness (€4.7 bn)

This is the most general part of the plan. It consists of policies from various institutional areas (e.g., the labour market, housing, and social protection) that should help the economy to recover from the pandemic. The first element of this component (A1) consists of measures that are aimed at reducing the impact of COVID-19 and the effects of the crisis on enterprises to the amount of more than €2 bn. Companies are the major direct beneficiaries of this element, but some public investment is also planned, including money for preparing land for greenfield investment and financing for the acceleration of spatial planning. In the second element (A2), activities for the development of the national innovation system are grouped. Although most of the €500 m earmarked for this purpose is to go to companies, there are also public projects here, such as the construction of a museum of architecture and design in Krakow. The third element (A3) is aimed at improving education and the lifelong learning system to match the skills of employees with what is needed within the economy. This part also covers a plan to spend €500 m on the creation of 120 industry vocational skills and career guidance centres, so as to promote education and training in general. The last element (A4) contains an increase in the structural adjustment, efficiency, and crisis resilience of the labour market. An important goal is to increase the professional activity of women, part of which involves investment in nurseries and daycare centres, especially outside large urban areas (€400 m). Significant amounts are also earmarked for improving the operation of employment offices and e-administration. In the loan part, €150 m will be earmarked for increasing the use of satellite data—for instance, for monitoring weather risks. The government also plans reforms to strengthen the stability and transparency of public finances, reduce the regulatory burden, and increase the role of public consultation in law-making.

Green energy and reduction of energy consumption (€14.5 bn)

This KPO component coincides with the EU's long-term financial perspective and the Just Transition Fund, which is aimed at helping communities affected by coal mining closures. The overall goal in this area is to transform key sectors of the economy to a low-carbon model, while maintaining competitiveness and energy security. The plan consists of three elements. The first (B1), worth €3.2 bn, is the improvement of energy efficiency. Much attention has been paid to supporting the transition to a less energy-intensive mix of heat generation in residential buildings. As far as the sphere of public investment is concerned, the most important thing is the thermal modernisation of schools envisaged in the plan. The second part (B2) focuses on increasing the use of renewable energy sources. A considerable amount of funds has been allocated to the development of transmission networks, development of hydrogen technologies, and intelligent infrastructure increasing energy consumption efficiency. By the end of 2024, an installation terminal for the construction of offshore wind farms is to be built and launched, and by 2026, offshore farms with a capacity of 2.6 GW and electrolysers to produce green hydrogen with a capacity of 400 MW will be completed. The last element (B3) includes activities aimed at adapting the Polish economy to climate change and limiting environmental devastation. It is planned, amongst other things, that degraded and post-industrial areas will be revitalised, including the cleaning of the bottom of the Baltic Sea. Additional funds will be allocated to facilitate the creation of "green" cities, e.g., those with limited traffic. Loans will be used to finance—in addition to offshore wind energy farms—green urban transformation, including "green multifamily housing". The government is planning to establish a Green Urban Transformation Fund co-managed by local governments. The loan component also includes support for sustainable water management in rural areas.

Digital transformation (€4.9 bn)

Poland will allocate 20.9% of the funds to digital transformation—only 0.9 pp more than the minimum set by the European Commission. That is, in our opinion, an important deficiency of the plan, as there are significant deficits in the field of digital competence in society and in the computerisation of state institutions in Poland. The first element of this component (C1) is aimed at improving access to high-speed internet (>30 Mb/s), with a goal of increasing the proportion of households that have such access from around 65% to more than 80% in 2026. In this element, state support for private investment activity is planned, especially in regions with lower population density. For example, the loan component will help to finance the construction of 5G networks by telecommunication companies. In turn, element C2 focuses on the development of digital services, also within public administration and between businesses, society, and the state. For example, the introduction of dozens of new e-services (e.g., e-invoicing and the digitalisation of construction permits) by public institutions is a planned development, as well as the creation of new communication platforms. Significant funds are to be spent on expanding the digital infrastructure of schools and improving teachers' competence, which should result in an increase in the overall level of digital skills in society. The last part of this component (C3) is devoted to investment in increasing digital security.

Efficiency, accessibility, and quality of the healthcare system (€4.5 bn)

This component is compliant with the Polish Deal—the government's newly published economic and social policy programmet—that also prioritises the improvement of healthcare services. The basis for reforms and investment in both documents is the Polish healthcare strategy for 2021–27. The EU funds will be used to expand the public healthcare infrastructure, especially in oncology, psychiatry, and geriatric care, and to digitise healthcare and provide financial support for the education of medical students. The government also wants to finance the development of medical research and the pharmaceutical industry—for example, by creating a research centre for epidemic safety in Poland. The loan component will be used to facilitate the development of the pharmaceutical sector, primarily the production of active substances—manufacturers will be able to apply for €300 m in loans. Initially, the government wanted to finance the purchase of COVID-19 vaccines (€1.4 bn) using RRF funds, but they were forced by the European Commission to drop this idea.

Green and smart mobility (€7.3 bn)

In this component, the government plans, amongst other things, to promote a low-carbon economy in private companies and zero-emission public transport—in part, due to the approaching Fit for 55—and aims to cover the costs of the sector with ETS. There is, for example, over €1 bn's worth of funds available for the purchase of EV buses and an additional €200 m for the purchase of new trams. Over half of the funds will be used to develop the Polish network of railway transport, including the modernisation of railway lines, purchases of new passenger rolling stock, and the construction of intermodal terminals. The government has also pledged to rewrite the e-mobility roadmap and increase the competitiveness of railways by reducing fees for access to infrastructure (charged by the railway network company PKP PLK). Almost all the expenses in this part of the plan will be procured by local governments.

5.4.3 Macroeconomic Impact of the National Recovery Plan

The disbursement of the funds according to the National Recovery Plan will have both direct and indirect effects on the economy. In the short term, it will stimulate aggregate demand and, through multiplier effects, increase employment, GDP, and tax income, speeding up the economic recovery. On the other hand, the programme might also lead to an increase in inflation, as companies are having supply-side problems with satisfying the fast-increasing demand, which provides incentives to increase prices in the wake of full capacity utilisation. In the long term, the disbursement of EU funds can stimulate the growth of the potential output by increasing the amount of working-age population in good health as well as boosting total factor productivity, thanks to higher energy efficiency, lower bureaucratic burden, and better labour skills.

According to baseline economic simulations of the Ministry of Finance, as presented to the European Commission in the regular update of the Convergence Programme (Ministry of Finance 2021), in the short term the implementation of the KPO will increase the real GDP level by 1.2% in 2024, compared to the baseline scenario without additional spending.

In the first three years of using the funds, the real economic growth rate will increase by an average of 0.56 pp compared to the baseline scenario. In 2027, the GDP level will be 1.3% higher than in the baseline scenario presented in the plan. The implementation of the KPO will also have a positive impact on the labour market. It is estimated that, after two years, 0.3% more jobs will be created, and after five years of using the funds in line with the KPO project, the number of jobs created will increase by 0.4% compared to the baseline scenario (see Table 2).

Table 2 Macroeconomic Impact of the National Recovery Plan

	2024	2027	2042
	difference to the no-policy change scenario		
GDP	+1.2%	+1.3%	+1.9%
Employment	+0.3%	+0.4%	+1.3%
General government balance	+0.3%	+0.3%	+0.9%

Source of data: Authors' own assumptions based on Ministry of Finance 2021 calculations.

The long-term effects (i.e., twenty years after the beginning of the programme) of using funds from the RFF are related mainly to reforms and investment in green transformation, digital transformation, and the healthcare system. Moreover, as the RFF will be distributed across the European Union, it will translate into the greater economic growth of Poland's main trade partners (on average, +0.9 in the EU27, according to the European Commission; European Commission 2020), boosting the external demand for goods produced in Poland. The Ministry of Finance estimates that introducing the KPO will yield a 1.9% higher GDP over the long term than in the baseline scenario. Of these, 1.3 pp will be the result of high labour supply and better matching of workers' skills (translating into lower natural unemployment rate), and the remaining 0.6 pp will result from the accumulation of productive capital.

In the long term, the main factors supporting Poland's economic growth under the influence of KPO, apart from the increase in productivity, will be favourable changes in the population resulting from the improvement of the efficiency, availability, and quality of the healthcare system, and the increase in labour market activity. According to the Ministry of Finance's forecast, the population in 2042 will increase by 303,000 inhabitants, and the economic activity rate will increase by 0.9 pp compared to the baseline scenario. As a result, along with the increasing qualifications of employees and the demand for labour, employment is expected to increase by 1.3% compared to the baseline scenario in the horizon of twenty years.

According to the European Commission, the disbursement of grants from the RRF will have a neutral impact on the public deficit path of EU member states (European Commission 2021b). In the case of debt, grant flows may have a temporary negative impact due to the mismatch in cash expenditure and receipts over time. In line with these assumptions, the Ministry of Finance expects that, despite some minor short-term negative effects, the KPO will increase the general government balance due to higher tax incomes and lower expenditure needs from domestic funds. In total, the public deficit will be reduced by 0.3 pp in the short term and 0.9 pp in the long term, providing additional fiscal space to stimulate the economy in times of a slowdown, making Poland more resilient to negative external shocks.

5.5 Conclusion

The long-term investment plans of the Polish government are ambitious. If they are accomplished, both society and the economy will benefit, as real convergence will be sustained, the adaptation to the new climate policy will be faster, and private investment outlays will flourish, being made more attractive by high infrastructure quality, low transaction costs, and a skilled labour force. However, there are many pitfalls that need to be avoided—there is the risk of overheating the economy in the case of demand growing too quickly, the risk of engaging in investment projects that are deemed to fail (as it is constantly the case with motorway construction contracts in Poland), and finally there is the risk of over-politicising the investment process, which in our opinion might be the biggest risk, taking into account the polarisation of the Polish political scene and the partisan cycle it induces (i.e. consecutive periods of radical policy U-turns).

Moreover, there are also some intrinsic risks stemming from the weaknesses of the current programmes, especially the National Recovery Plan. Its text exhibits a lack of significant measures to increase the economic activity of the elderly and the disabled, and it leaves us with doubts regarding the achievability of the goals in society's "digital" activation. For example, providing wider access to education does not always translate into the improvement of skills, if proper incentives and nudges are not provided simultaneously. In turn, long-term effects of the KPO are strongly dependent on the way in which the available money will be spent. As the disbursement of EU budget funds shows, the selection of qualified projects—as well as tender design—can largely affect the quality and adequacy of public investment outlays. There is also a political risk the KPO is exposed to. In the event of an escalation of disputes with the European Commission over the rule of law, access to funds may be suspended—which would mean immeasurable economic damage.

References

Darvas, Z. (2020) "Will European Union Countries Be Able to Absorb and Spend Well the Bloc's Recovery Funding?" *BlogPost Bruegel* (24.9.2020), https://www.bruegel.org/2020/09/will-european-union-countries-be-able-to-absorb-and-spend-well-the-blocs-recovery-funding/ .

European Commission (2020) *European Economic Forecast, Autumn 2020*, https://doi.org/10.2765/878338 .

European Commission (2021a) *European Economic Forecast, Spring 2021*, https://ec.europa.eu/economy_finance/forecasts/2021/spring/ecfin_forecast_spring_2021_pl_en.pdf .

European Commission (2021b) *Debt Sustainability Monitor 2020*, https://ec.europa.eu/info/publications/debt-sustainability-monitor-2020_en .

Eurostat (2021a) *Real GDP per Capita*, https://ec.europa.eu/eurostat/databrowser/view/sdg_08_10/default/table?lang=en .

Eurostat (2021b) *Europop 2019: Population Projections at National Level 2019–2100*, https://ec.europa.eu/eurostat/databrowser/view/proj_19np/default/table?lang=en .

Grata, P. (2019) "Central Industrial District as an Attempt to Implement the Principles of Sustainable Development in the Inter-War Period Poland", *European Journal of Sustainable Development* 8(5), European Center of Sustainable Development: 137, https://doi.org/10.14207/ejsd.2019.v8n5p137 .

Komornicka, A. (2020) "From 'Economic Miracle' to the 'Sick Man of the Socialist Camp': Poland and the West in the 1970s", *European Socialist Regimes' Fateful Engagement with the West: National Strategies in the Long 1970s*, 78–106. Taylor and Francis, https://doi.org/10.4324/9780429340703-5 .

KPRM (2017) *Strategia Na Rzecz Odpowiedzialnego Rozwoju Do 2020 (z Perspektywą Do 2030 r.)*, https://www.gov.pl/documents/33377/436740/SOR.pdf .

MFiPR (2020) *Raport: Inwestycje w Polsce. Okres: I Kw. 2018—4 Kw. 2019*, https://www.ewaluacja.gov.pl/media/93243/DSR_Raport_Inwestycje2018_IV2019_web2.pdf .

Ministry of Finance (2021) *Convergence Programme 2021 Update*, https://www.gov.pl/web/finance/convergence-programme .

Nölke, A. and A. Vliegenthart (2009) "Enlarging the Varieties of Capitalism: The Emergence of Dependent Market Economies in East Central Europe", *World Politics* 61 (4): 670–702, https://doi.org/10.1017/S0043887109990098 .

6. Trends and Patterns in Public Investment in Spain

An Update

José Villaverde and Adolfo Maza

Introduction

After a good deal of both theoretical and empirical analysis on the issue, it is pretty obvious that there is a general consensus about the positive effects of public investment on the economy (for a recent survey, see Bom and Ligthart 2014). GDP, employment, and private investment trends are closely related to that of public investment, although the value of the corresponding multipliers is still a matter of certain debate. As is well known, it depends on a number of factors such as, for instance, the level of development and the stage of the economic cycle (for an analysis on influential factors, see, e.g., Gechert 2015). This direct and positive link between public investment and, amongst other things, the three aforementioned macrovariables, becomes particularly important in times of economic crisis, such as during the Great Recession of 2008 and the current COVID-19 pandemic.

In this update of our previous paper (Villaverde and Maza 2020), we pay attention to the key characteristics related to the evolution of public investment in Spain between 2000 and 2020. Specifically, although we have to admit the data is very scant and the period still too short, in Section 6.1 we focus our attention on the new economic crisis unleashed by the pandemic and, more precisely, try to shed some light on its effects on public investment. In the next part of the paper, Section 6.2, we make a brief reference to what Next Generation EU funds may imply for public investment in the country. Finally, in Section 6.3, we present the main conclusions from our research.

6.1. Public Investment in Spain: 2000–20

When evaluating the relevance and evolution of anything (be this a plant, an animal, an idea or an economic variable), the judgement critically depends on what or who we

https://doi.org/10.11647/OBP.0280.06

are comparing with. As for economic variables in the case of Spain, it seems natural to start, very briefly, by comparing them with those of Spain's main partners and competitors, namely the EU countries.

According to its GDP, Spain is (after Germany, France, and Italy) the fourth largest economy in the EU, fifth before Brexit took place. In terms of public investment specifically, it is also the fourth European economy, and although its evolution from 2000 onwards has followed a similar path to that of the average of the EU, there is no doubt that it has also experienced much larger fluctuations. This is indeed true for each one of the three main subperiods we can split the period of 2000–19 into and, to a certain extent, for the year 2020. During the expansion period 2000–08, Spain registered, in 2015 constant prices, one of the highest increases in public investment among the EU countries, a rate (about 6% per year) much higher than that of both the EU and Eurozone averages (2.7%). The Global Financial Crisis that hit the EU, and the whole world, in 2008 and successive years had a very negative impact on Spanish public investment. More precisely, with a fall of around 12% per year between 2008 (€46.2 bn) and 2014 (€22.6 bn), Spain was, by far, the country that suffered the deepest decline among the big four. Not only this, but it also experienced a much larger drop than the EU and Eurozone (the annual drop was 3.2 and 2.1%, respectively). In 2014, however, the economic situation in Spain began to improve at a greater speed than in the EU; this is most probably the reason why Spanish public investment between 2014 and 2019 not only returned to positive rates of growth (see further below), but also its growth rate was, on average, much higher than that of the EU. Although quite understandable, the pro-cyclical performance of Spanish public investment is counterproductive in terms of stability, as this variable is supposed to play, at least in cases of severe recessions, an anti-cyclical role to limit the pressures from the economic cycle. Fortunately, and as stressed later on, this seems to be the case in the year 2020, when the health, social, and economic crisis hit the country most acutely.

The aforementioned pro-cyclical role of public investment is depicted in Figure 1. As can be seen, public investment (measured in bn euros, 2015) exhibited a relatively steady upward path from 2000 to 2009, declined sharply from then to 2014, and has remained relatively stable afterwards. There are, however, two relevant exceptions to this pro-cyclical path. The first one refers to 2009: although this is a year of clear, huge recession in Spain, public investment grew even more rapidly than in previous years, most likely as a government's attempt to reduce the depth of the crisis that erupted in 2008. The second exception refers precisely to 2020, the year of the COVID-19 outbreak, in which the Spanish government also tried to soften the effects of the pandemic on both GDP and employment. As depicted in the green line of Figure 1, the public-to-total (P/T) ratio grew very sharply, much more than in any other year of our sample period, both in 2009 and 2020.

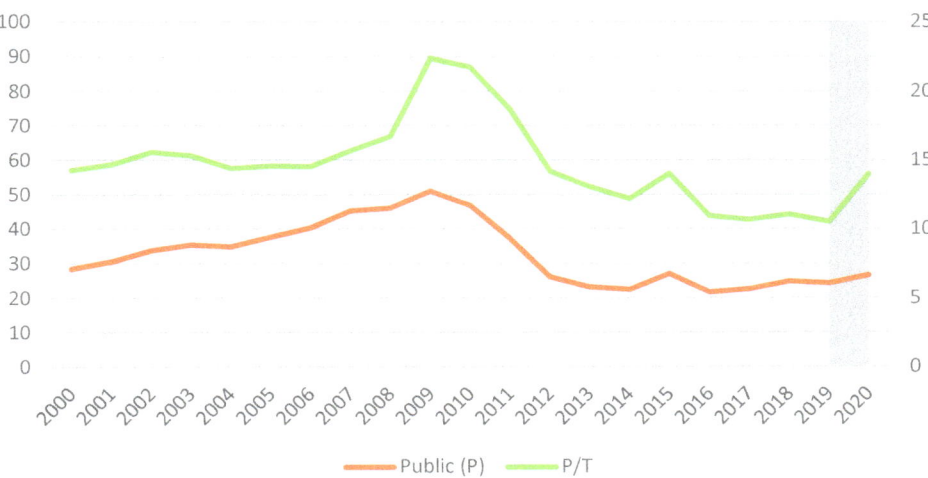

Fig. 1 Public Investment.

Source of data: AMECO database. Figure created by the authors.

Note: Public investment is given in 2015 € bn. The ratio P/T is measured (in pp) on the right-hand axis.

Be that as it may, the pro-cyclical role of public investment in Spain can be seen even more clearly in Figure 2, in which the period under consideration has been split into expansion and contraction subperiods. Concerning the expansion ones and in line with previous comments, it is observed that public investment grew at a very high rate (6% per year) between 2000 and 2008 and, once again, although at a much lower one (1.5% on an annual basis), between 2014 and 2019. As for the contraction subperiods, it is shown that, despite the significant growth in 2009 noted above, public investment experienced a severe decline during the 2008–14 subperiod, with an average yearly rate of -11.5%. The revival of public investment in 2020, with an increase of 9.5%, effectively illustrates, and confirms, the second exception to the pro-cyclical tendency mentioned in the previous paragraph.

To conclude with the public investment evolution, we think another additional trait needs to be highlighted: expressed in 2015 constant euros, public investment in Spain declined over the 2000–20 period at an average annual rate of -0.3% (Figure 2), a fact that explains why its level in 2020 is lower than that in 2000 (Figure 1).

An indirect but complementary, as well as quite significant, way of analysing the evolution of public investment is by paying attention to the investment effort made by the government. Measured through the ratio "public investment/GDP (in pp)", Figure 3, apart from confirming what was previously reported, shows that Spain made a great investment effort during the first boom subperiod 2000–08 (4.3% per year) and the first year of the Great Recession, 2009 (5.3%). Afterwards, and due to the guidelines issued from Brussels regarding the consolidation of public finances, the

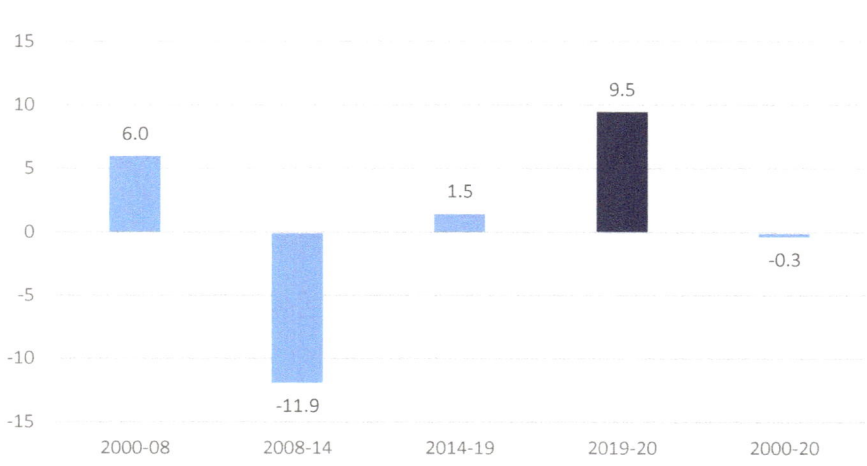

Fig. 2 Public Investment: Growth Rate (%).

Source of data: AMECO database. Figure created by the authors.

investment effort dropped very sharply until 2014, and then remained more or less stable at a level of just over 2%. Fortunately, in 2020, and because of the more relaxed and anti-cyclical policy stance emanating from Brussels, the investment effort grew once more, but to a meagre 2.6%; in any case, it is evident that it falls far short of what is needed, since its level in 2020 is around 50% lower than the average between 2000 and 2009.

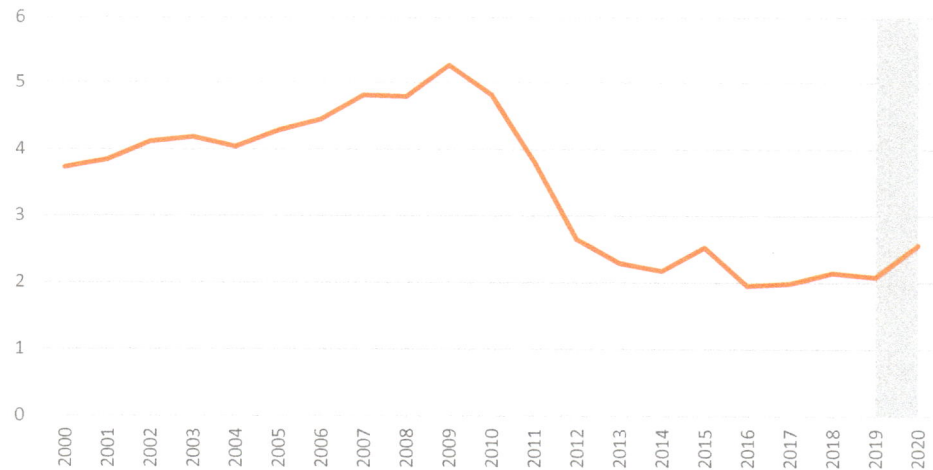

Fig. 3 Public Investment Effort: Public Investment over GDP (%).

Source of data: AMECO database. Figure created by the authors.

Up to now, we have referred to public investment without considering the level of government that acts as the effective investor. This might not be relevant for a country with a highly centralised way of governing, but it is important for a country, such as Spain, with a very decentralised one (for an analysis of fiscal policy across levels of government, see OECD 2010). In this respect, Figure 4—in which, for the sake of clarity, we once again split the whole period into expansion and contraction subperiods—shows the shares corresponding to the three tiers (central, state or regional, and local) of government, plus the social security share. Three features need to be highlighted: first, that the state governments are the main public investors in Spain; second, that their share in total public investment increased over time; and third, that this share has peaked up precisely in 2020, reaching a value of 45%. On average, more than 42% of public investment in Spain comes from state governments, around 31% from the central government, and 26% from local governments; as expected, the share corresponding to social security has been almost negligible (less than 1%).

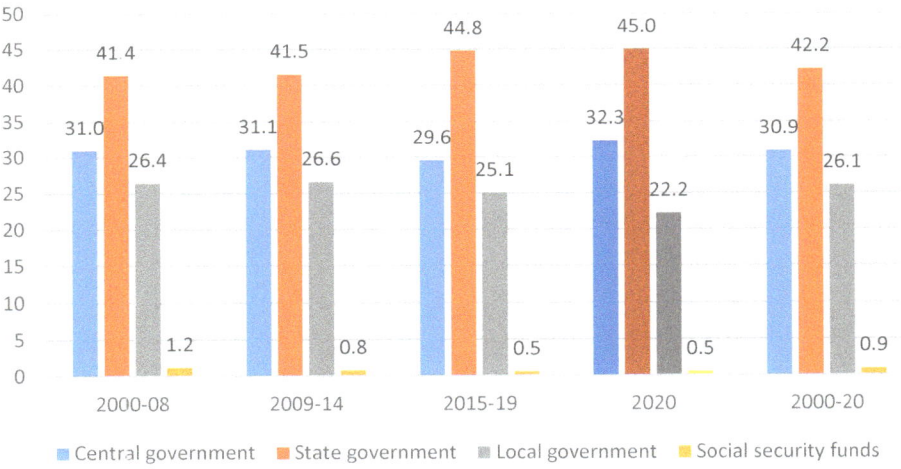

Fig. 4 Distribution of Public Investment by Government Level (%).

Source of data: EUROSTAT database, along with an extension for the year 2020 based on IGAE data (IGAE stands for 'Intervención General de la Administración del Estado'). Figure created by the authors.

Finally, it is important to note that just as relevant as the level and evolution of public investment is its composition, the areas in which public funds are being invested. According to Table 1—which only covers the period 2000–19, because there is no official, reliable data about 2020—it is obvious that, making use of the so-called Classification of the Functions of Government (COFOG), the share devoted to "economic affairs" (which includes subheadings such as general economic, business, and labour affairs; agriculture, forestry, fishing, and hunting; fuel and energy; mining, manufacturing, and construction; transportation; communications; other activities; and R&D related to economic affairs) is always the most relevant, with figures accounting for more than 40% of the total. As can be seen by looking at the three subperiods, and in what may be considered as a government attempt to play, to a certain extent, an anti-cyclical role, the amount of investment in "economic affairs" reached its maximum share during the huge economic contraction that took place between 2009 and 2014. As for the rest of assets, it is worth mentioning that the second position in the ranking always corresponds, and with increasing values, to the "general public services" (including subheadings such as executive and legislative bodies; financial, fiscal, and foreign affairs; foreign economic aid; general services; basic research; R&D related to general public services; public debt operations; and general intergovernmental transfers). The third position is occupied by either "health", also with increasing values, or "housing and community amenities", in this case with decreasing ones. Although, as mentioned before, there is no information about what happened in 2020 from this perspective, it is very likely that, due to the efforts made to overcome the severity of the COVID-19 crisis, the share devoted to investment in health had reached a new peak. Even being higher, this new peak will not probably be much higher than the previous one, considering that most of the spending in this area was current and not capital spending.

Table 1 Distribution of Public Investment by Type of Asset (%)

	2000–08	2009–14	2015–19	2000–19
General public services	11.00	12.58	16.59	12.54
Defence	7.00	5.32	8.26	6.69
Public order and safety	3.09	2.86	3.07	3.01
Economic affairs	41.52	45.27	40.71	42.59
Environmental protection	5.67	4.75	4.56	5.17
Housing and community amenities	9.82	6.93	4.65	7.94
Health	6.67	8.21	9.82	7.75
Recreation, culture, and religion	6.92	6.26	4.97	6.35
Education	6.50	6.09	6.34	6.34
Social protection	1.79	1.73	1.01	1.63

Source of data: EUROSTAT database following COFOG. Figure created by the authors.

6.2. Next Generation EU: Some Insights from Spain

As is well known, due to the severe economic crisis caused by the COVID-19 pandemic, the EU institutions (the European Commission, the European Parliament, and the European Council) launched a recovery plan, branded Next Generation EU (NGEU). This plan, which breaks with the rules of no common debt issuance (de la Porte and

Jensen 2021), aims to stimulate the economic recovery of the EU member countries by laying the foundations for a modern and more sustainable Europe, agreed on a European recovery fund of up to €750,000 m (in 2018 constant prices). Spain, the EU country hardest hit in economic terms, is expected to receive, over the period 2021–26, up to €140,000 m, about half of them in direct transfers and the other half in soft credits. However, at the time of writing, and due to the uncertainty and the difficulty of setting actions for a longer period, the current Spanish recovery plan—the so-called "RTRP", which stands for Recovery, Transformation, and Resilience Plan (see Spanish Government Agenda 2030)—revolves around the reforms and investment to take place between 2021 and 2023 only.

Regarding public investment, it is important to note that, as pointed out in the RTRP, without the support of direct transfers from the European funds, it would be practically nil because of a context of limited fiscal space and a great need for current spending on health and education. In a trend scenario, it would mean, in practice, assuming a continued deterioration of the capital stock, as can be seen in Figure 5, since the tendency line (referred to as "no-policy change") is below the "replacement" line. There is no doubt this situation would have a negative effect on long-term growth and, consequently, on social and territorial cohesion (since many of these public investments are territorialised). However, the investment foreseen in the RTRP (represented by the "plan" line in Figure 5), with its additive nature, will make it possible to reach an investment effort of around even 4% of GDP some years and always appreciably higher than the "no-policy change" scenario; this will not only imply closing the gap with the EU average, but also allow net investment to be positive for the first time since 2011.

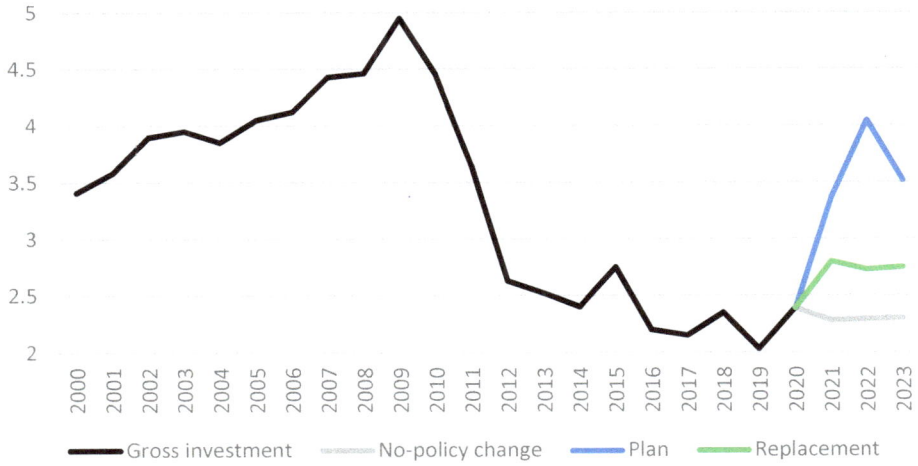

Fig. 5 Investment Recovery: Gross Public Investment (% GDP).

Source of data: Valencian Institute of Economic Research (IVIE) dataset and AMECO dataset. The figure is an adaptation created by authors of the original published in Spanish Government Agenda 2030 (2021).

As shown in Table 2, the nearly €70,000 m of investment from direct transfers will be mainly devoted to two large areas, in line with the EU climate and digitalisation agendas: green transition and digital transformation. Human capital formation and R&D are two other important areas in which a large amount of the European funds will be invested. The main aim of this investment is to boost productivity and, in so doing, to increase the potential growth rate of the economy. In short, its purpose is to make the Spanish economy more modern, more resilient, and more competitive.

More specifically, in the classification by investment levers (again, see Table 2), the lever related to the modernisation and digitalisation of industry stands out (23.1% of total investment), which includes the development of the Spain 2030 Industrial Policy, strategies to enhance small and medium-sized enterprises, the plan for the modernisation and competitiveness of the tourism sector, and the promotion of digital connectivity and 5G. Another very important target of the funds will be the development of a rural and urban agenda that will, among other things, modernise agriculture and promote territorial cohesion (20.7%). It includes, amongst other things, an action plan for sustainable mobility in urban and metropolitan environments, housing rehabilitation and urban regeneration, and the environmental and digital transformation of agriculture and fisheries. The third investment lever we want to highlight is that devoted to the development of resilient infrastructures and ecosystems (15%). Given the structural impact that infrastructures can have on the economy and on society, the aim is to develop nature-based solutions and strengthen their capacity to adapt to climates—and, thus, their resilience. To this end, investment will focus on the conservation and restoration of ecosystems and biodiversity, the preservation of the coastal zone and water resources, and, again, progress in terms of sustainable, safe, and connected mobility.

Table 2 Investment Allocation

Lever Policies	Amount (%)
I. Urban and rural agenda, territorial cohesion, and modernisation of agriculture	14.407 M€ (20.7%)
II. Resilient infrastructures and ecosystems	10.400 M€ (15.0%)
III. A fair and inclusive energy transition	6.385 M€ (9.2%)
IV. An administration for the 21st century	4.315 M€ (6.2%)
V. Modernisation and digitalisation of industry and SMEs, entrepreneurship and business environment, recovery and transformation of tourism and other strategic sectors	16.075 M€ (23.1%)
VI. Promotion of science and innovation and strengthening of the capabilities of the National Health System	4.949 M€ (7.1%)

Lever Policies	Amount (%)
VII. Education and knowledge, lifelong learning, and capacity building	7.317 M€ (10.5%)
VIII. The new care economy and employment policies	4.855 M€ (7.0%)
IX. Promotion of the culture and sports industry	825 M€ (1.2%)
X. Modernisation of the tax system for inclusive and sustainable growth	-
Total	69.528 M€

Source of data: The table is an adaptation created by authors of a figure published in Spanish Government, Agenda 2030 (2021).

According to the RTRP, it is foreseen that this new stream of public investment will give, on average, an approximate boost to the GDP of 2 pp per year, something that, hopefully, will allow Spain to return to its pre-COVID-19 GDP growth trend by, approximately, the end of 2022 (GDP forecast can be seen in Figure 6). As for the labour market, it is expected that, in aggregate terms, the employment generated by the RTRP could exceed 800,000 jobs at the end of the plan´s execution period. Not only this, but they will be quality jobs which, in principle, should increase the productivity of the Spanish economy, one of its well-known weaknesses. Finally, and in a similar vein, although admittedly a little more difficult to assess, it is also foreseeable that the investment from the RTRP will affect Spanish foreign trade positively. More precisely, a 0.2 pp increase in the long-term growth rate of exports is expected.

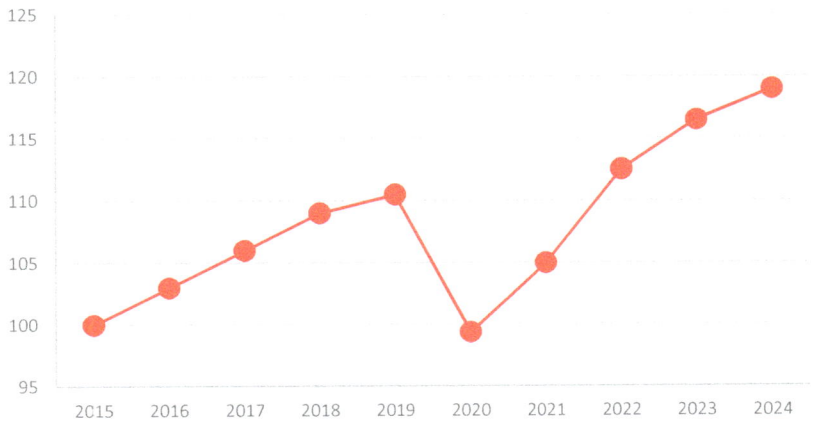

Fig. 6 Macroeconomic Impact (GDP Forecast 2015 = 100).

Source of data: National Statistical Institute of Spain, Ministry of Economic Affairs and Digital Transformation. The figure was taken from Spanish Government Agenda 2030 (2021).

6.3. Conclusion

The aim of this chapter, apart from summarising the main findings of a previous one (Villaverde and Maza 2020), was twofold. First, to present new evidence on the evolution of public investment since 2000 and, above all (and despite the fact that in this case the evidence is necessarily partial due to the scarcity of data), to present evidence from during the COVID-19 pandemic. Second, to briefly discuss the key points of the content of the Spanish recovery plan, the RTRP. By doing so, the paper has reached some interesting conclusions.

First, and contrary to what is expected, public investment in Spain has mainly played a pro-cyclical role in the new century. There were just two exceptions to this general trend: the years 2009 and 2020, precisely when the two recent economic recessions were at their strongest.

Second, the investment effort made by the public authorities in Spain has been very volatile and, on average, lower than that of the EU. After the outbreak of the pandemic, nevertheless, it has increased markedly and is expected to continue in the same vein.

Third, state (regional) governments have not only carried out most of the public investment in the country, but also their share of total public investment has grown over time, even after the outbreak of the COVID-19 pandemic. In any case, the largest increase in public investment in 2020 corresponded to the central government.

Fourth, the economic affairs category of the Classification of the Functions of Government (mainly infrastructure) is the one that received the lion's share of Spanish public investment—on average, more than 40% of the total. Although we are unable to give precise figures due to the paucity of data, it seems clear that we can point to the existence of a strong increase, yet to be quantified, in health investment during the current COVID-19 crisis.

Fifth, between 2021 and 2023, in the context of the NGEU plan and as a way to promote economic recovery, Spain will receive an amount close to €70,000 m in the form of direct transfers. According to the RTRP, this will bring net public investment back into positive figures for the first time since 2011.

Sixth, this additional public investment spending will hopefully give an important boost to the Spanish economy, namely to GDP (an additional increase of 2% per year) and employment (about 800,000 new jobs by 2024).

Although very promising, we consider that the positive expectations for the future of the Spanish economy linked to the European funds are a bit too optimistic and, therefore, have to be tempered. This opinion is based, on the one hand, on the foreseeable delays in the implementation of the NGEU plan and, therefore, in the effective delivery of funds to Spain and, on the other, on the fact that the investment projects that will benefit from these funds are not yet sufficiently detailed. In any case, there is no doubt that the arrival of the EU funds (the sooner the better) will give a big push to the economy, helping it, as mentioned before, to become more modern (productive), resilient, and competitive. This is an opportunity that Spain cannot afford to miss.

References

Bom, P.R. and J.E. Ligthart (2014) "What Have We Learned from Three Decades of Research on the Productivity of Public Capital?", *Journal of Economic Surveys* 28: 889–916, https://doi.org/10.1111/joes.12037.

De la Porte, C. and M. Jensen (2021) "The Next Generation EU: An Analysis of the Dimensions on Conflict behind the Deal", *Social Policy and Administration* 55(2): 388–402, https://doi.org/10.1111/spol.12709.

Gechert, S. (2015) "What Fiscal Policy is Most Effective? A Meta-Regression Analysis", *Oxford Economic Papers* 67(3): 553–80, https://doi.org/10.1093/oep/gpv027.

OECD (2010) "Fiscal Policy across Levels of Government in Times of Crisis", COM/CTPA/ECO/GOV/WP 12, OECD, Paris.

Spanish Government, Agenda 2030 (2021) *Plan de Recuperación, Transformación y Resiliencia (Recovery, Transformation and Resilience Plan)*. Madrid, https://www.lamoncloa.gob.es/presidente/actividades/Documents/2021/130421-%20Plan%20de%20recuperacion%2C%20Transformacion%20y%20Resiliencia.pdf.

Villaverde, J. and A. Maza (2020) "Trends and Patterns in Public Investment in Spain". In F. Cerniglia and F. Saraceno (eds), *A European Public Investment Outlook*, Cambridge: Open Book Publishers, pp. 83–95, https://doi.org/10.11647/obp.0222.05.

PART II

CHALLENGES

7. Crowding In-Out of Public Investment[1]

Luigi Durand, Raphael Espinoza, William Gbohoui, and Mouhamadou Sy

Introduction

Public investment stands apart as a fiscal instrument to boost growth. Not only can it boost economic activity in the short term, it can also increase the productive potential of the economy by raising the capital stock and thus productivity. This is particularly important for countries that seek to support economies through crises but that, at the same time, need to boost long-term growth and thus, protect fiscal space (IMF 2020). This is the situation many advanced economies face as they seek to kickstart their economies, after having shut them down in order to prevent the propagation of COVID-19. In Europe, the EU Recovery Fund is a €750 bn plan, financed at the EU-level, that has a strong focus on public investment.

This modern view of the effect of public investment owes a lot to Keynes. Prior to the publication of *The General Theory of Employment, Interest and Money* in 1936, the conventional wisdom was that an increase in public investment would lead to an equivalent decrease in private investment, so that the level of aggregate output would be unchanged. This concept of "crowding out" was challenged by Keynes: when prices are rigid in the short run, aggregate demand determines the level of output, and markets adjust via quantities rather than prices. Under this model, there is room for governments to support economic activity by increasing public investment. This argument is summarised by the concept of the "fiscal multiplier":[2] "when there is

---

1   The views expressed in this chapter are those of the authors and do not necessarily represent the views of the Central Bank of Chile or its Board members, the IMF, the IMF Executive Board or IMF management.

2   Even if the concept of multiplier is associated with Keynes, it was first was developed first by Kahn (1931). However, Kahn's focus was on the "employment multiplier": by how much does aggregate employment increase when public investment increase? See Kahn (1931) and Snowdon and Vane (2005).

          https://doi.org/10.11647/OBP.0280.07

an increment of aggregate investment, income will increase by an amount which is k times the increment in investment" (Keynes 1936, p. 115).

The public "investment multiplier" can thus be defined as the ratio between the variation in output and the variation in public investment. In *The General Theory*, the main determinant of the multiplier is the marginal propensity to consume (MPC);[3] that is, how much of their extra euros of disposable income households spend on consumption. When the MPC is close to unity, small changes in investment lead to large increases in economic activity because spending (and thus employment and workers' incomes) reacts strongly to income. However, if the MPC is close to zero, the multiplier is low. Keynes thought that the MPC would fall between these two bounds but be closer to unity, which would imply a large public investment multiplier.

Arguments that run counter to this Keynesian view also have a long tradition, and include: the "Treasury view" of crowding out, according to which government borrowing to finance fiscal expansion would lead to a full crowding out of private investment,[4] which is why deficits should be reduced to boost confidence (this view is echoed in the current debate on expansionary fiscal consolidation; see Alesina et al. 2019); the "Monetarist view" of Friedman (1957), according to which consumers respond only to changes in permanent income, and thus the impact of an unexpected temporary increase in income is going to be small; and the "Classical view", according to which an expansionary fiscal policy cannot boost aggregate demand, because private agents have rational expectations and increase their savings in anticipation of a rise in future taxes (the "Ricardian equivalence"; see Ricardo 1820, and Barro 1974).

However, the Keynesian view has been mostly supported by the data, as this chapter will show. Section 2 of the chapter gives a few examples of the existing literature and reports the results of a meta-analysis of Gechert and Rannenberg (2018). Section 3 will present some of the conditions that can lead to strong crowding in. Section 4 provides information on EU structural funds and the EU Recovery Fund, and discusses, in light of the recent literature, whether the EU Recovery Fund is likely to crowd in private investment and private activity in the sectors most hit by the COVID-19 crisis.

7.1 Modern Estimations of the Fiscal Multiplier

The empirical literature of the effect of fiscal policy on growth has bloomed since the 2008 Global Financial Crisis (GFC). The renewed interest is due to the fact that many governments launched recovery plans to boost their economies during the GFC. Responses to the COVID-19 pandemic are benefiting from this experience (IMF 2020). Recent empirical estimations (summarised in the meta-analysis of Gechert and

---

3    $MPC = 1 - 1/k$
4   Ralph G. Hawtrey (1925), then a senior official at the Treasury, harshly repopularised the Treasury view: "The public works are merely a piece of ritual, convenient to people who want to be able to say that they are doing something, but otherwise irrelevant".

Rannenberg (2018); see Figure 1) find that the fiscal multiplier is relatively high for public investment, possibly because public investment has the potential to crowd in private investment and support long-term productivity growth. For instance, Abiad et al. (2016) use investment forecast errors produced by the IMF to identify the effect of government investment, and find that increasing public investment by 1% of GDP increases GDP by about 0.4 in the short term and by 1.4 in the medium term (i.e., a short-run multiplier of 0.4 and a medium-run multiplier of 1.4).

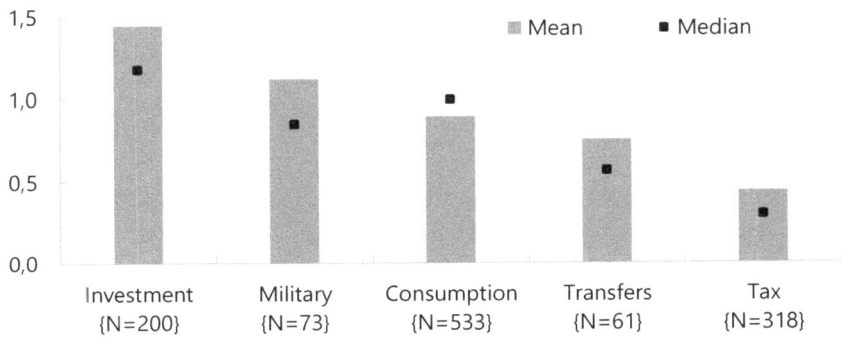

Fig. 1 Reported Fiscal Multipliers.
Source of data: Gechert and Rannenberg (2018).
Note: n denotes the number of papers.

Eden and Kraay (2014) estimated the causal effect of public investment on private investment by using the variation in loan disbursements from official creditors in thirty-nine low-income countries. They found that one additional dollar of public investment leads to an increase in private investment by about two dollars. Some estimations based on subnational data also found large fiscal multipliers for public investment. Leduc and Wilson (2012) use US state-level funding for highways and estimate a multiplier of public infrastructure of about 1.7. Coelho (2019) finds that EU structural funds have a multiplier of around 1.7.

7.2 Conditions under Which Crowding In Is More Likely

The above summary hides several factors that can affect the extent of crowding-in. Keynes had anticipated some of them: (i) in an open economy, part of the benefits of investment will accrue to foreign economies, lessening the effect of the multiplier on domestic economic activity; (ii) following a fiscal expansion, the increase in "confidence" could increase the preference for liquidity and thus decrease the MPC; (iii) when firms have limited capacity, any attempt to increase investment is likely to lead to an increase in inflation; and (iv) the central bank may respond by tightening monetary policy, which would reduce private investment.

Recent research has emphasised the role of business cycles and monetary conditions. A fiscal stimulus may be less effective during expansions, because at full capacity, the short-term effects of an increase in public investment on output are limited, leading to crowding out of private investment and private demand, and higher prices. Moreover, in times of recession, the proportion of credit-constrained households and firms which can adjust spending in response to a change in disposable income is higher. Most of the literature finds that fiscal multipliers are larger during recessions, when there is economic slack, than during expansions (Gechert and Rannenberg 2018; Baum et al. 2012; Auerbach and Gorodnichenko 2013). Auerbach and Gorodnichenko (2013) reported a fiscal multiplier of up to 3.5 during downturns and a statistically insignificant multiplier during upturns, in a sample of OECD countries over the period from 1985 to 2010.

Public investment multipliers also tend to be larger when monetary conditions are accommodative (Erceg and Lindé 2014; Christiano, Eichenbaum, and Rebelo 2011; Coenen et al. 2012). In particular, multipliers are larger when interest rates do not increase in response to the fiscal expansion (for instance, because the economy would need negative interest rates that are much below the feasible policy interest rate, which is, in practice, close to zero). The literature on the effect of temporary government purchases suggests that accommodative monetary conditions increase the size of fiscal multipliers by a factor of two to three. Relatedly, multipliers tend to be larger in countries that follow a fixed exchange rate regime (which includes members of a currency union), because monetary policy does not offset the fiscal policy shock, thus remaining more accommodative. Empirical estimates find that countries that follow a fixed exchange rate regime have long-run fiscal multipliers that are larger by a third (Born et al. 2013; Ilzetzki et al. 2013; Karras 2011).

In periods of high macroeconomic uncertainty, public investment can also crowd in private investment if it affects private sector confidence. This is important at the current juncture, as the medium-term economic outlook crucially hinges on the race between a mutating virus and the deployment of effective vaccines. Uncertainty has been found to reduce firm-level investment (see Guiso and Parigi 1999, or Bloom 2014, for a review), and some have suggested that high levels of uncertainty could also make firms and consumers less responsive to fiscal stimulus (Bloom et al. 2018; Alloza 2018). At the same time, uncertainty could increase the fiscal multiplier if public investment shocks improve private agents' expectations about the economic outlook, thereby generating a positive and stronger private response (Farmer 2010; Bachmann and Sims 2012). Indeed, Gbohoui (forthcoming) finds that public investment shocks boost private sector confidence during periods of high uncertainty, leading to large multipliers of up to 2.7 over two years, compared to a multiplier of 0.6 in a linear version of the model (Figure 2). The crowding in of private investment is also stronger

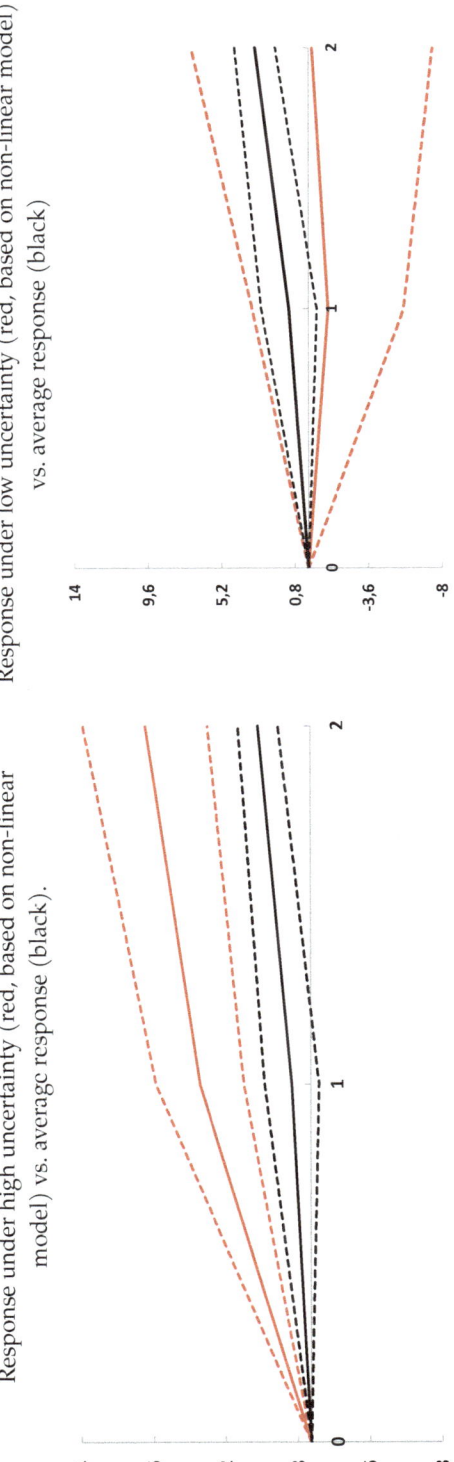

Fig. 2 Uncertainty and Crowding-In Effects: Public Investment on Private Investment.

Source of data: Gbohoui (forthcoming, IMF Working Paper).

Note: Macroeconomic uncertainty is measured by the standard deviation of GDP growth rate forecasts across professional forecasters as published by Consensus Economics, using the spring vintage for each year. Investment shocks are identified as forecast errors of public investment spending relative to GDP. t=1 is the year of the shock; non-linear (linear) estimates are plotted in red (black); dashed lines denote 90% confidence bands. The effects represent the response, in percentage change, to an unexpected increase of public investment by 1% of GDP.

in periods of high uncertainty. Private investment increases by more than 10% over a period of two years, after an initial public investment increase of 1% of GDP. A possible reason behind this result is that public investment shocks signal future improvement in productivity, driving up the private sector's expectations about future growth, which leads to higher private investment. During periods of low uncertainty, public investment shocks do not seem to have effects on the economy. These results extend to a panel of countries, the findings by Arčabić and Cover (2016) for the US, and Berg (2019) for Germany, that reported fiscal multipliers larger than two during periods of high uncertainty.

The composition of the investment package also matters for its effect on private investment, especially in the long run. For instance, crowding-in effects can be larger if the package prioritises sectors with large positive externalities (Arrow 1962; Romer 1986) or if it fosters innovation (Moretti et al. 2019; Agenor et al. 2015). From a theoretical standpoint, the private sector's response to increases in public investment should be larger when newly installed public capital complements private capital (Aschauer 1989). For example, Fernald (1999) found that US industries that are more vehicle intensive have a disproportionate increase in productivity after the construction of roads (see also Lanau 2017). In recent years, the literature also suggests that public spending on environmentally friendly investment is likely to crowd in more private investment. Batini et al. (2021), for instance, find an impact multiplier of 1.2 for renewable energy investment and of 4.1 for nuclear energy investment, but the multiplier is only 0.65 for "brown" energy investment.

The quality of public investment, which will depend on the institutional, legal, and regulatory frameworks, is also fundamental. Short-term multipliers are likely to be lower when resources are diverted—for instance, because of corruption—and public inefficiencies in project planning, allocation, and implementation can result in less productive public capital in the long term.[5] Even though there is no fully satisfactory metric of public investment "quality", several measures and indexes are commonly employed. Among these, the IMF Public Investment Management Assessment (PIMA) score summarises information on institutional designs drawn from all three stages of the investment cycle (planning, allocation, and implementation), while the IMF Public Investment Efficiency Indicator (PIE-X) estimates the relationship between the public capital stock and indicators of access to and the quality of infrastructure assets.[6] The empirical literature has confirmed that fiscal multipliers are higher in countries with

---

5   However, Berg et al. (2019) note that the relationship between fiscal multiplier and the efficiency of public investment is complicated in theory, because the marginal productivity of capital should be increasing in investment inefficiencies if one realises that inefficient investment results in less capital, and thus a higher marginal product of capital.

6   Other measures that can be used to quantify public investment quality measures include the International Country Risk Guide (ICRG) indexes, the World Economic Forum Global Competitiveness Report survey on the wastefulness of government spending, the IMF Tax Administration and Diagnostic Assessment Tool (TADAT), the Public Expenditure and Financial Accountability (PEFA), and the IMF Fiscal Transparency Code (FTI).

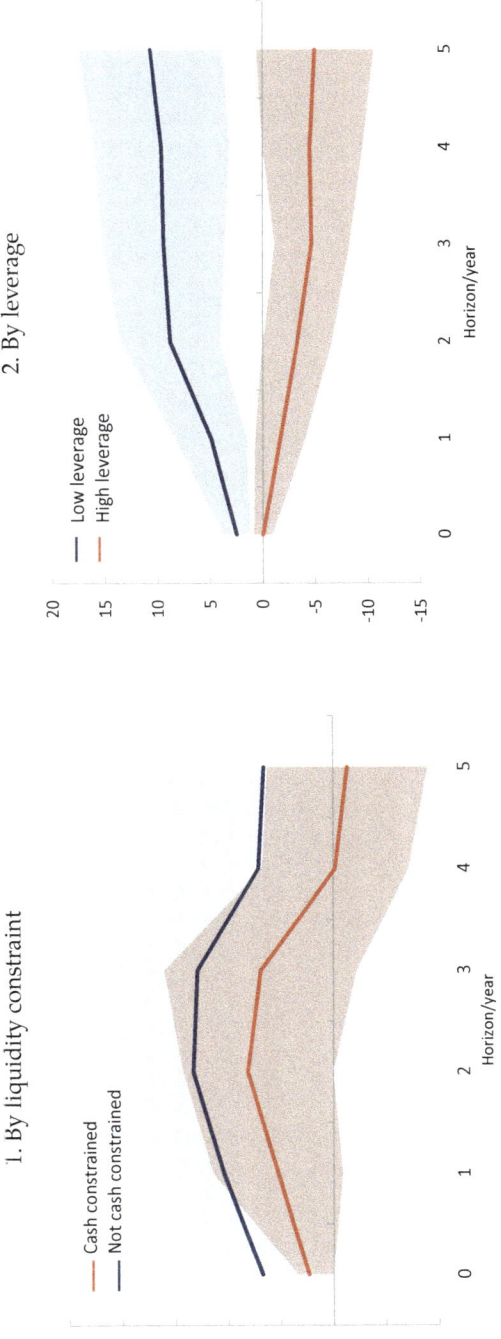

Fig. 3 Effect of Public Investment on Private Firms' Net Investment (in Percentage Change of an Increase of Public Investment by 1%)

Source of data: Espinoza, Gamboa-Arbelaez, and Sy (2020).

strong public investment management (Abiad, Furceri, and Topalova 2016; Myamoto et al. 2020).

In addition, recent research has noted that crowding in is unlikely to materialise if public or private balance sheets are weak. A higher level of public debt is associated with low or even negative fiscal multipliers in the long run, a result obtained at both the country level (Ilzetzki et al. 2013) and the subnational level (Huang et al. 2020). Using firm-level data across sixty-nine countries, Huang et al. (2018) documented a negative correlation between public debt and corporate investment. One possible explanation is that public debt increases the correlation between investment and cashflow for firms that are credit constrained.

Finally, the effect of an increase in public investment on private investment also depends on the strength of corporate balance sheet. Espinoza, Gamboa-Arbelaez, and Sy (2020) show that financial constraints matter for the effect of public investment on corporate investment. In particular, the authors find that an increase of public investment by 1% is associated with an increase in net investment rate of private firms by 2.3% on average, but for firms that are not liquidity constrained, net investment increases by 6.7%. Similarly, high leverage can discourage firms to invest, because new investment financed by additional debt could induce future low cashflows (Myers 1977), a theory confirmed by the data (Figure 3).

7.3 Lessons for the European Union

7.3.1 Public Investment and EU-Financed Investment in the Post-COVID Recovery

The pivotal role of the European funds in directing and supporting economies and investment has recently gained the spotlight, with the finalisation, in 2020, of a Recovery Fund (Next Generation EU, NGEU) to both buffer the negative effects of the COVID-19 pandemic, and to promote a transition towards more sustainable and more efficient means of production, through the disbursement of loans and grants. Given the heterogeneity in the intensity of the impact of the COVID-19 pandemic across countries and regions, the current programme sits well within the Cohesion Policy objective of ensuring medium-term income convergence in the EU. The concern is that the pandemic had highly asymmetric regional effects (OECD 2020), which have depended on the degree of exposure to tradable sectors and global value chains, and the reliance on the tourism industry. Of particular relevance is the disruption suffered by the agri-food sector (European Parliament 2020a), which exemplifies the fragility of complex production networks in the face of a systemic shock. Importantly, the crisis is showing that peripheral (still-converging) regions are suffering more than others (European Commission 2020a).

The NGEU offers an unprecedented mechanism to counteract a major crisis episode (through the Recovery and Resilience Facility, RFF), both in terms of resources and characteristics; for instance, the firepower of NGEU amounts to approximately €750 bn, committed over a period going from 2021 to 2024, which adds to the planned 2021–27 EU budget, for a total sum of around €1.85 tn (approximately 13% of EU GDP). NGEU is financed by borrowing on capital markets, in stark contrast with the regular EU budget, which has historically been funded using the EU's own resources. The European Commission projects the total economic impact generated by the RRF to be approximately 1.2% of 2019 EU real GDP, over the 2021–22 forecast horizon (European Commission 2021).

NGEU financing is primarily tilted towards public investment, which constitutes 87% of the total allocated expenditure (D'Alfonso 2020). NGEU could thus push future private investment towards economic sectors that are likely to be essential to ensure resilience and prosperity, such as digital communication, transportation infrastructure, sustainable farming, and clean energy. In this sense, the current crisis offers an unprecedented opportunity for public policy to advance its footprint on fundamental challenges, such as climate change and the erosion of natural ecosystems, by steering the national investment away from a production system strongly unbalanced toward polluting and unsustainable activities (see European Energy Agency 2021).

NGEU adds to the funds that the EU traditionally employs to reduce disparities between development levels and to promote the catch-up of lagging regions. As of today, the EU relies on five major funds: the European Regional Development Fund (ERDF), the European Social Fund (ESF), the Cohesion Fund (CF), the European Agricultural Fund for Rural Development (EAFRD), and the European Maritime and Fisheries Fund (EMFF). Together, these funds currently make up over half of the EU funding budget, and they are commonly referred as the European Structural Investment (ESI) Funds. Importantly, these funds finance both public investment and private investment.

ESI Funds are allocated under different "banners". The lion's share of ESI payments is classified under three objectives: payments associated with the Convergence Objective (formerly known as Objective 1) are aimed at stimulating growth in lagging regions (and can only be allocated in regions with a GDP per capita below 75% of the EU average), while payments associated with the Regional Competitiveness and Employment Objective (formerly known as Objective 2) are allocated to regions in structural decline; finally, payments associated with the European Territorial Cooperation Objective (formerly known as Objective 3) are disbursed to support education and employment policies in regions not included under Objective 1. ESI Funds are integrated into an overarching cohesion policy, dating back to 1988. Since then, the EU has gone through five programming periods (Multiannual Financial Frameworks, MFF), that usually lasted seven years each. In the case of the last programme (2014–20), the total budget (including EU financing and national co-financing) equalled approximately €650 bn—around 4% of EU GDP—of which €450 bn was from the EU only.[7]

---

7   European Commission (2021x) "European Structural and Investment Funds 2014-2020. 2020 Summary report of the programme annual implementation reports covering implementation in 2014-2019." European Commission Strategic Reports.

Figure 4 describes the evolution of ESI Funds' (modelled) expenditures across all MFFs to date. The figure highlights the extension of payments beyond the end of each MFF, a feature which stems from a decommitment rule, which allows the recipients to spend the funds after each programme's end date. Interestingly, the 2014–20 period shows a significant slowness in disbursements. Despite this trend, 94% of the budgeted European Structural and Investment Funds (ESIF) had been allocated by the end of June 2020, and 47% had already been spent, on average.[8] Figure 5 summarises these dynamics, by showing the share of EU funds payments as a percentage of the planned amount, for all EU countries. The issue of slow spending of EU funds can be attributed to several factors, including low project approval rate and delays in execution in some countries, but also the decommitment rule itself; these patterns are relevant from a policymaker perspective, since they raise concerns on the effectiveness of ESI Funds to provide an effective short-term stabilisation tool against unexpected adverse macroeconomic shocks (see Carrion Alvarez 2020).

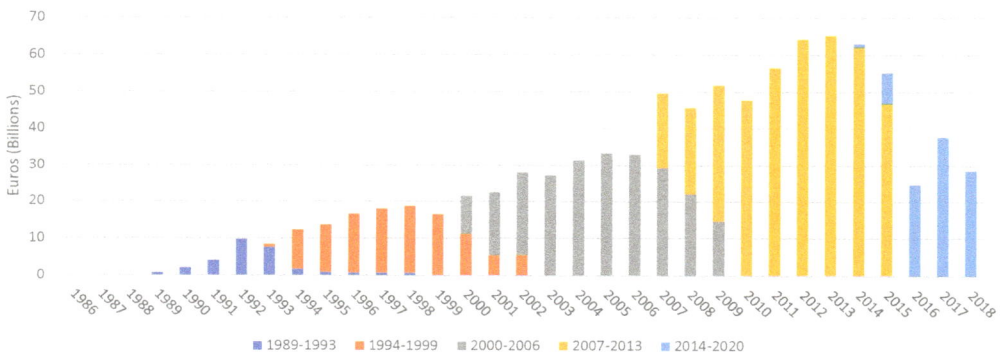

Fig. 4 ESI Funds Modelled Expenditures.

Source of data: Annual EU budget payments (EUR) made by programme period, available at https://cohesiondata.ec.europa.eu/Other/Historic-EU-payments-regionalised-and-modelled/tc55-7ysv.

Within the context of the ongoing pandemic, many regulations surrounding the use of EU funds have been amended to allow for more flexibility and to increase the speed of project implementation (European Parliament 2020b). Among the major amendments is the temporary suspension of the principle of additionality, which originally required ESI Funds not to replace the national or equivalent expenditure by a member state. While co-financing might prevent crowding out of private capital in normal times, this concern is unwarranted in a crisis, when private investment is depressed because of ongoing uncertainty. Thus, the NGEU framework does not include the need for co-financing. Other amendments to ESI Funds include the exemption from the need to comply with thematic concentration requirements and the possibility of receiving EU

---

8   See the EU Open Data Portal here: https://cohesiondata.ec.europa.eu/overview.

support on expenditures related to operations fostering crisis-response capacity to the COVID-19 outbreak.

Fig. 5 Historical ESI Funds Payments as a % of Planned Amounts.

Source of data: Author's calculations.

Note: Absorption rates for the 2007–13 MFF are from the Commission's "SF 2007–2013 Funds Absorption Rate" dataset available at https://cohesiondata.ec.europa.eu/2007-2013-Finances/SF-2007-2013-Funds-Absorption-Rate/kk86-ceun/data; the 2014–20 data is based on the Commission's "Regional Policy 2014–2020 EU Payment Details by EU Countries" dataset available at https://cohesiondata.ec.europa.eu/2014-2020-Finances/Regional-Policy-2014-2020-EU-Payment-Details-by-EU/vs2b-dct3/data.

7.3.2 The Crowding In Effects of EU Funds

Given the size and scope of the EU investment policy for growth and regional convergence, it is essential to quantify the impact of such programmes on growth and both private and total investment; indeed, a requirement for accessing the EU Recovery and Resilience funds has been that member states provide detailed plans that also include a description of how the EU funds will contribute to promoting the EU's economic, social, and territorial cohesion and also mitigate the social and economic impact of the crisis (see European Commission 2020b).

A large literature has estimated the growth effects of EU funds at a regional level; for example, Hagen and Mohl (2010) estimated that a 1% increase of Objective 1 payments leads to a small but positive impact on the regional GDP per capita by approximately 0.5%. A more positive assessment was provided by Becker, Egger, and Von Ehrlich (2010), who found that for every euro spent on Objective 1 transfers, GDP increases by €1.20. A common denominator in both studies is that having access to Objective 1 status does not immediately lead to higher growth, and several years are needed to show significant effects. Coelho (2019) analysed the response of output to Objective 1 EU funds, at the regional level, over the period 2000–13 and found large regional output multipliers, averaging 1.7 on impact in the poorest regions, and with a cumulative effect reaching a value of 4 after three years (after adjusting for co-financing). Canova and Pappa (2021) offered a more nuanced approach by studying ERDF and ESF funds separately, and finding that, on average, in the case of ERDF (ESF), an increase corresponding to 1% of regional GVA, increased GVA cumulatively by 1 (5.1)%, employment growth by 0.9 (1.6)%, and investment growth by 1.3 (4.3)%, cumulatively over a three-year horizon. The authors also underscored how these average figures hide significant heterogeneities across time and space.

In this respect, the literature also highlighted that these multipliers depend on the initial level of economic development. Becker, Egger, and Von Ehrlich (2013), for example, concluded that only in regions where there is sufficient human capital, and enough institutional quality, do transfer programmes increase growth (see also Breidenbach, Mitze, and Schmidt 2016, and Ederveen, De Groot, and Nahuis 2006).

There are very few studies that move beyond regional multipliers to estimating national multipliers of EU funds. In Durand and Espinoza (2021), which uses national data to assess the crowding-in effect of ESI Funds,[9] shocks to investment are computed using associated disbursements from all ESI Funds, following an identification strategy based on an instrumental variable approach first proposed by Kraay (2014), which exploits the time lags between commitments and disbursements of funds. The study also investigates country heterogeneity by looking at crowding-in effects in a selected group of CEE countries where the multiplier would be expected to be large given the fixed exchange rate regime and high quality of institutions.[10] The results, presented in Figure 6, summarise the main findings for the EU. The figure shows that ESIF funds crowd in private investment, increase total investment and GDP (with a multiplier of around 1.2), but do not increase employment.[11]

In addition to analysing aggregate multipliers, Durand and Espinoza (2021) further highlight significant heterogeneities in estimated multipliers across economic sectors. Understanding the heterogeneous impact of EU funds is particularly pressing in the context of both the NGEU and the MFF. Figure 7 reports the responses of EU total investment following ESI Funds shocks, by highlighting only those economic sectors where either the contemporaneous or 1Y multipliers are found to be statistically significant (at the 10% level).

---

9   In Durand and Espinoza (2021) ESI disbursements are computed using data from the major funds throughout the sample years starting in 1989, depending on data availability. This is in contrast with much of the previous literature, which instead focuses only on specific funds.

10 This group is composed of Croatia, the Czech Republic, Estonia, Latvia, and Slovenia. Durand and Espinoza (2021) show that in this group of countries, multipliers on investments and total investments are relatively higher when compared to the EU-wide multipliers.

11 Notice that all coefficients are subject to uncertainty, as illustrated by the bars surrounding the point estimates in Figure 6. In Durand and Espinoza (2021), the estimated multipliers also include the effects driven by co-financing, which is approximately equal to 40% on average.

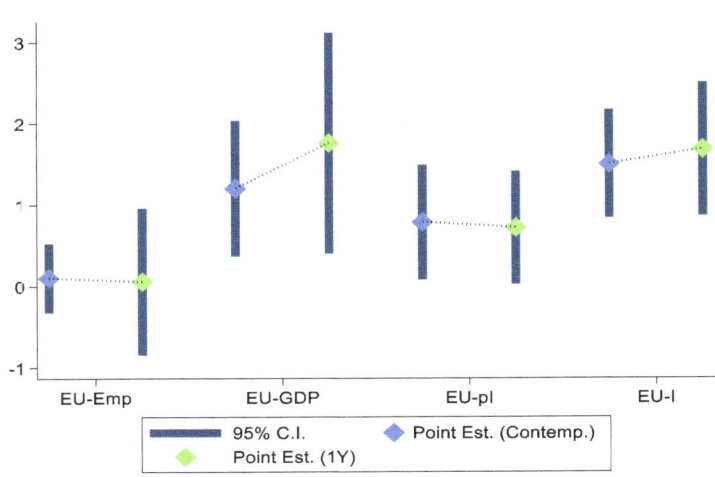

Fig. 6 ESI Funds Multipliers in EU.

Source of data: Durand and Espinoza (2021), and author's calculations.

Note: EU-GDP refers to the EU-wide impact of a 1% increase in ESI Funds disbursements on GDP. Similar interpretations apply for the case of total investment (I) and private investment (pI). The coefficients are subject to uncertainty, as illustrated by the bars surrounding the point estimates.

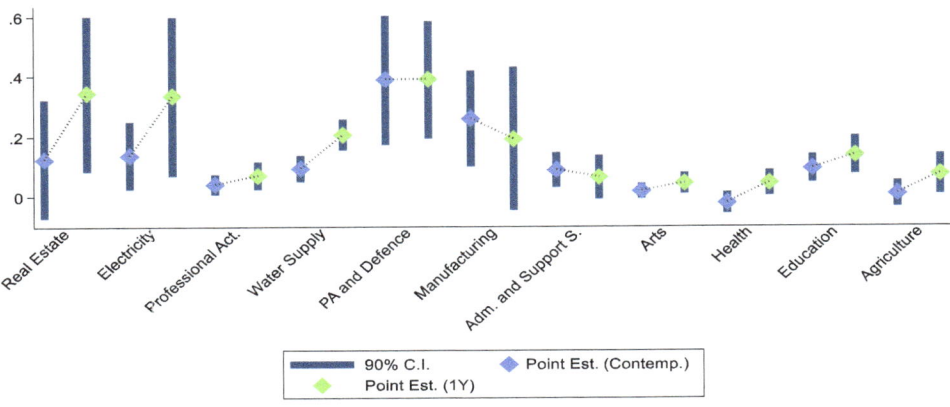

Fig. 7 Total Investment ESI Funds Multipliers in EU across Economic Sectors.

Source of data: Durand and Espinoza (2021), and author's calculations.

Note: The figure shows the EU-wide impact of a 1% GDP increase in ESI Funds disbursements on total investment across economic sectors (based on the NACE Rev. 2 classification); as an example, the figure suggests that a 1% GDP increase in ESI Funds contemporaneously increases investment in Water Supply by approximately 0.2% of GDP, after one year. The figure only includes the list of economic sectors which contain statistically significant multipliers. The sectors are ordered from left to right based on the degree of labour intensity (defined as sectoral employment/sectoral Gross Value Added). The coefficients are subject to uncertainty, as illustrated by the bars surrounding the point estimates.

An interesting result is that, overall, the list of economic sectors includes many labour-intensive activities such as agriculture, manufacturing, education, and health, which were all hit by the pandemic.

The composition of the funding package itself is also likely to affect crowding in. This is particularly relevant, given that the EU resources are allocated toward a wide variety of economic sectors, with different potentials for crowding in; reassuringly, the NGEU funding programme is well aligned with the theoretical arguments that we reviewed in the previous sections, by focusing on financing activities with potentially large externalities for the rest of the economy, and those that can foster innovation. More precisely, the package supplements short-term support to crisis-stricken sectors, such as manufacturing and health, with longer-term packages, which are tilted towards research and innovation (via Horizon Europe), digital transition (Digital Europe Programme), transportation and energy efficiency (Connecting Europe Facility), and addressing market failures in investment (InvestEU). In parallel to these programmes, the EU will remain engaged in more traditional themes such as regional cohesion (also through REACT-EU), recovery and resilience, security and defence, border and migration, and an efficient European public administration (European Council 2020).

The EU is also extensively engaged in climate actions, as exemplified by the 2030 climate target and the 2050 climate neutrality goal, as part of the so-called European Green Deal. Concerning climate change, the EU recently established a rule that programmes and instruments should contribute to mainstream climate actions and to the achievement of an overall target of at least 30% of the total amount of the EU's budget and of NGEU expenditures supporting climate objectives.[12] In this respect, the EU also established a Just Transition Fund to address the social and economic consequences of the objective of reaching EU climate neutrality. By implementing these directives, the EU is on the right track towards achieving strong multipliers.[13]

To better appreciate the importance of the composition of the stimulus package, it is useful to review what the existing empirical evidence suggests with respect to sectoral public investment shocks. Durand and Espinoza (2021) follow the Classification of the Functions of Government (COFOG) to study the impact of sectoral public investment on aggregate outcomes, including total investment, in the EU. Their analysis shows strong crowding-in effects across a broad range of sectors (in fact, out of ten COFOG categories, only the category "GF10: Social Protection" does not display significance at both horizons). Importantly, it also suggests that the upcoming NGEU and 2021–27 MFF, with its focus on key themes such as environmental protection and health, is well positioned to give rise to strong multiplier effects.

---

12   See questions and answers on the MFF and Next Generation EU, available at: https://ec.europa.eu/commission/presscorner/detail/en/qanda_20_935.

13   This argument is further backed by the results from an international survey of experts, including senior officials from finance ministries and central banks, who expressed the desirability of green projects in creating more jobs and delivering higher short-term returns, when compared to more traditional fiscal stimulus (see Hepburn et al. (2020)).

7.4 Conclusion

The literature and the new results presented in this chapter lend support to the view that the 2021–27 European Multiannual Financial Framework and the recovery packages will be effective in boosting the post-pandemic economy. However, policymakers should remain aware of the long-term implications of public investment, as well as of the potential drawbacks of a governance framework which, given the historical levels of slow absorption, inevitably limits the timely availability of these resources to address unexpected shocks (Bruegel 2020).

These two observations give rise to a tension between efficiency and speed; in particular, policymakers must recognise that increasing absorptions of EU funds should not come at the cost of lower consideration for the value of money being spent, as seems to have been the case in recent years (see European Court of Auditors 2018). Importantly, while speed might be crucial during a time of crisis, the magnitude of the EU funds (especially when giving rise to further debt, as is the case with the NGEU) will inevitably bring long-term implications, both in terms of fiscal sustainability and in terms of long-term economic growth and development, and resilience against future crises. Although it is possible to optimise that trade-off by financing first maintenance spending and smaller and simpler projects (IMF 2020), transformational projects will take more time to implement, and the portfolio of investments will thus have to be carefully balanced to take into consideration the timeliness of an investment stimulus.

References

Abiad, A., D. Furceri, and D. Topalova (2016) "The Macroeconomic Effects of Public Investment: Evidence from Advanced Economies", *Journal of Macroeconomics*, 50(C): 224–40.

Agénor, P.-R. and K. Neanidis (2015) "Innovation, Public Capital, and Growth", *Journal of Macroeconomics*, 44(C): 252–75.

Alesina A., C. Favero and F. Giavazzi (2019) *Austerity: When It Works and When It Doesn't*. Princeton: Princeton University Press.

Alloza, M. (2018) *Is Fiscal Policy More Effective in Uncertain Times or during Recessions?* Banco de España Working Papers No 1730.

Arčabić, V. and J. Cover (2016) *Uncertainty and the Effectiveness of Fiscal Policy*. EFZG Working Papers Series No 1611, Faculty of Economics and Business, University of Zagreb.

Arrow, K. (1962) "Economic Welfare and the Allocation of Resources for Invention". In National Bureau Committee for Economic Research, Committee on Economic Growth of the Social Science Research Council (eds), *The Rate and Direction of Inventive Activity: Economic and Social Factors*, pp. 609–26. Princeton University Press.

Aschauer, D. A. (1989) "Does Public Capital Crowd-Out Private Capital?", *Journal of Monetary Economics*, 24(2): 171–88.

Auerbach, A., and Y. Gorodnichenko (2013) "Fiscal Multipliers in Recession and Expansion", in A. Alesina and F. Giavazzi (eds), *Fiscal Policy after the Financial Crisis*, pp. 63–98. University of Chicago Press.

Bachmann, R. and E.R. Sims (2012) "Confidence and the Transmission of Government Spending Shocks", *Journal of Monetary Economics*, 59 (3): 235–49.

Batini, N., M. Di Serio, M. Fragetta, G. Melina and A. Waldron (2021) *Building Back Better: How Big Are Green Spending Multipliers?*, IMF Working Paper 2021/087.

Barro, R.J. (1974) "Are Government Bonds Net Wealth?", *Journal of Political Economy*, 82(6): 1095–117.

Baum, A., M. Poplawski-Ribeiro and A. Weber (2012) *Fiscal Multipliers and the State of the Economy*, IMF Working Paper 2012/286.

Becker, S.O., P.H. Egger and M.V. Ehrlich (2010) "Going NUTS: The Effect of EU Structural Funds on Regional Performance", *Journal of Public Economics*, 94(9–10): 578–90.

Becker, S.O., P.H. Egger and M.V. Ehrlich (2013) "Absorptive Capacity and the Growth and Investment Effects of Regional Transfers: A Regression Discontinuity Design with Heterogeneous Treatment Effects", *American Economic Journal: Economic Policy*, 5.4 (2013): 29–77.

Berg, T. (2019) "Uncertainty and the Effectiveness of Fiscal Policy in Germany", *Macroeconomic Dynamics,* 23(4): 1442–470.

Berg, A., E.F. Buffie, C. Pattillo, R. Portillo, A.F. Presbitero and L.F. Zanna (2019) "Some Misconceptions about Public Investment Efficiency and Growth", *Economica*, 86(342): 409–30.

Bloom, N. (2014) "Fluctuations in Uncertainty", *The Journal of Economic Perspectives*, 28(2): 153–75.

Bloom, N., M. Floetotto, N. Jaimovich, I. Saporta-Eksten and S.J. (2018) "Really Uncertain Business Cycles", *Econometrica*, 86(3): 1031–065.

Born, B., F. Juessen and G.J. (2013) "Exchange Rate Regimes and Fiscal Multipliers", *Journal of Economic Dynamics and Control,* 37(2): 446–65.

Breidenbach, P., T. Mitze and C.M. Schmidt (2016) "EU Structural Funds and Regional Income Convergence: A Sobering Experience", *RUHR Economic Papers n.608.*

Bruegel (2020) *Will European Union Countries be Able to Absorb and Spend Well the Bloc's Recovery Funding?* Bruegel Blog Post, written by Zsolt Darvas, https://www.bruegel.org/2020/09/will-european-union-countries-be-able-to-absorb-and-spend-well-the-blocs-recovery-funding/.

Canova, F. and E. Pappa (2021) *What are the Likely Macroeconomic Effects of the EU Recovery Plan?* Pompeu Fabra University.

Carrión Á. M. (2020) *What the Absorption of Structural Funds says about the EU Recovery Plan.* Funcas Europe, https://www.funcas.es/articulos/what-the-absorption-of-structural-funds-says-about-the-eu-recovery-plan/ .

Christiano, L., M. Eichenbaum and S. Rebelo (2011) "When Is the Government Spending Multiplier Large?", *Journal of Political Economy*, 119(1): 78–121.

Coelho, M. (2019) "Fiscal Stimulus in a Monetary Union: Evidence from Eurozone Regions", *IMF Economic Review*, 67(3): 573–617.

Coenen, G., C. Erceg, C. Freedman, D. Furceri, M. Kumhof, R. Lalonde, D. Laxton, J. Lindé, A. Mourougane, D. Muir, S. Mursula, C. de Resende, J. Roberts, W. Roeger, S. Snudden, M. Trabandt and J. in't Veld (2012) "Effects of Fiscal Stimulus in Structural Models", *American Economic Journal: Macroeconomics*, 4(1): 22–68.

D'Alfonso, A. (2020) *Next Generation EU—A European Instrument to Counter the Impact of the Coronavirus Pandemic*. European Parliamentary Research Service Briefing.

Durand, L. & R. Espinoza (2021) *The Fiscal Multiplier of European Structural Investment Funds: Aggregate and Sectoral Effects with an Application to Slovenia*, IMF Working Paper 2021/118.

Eden, M. and A. Kraay (2014) *Crowding In and the Returns to Government Investment in Low-Income Countries*, Policy Research Working Papers, World Bank. WPS6781.

Ederveen, S., H. L. F. De Groot and R. Nahuis (2006) "Fertile Soil for Structural Funds? A Panel Data Analysis of the Conditional Effectiveness of European Cohesion Policy". *Kyklos* 59(1): 17–42.

European Council (2020) *Special Meeting of the European Council—Draft Conclusions*, https://www.consilium.europa.eu/media/45109/210720-euco-final-conclusions-en.pdf.

European Court of Auditors (2018) *Commission's and Member States' Actions in the Last Years of the 2007–2013 Programmes Tackled Low Absorption but Had Insufficient Focus on Results*, Special Report 17/2018.

European Commission (2021) *European Economic Forecast, Spring 2021*, Institutional Paper 149, May 2021.

European Commission (2020a) *Identifying Europe's Recovery Needs*, Commission Staff Working Document.

European Commission (2020b) *Guidance to Member States—Recovery and Resilience Plans*, Commission Staff Working Document.

European Energy Agency (2021) *Industrial Production in Europe*, Indicator Assessment, https://www.eea.europa.eu/data-and-maps/indicators/industrial-pollution-in-europe-3/assessment.

European Parliament (2020a) *Protecting the EU Agri-Food Supply Chain in the Face of COVID-19*. Brief-European Parliamentary Research Service.

European Parliament (2020b). *Specific Flexibility Measures for ESI Funds in Response to the Coronavirus Outbreak*. European Parliamentary Research Service.

Erceg, C. and J. Lindé (2014) "Is There a Fiscal Free Lunch in a Liquidity Trap?", *Journal of the European Economic Association*, 12(1): 73–107.

Espinoza R., J. Gamboa-Arbelaez and M. Sy (2020) *The Fiscal Multiplier of Public Investment: The Role of Corporate Balance Sheet*, IMF Working Paper 2020/199.

Farmer, R. (2010) "10 Questions: Economist Roger Farmer", *UCLA Today*.

Fernald. J.G. (1999). "Roads to Prosperity? Assessing the Link between Public Capital and Productivity", *American Economic Review*, 89(3): 619–38.

Friedman, M. (1957). *A Theory of the Consumption Function*. Princeton University Press.

Gechert, S. and A. Rannenberg (2018) "Which Fiscal Multipliers Are Regime-Dependent? A Meta-Regression Analysis", *Journal of Economic Surveys*, 32(4): 1160–182.

Gbohoui, W., forthcoming. *The Fiscal Multiplier of Public Investment: The Role of Economic Confidence*. IMF Working Paper.

Guiso, L. and G. Parigi (1999). "Investment and Demand Uncertainty", *Quarterly Journal of Economics*, 114: 185–227.

Hagen, T. and P. Mohl (2010) "Do EU Structural Funds Promote Regional Growth? New Evidence from Various Panel Data Approaches", *Regional Science and Urban Economics*, 40(5): 353–65.

Hawtrey, R. G. (1925). "Public Expenditure and the Demand for Labour", *Economica*, 13(1925): 38–48.

Hepburn, C., B. O'Callaghan, N. Stern, J. Stiglitz, and D. Zenghelis (2020) "Will COVID-19 Fiscal Recovery Packages Accelerate or Retard Progress on Climate Change?", *Oxford Review of Economic Policy*, 36(Supplement_1): 359–81.

Huang Y., U. Panizza and R. Varghese (2018). "Does Public Debt Crowd Out Corporate Investment? International Evidence", *CEPR Discussion Paper 12931*.

Huang Y., M. Pagano and U. Panizza (2020), "Local Crowding Out in China", *Journal of Finance*, 75(6): 2855–898.

Ilzetzki, E., E. Mendoza and C. Vegh (2013) "How Big (Small?) are Fiscal Multipliers?", *Journal of Monetary Economics*, 60: 239–54.

International Monetary Fund (2020). "Policies for the Recovery", *International Monetary Fund, Fiscal Monitor*, Washington, D.C.

Kahn, R.F. (1931) "The Relation of Home Investment to Unemployment", *Economic Journal*, June.

Karras, G. (2011) "Exchange-Rate Regimes and the Effectiveness of Fiscal Policy", *Journal of Economic Integration*, 26(1), 29–44.

Keynes, J.M. (1936) *The General Theory of Employment, Interests and Money.* London: Macmillan.

Kraay, A. (2014) "Government Spending Multipliers in Developing Countries: Evidence from Lending by Official Creditors". *American Economic Journal: Macroeconomics*, 6(4): 170–208.

Lanau, S. (2017) *The Growth Return of Infrastructure in Latin America*, IMF Working Paper 17/35.

Leduc, S. and D. Wilson (2012) "Roads to Prosperity or Bridges to Nowhere? Theory and Evidence on the Impact of Public Infrastructure Investment", *NBER Macroeconomics Annual*, 27: 89–142.

Miyamoto, H., N. Gueorguiev, J. Honda, A. Baum and S. Walker (2020) "Growth Impact of Public Investment and the Role of Infrastructure Governance", in G. Schwartz, M. Fouad, T. Hansen and G. Verdier (eds), *Well Spent: How Strong Infrastructure Governance Can End Waste in Public Investment.* Washington, DC: International Monetary Fund.

Moretti E., C. Steinwender and J.V. Reenen (2019) *The Intellectual Spoils of War? Defense R&D, Productivity and International Spillovers*, NBER Working Papers 26483.

Myers, S. (1977) "Determinants of Corporate Borrowing", *Journal of Financial Economics*, 5(2): 147–75.

OECD (2020) *The Territorial Impact of COVID-19: Managing the Crisis across Levels of Government*, OECD Policy Responses to Coronavirus (Covid-19) Policy Paper.

Ricardo, D. (1820). *The Essay on the Funding System.* Timeless Books.

Romer, P. (1986). "Increasing Returns and Long-Run Growth", *The Journal of Political Economy*, 94(5): 1002–037.

Snowdon B. and H. R. Vane (2005) *Modern Macroeconomics*. Cheltenham; Northampton, MA. Edward Elgar Publishing, Inc.

Wolff, G. B. (2020) Without Good Governance, the EU Borrowing Mechanism to Boost the Recovery Could Fail. Bruegel Opinion Piece, https://www.bruegel.org/2020/09/without-good-governance-the-eu-borrowing-mechanism-to-boost-the-recovery-could-fail/.

8. Investing in Health

Pierre-Yves Geoffard

Introduction

Broadly speaking, any healthcare intervention that improves patients' health may be qualified as an investment. Good health, a major component of individual welfare, may also increase labour supply, especially during older age, as well as increasing labour productivity. In that sense, health is a key component of human capital. In the words of the European Commission (2014), "the Commission adopted the SWD "Investing in health" (as part of the Social Investment Package, SIP) which presents health as a value in itself and as a "growth-friendly" investment." In line with this definition, the Commission recommended in 2014 "investing in three key areas: health systems sustainability, people's health as a human capital, and reducing health inequalities."

However, such an approach raises many issues. Not every good or service that improves welfare may be qualified as an investment. Many healthcare treatments may alleviate pain, and improve or restore the autonomy of the patient treated, without increasing their future productivity. The value of healthcare cannot be reduced to the effect it may have on future production, and benefit/cost analysis now defines the benefit of healthcare as the gain it provides in terms of quality of life or longevity. We choose, in this chapter, to focus on a narrower definition of health investment: current expenditures that may improve the future production of health. Such a definition encompasses the prevention of diseases, human capital investment in healthcare and the long-term care labour force, and capital expenditure in healthcare. Put differently: "How much a country invests in new health facilities, the latest diagnostic and therapeutic equipment and information and communications technology (ICT) can have an important impact on the capacity of a health system to meet the health needs of the population and thus contribute to better outcomes" (OECD 2019).

When we talk about health and healthcare, some contextual elements are important to keep in mind.

8.1 Health

After decades of constant improvement, the decrease of mortality in most European countries, especially the richest ones, has been slowing down in the recent period.

 https://doi.org/10.11647/OBP.0280.08

Indeed, in 2015, overall mortality even increased across Europe, due to a severe influenza outbreak which killed many elderly individuals. Overall, population ageing and increases in obesity and diabetes slow down the decreasing trend of mortality by stroke or heart disease. Chronic diseases not only increase mortality, but they also reduce quality of life, especially at older ages. Population ageing also raises important issues in terms of health and long-term care, as in many countries, gains in life expectancy are no longer associated with gains in life expectancy with good health. Moreover, in all countries, individual health is strongly associated with socioeconomic status: the richer and the better educated live longer, and in better health, than the poorest and the least educated. Last but not least, the COVID-19 pandemic has induced, between March 2020 and June 2021, more than 735,000 deaths in the European Union alone.

In short, there have been as many important progresses as there are challenges ahead. Medical innovation has been incredibly successful in discovering several vaccines against COVID-19 in a few months, but better treatments for acute cases are still needed. More generally, as chronic diseases are becoming more and more prevalent, and as more and more hospital treatments can now be administered in ambulatory care units, healthcare systems need to evolve from hospital-centered organisations to more decentralised ones, which raises important issues in terms of coordination of care. The increase in "behaviour-related" diseases—such as those induced by lack of physical activity, alcohol or other drug consumption, and unhealthy diets—require public health interventions, all the more so as these diseases and these behaviors reveal strong social inequalities. Other evolutions of healthcare also impact investment, both actual and needed. New medical treatments, especially gene therapies and recent advances in oncology, often come at a very high unit cost. Finally, the digitalisation of health and healthcare information creates new possibilities for improving patients' follow-ups and healthcare coordination.

8.1.1 Healthcare and Investment in Healthcare

Overall, in 2018 European Union countries spent 10% of their GDP on healthcare,[1] and this figure varies from 5.7% in Luxemburg to 11% in Germany, France, or Sweden. Hospital care accounted for 36% of healthcare expenditures, ambulatory care for 25.5%, and drugs and medical devices represented 17.6%. Labour costs represent about three quarters of hospital and ambulatory care costs, and an even larger share of long-term care costs.

Investment in healthcare capital typically represents a small share of healthcare expenditures, highly variable across countries and time (Figure 1).

---

1   https://ec.europa.eu/eurostat/statistics-explained/index.php?title=Healthcare_expenditure_
    statistics.

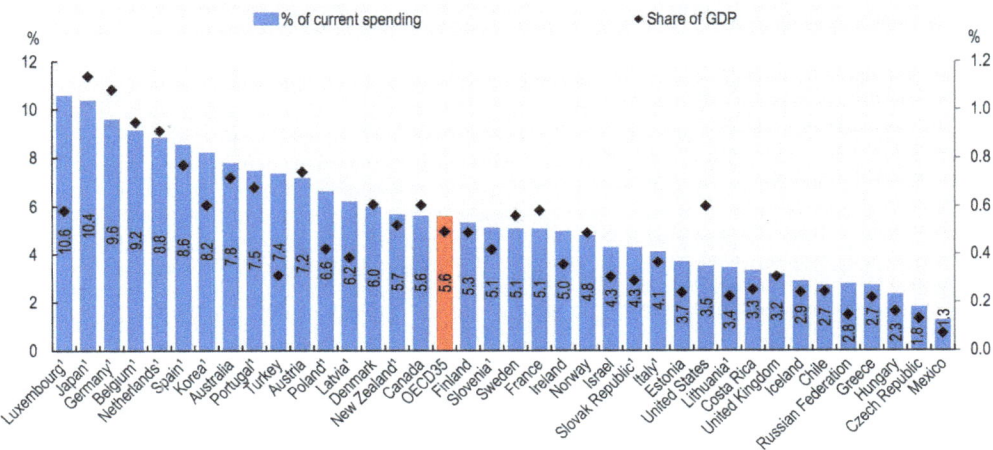

Fig. 1 Investment in Healthcare Capital as a Share of Current Health Expenditure, 2017 (or Nearest Year).

Source of data: OECD 2021, Health at a Glance.

8.1.2 Recent Crises

The Global Financial Crisis of 2008 induced tension on public budgets, including healthcare financing, due to a decrease in revenues following a decrease in economic activity. Given the high share of labour costs in healthcare, and given that these costs are mostly fixed in the short run, the pressure on healthcare budgets led to a substantial drop in investment in some countries, especially Greece and the UK.

The COVID-19 pandemic induced high-excess mortality among the elderly. The large number of patients requiring intensive care for unusually long hospital stays put tremendous pressure on hospitals. In order to cope with an exceptionally large number of COVID patients, most hospitals postponed non-urgent care for other diseases, which increased treatment delays. The structure of healthcare expenditures changed, with a sharp decrease in ambulatory care, important changes in medical drug consumption, and (of course) increases in hospital care costs; given these rapid and contrasted evolutions, it is still too early to say how much total healthcare expenditure has increased by. However, the sharp drop in GDP, induced both by individual responses to the risk of infection and by policy interventions such as lockdowns and other restrictions on social and economic activity, led to a sharp decrease in healthcare financing revenues, which are highly sensitive to GDP. As for public budgets, healthcare financing experienced in 2020 a historical deficit, contributing to a strong increase in the "social debt".

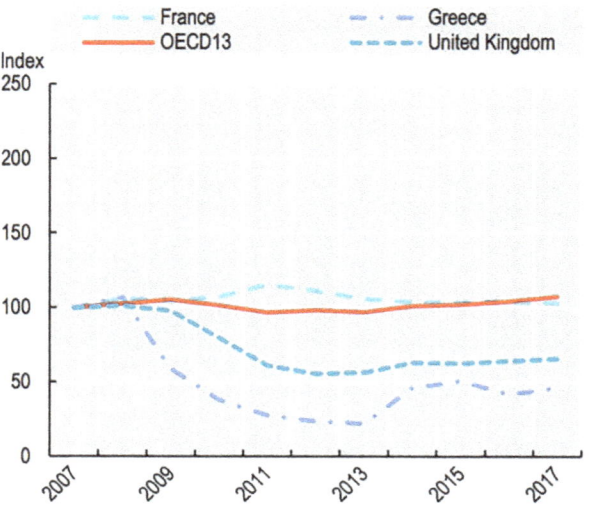

Fig. 2 Trends in Healthcare Capital Expenditure.
Source of data: OECD Health Statistics 2019, OECD National Accounts.

8.2 Relevant Investment in Health and Healthcare

However, it may be worth reminding that investment decisions should be based on the balance between current costs and the prospect of future benefits, and not on currently available budgets. This section suggests some areas in which investing resources may improve healthcare systems in the future, including investment in preventing future diseases. These suggestions are highly subjective, and each of them would require a thorough benefit/cost analysis which would go way beyond the scope of this brief.

8.2.1 Human Capital

As stated above, healthcare principally involves labour. Training medical staff usually takes up to ten years or more, taking into account medical school, internships, residencies, and specialisation. In a context in which healthcare organisations, due to digitalisation, switch from hospital to ambulatory care, and in which there is growing importance of chronic and older-age diseases, investment has to be made now to train the physicians that we will need in ten years. In addition, medical doctors are not the only workers in the health sector. Population ageing, given the uncertainty about the health condition in which individuals will spend the last years of their life, will induce a strong increase in long-term care needs. Many countries, not only in Europe, already face difficulties in hiring well-trained professionals. As suggested by some[2],

---

2   OECD (2020) *Who Cares? Attracting and Retaining Care Workers for the Elderly* https://www.oecd.org/health/who-cares-attracting-and-retaining-elderly-care-workers-92c0ef68-en.htm

this challenge may be solved by selective immigration. However, high unemployment rates, especially among women, may also suggest that an increase in training capacities may contribute to solving this challenge. Indeed, if we fail to increase labour in long-term care facilities, the elderly who suffer some loss of autonomy will be taken care of by their relatives—in practice, most of the time by their daughters or daughters in law, some of whom may have to reduce labour force participation in order to be able to devote sufficient time to their parents. Investing in training for long-term care jobs may therefore not only impact long-term care itself, but also female employment in many sectors.

8.2.2 Digital Transformations

Information is central to healthcare production. An episode of care starts with a medical visit in which a physician has to transform some information (symptoms, biological tests, past medical history, etc.) into another form of information (diagnosis). Given the rapid expansion of medical knowledge, every physician has to spend a substantial and growing share of their time learning about new therapeutic opportunities. Information technologies can be of great help, by offering computer assistance to medical decision-making. In some areas (e.g., radiology), systems based on artificial intelligence, relying on the standardised analysis of thousands or more past cases, can produce a highly reliable diagnosis. It is hard to believe that such technologies will not provoke dramatic changes in medical care, and increase healthcare productivity. Such systems are still in their infancy, and will need important investment to generate their full potential.

What is true for medical decision-making is also true for surgery. Surgeons increasingly rely on robots, not as substitutes of their own practice, but as a complement to it. For instance, a high-speed connection may allow a surgeon to command a surgical robot at long distance. Additionally, a robot commanded by a surgeon can be more precise than the same surgeon's hand in executing very precise surgical gestures. Again, such technologies will experience major improvements in the years to come, if they benefit now from relevant investment.

Electronic health records constitute another opportunity for improving healthcare. A typical healthcare episode, especially when it includes some hospital care, involves several physicians, and even more other healthcare professionals. Electronic health records may contribute to a better coordination of all. This is easier to say than to do, however, as many attempts to set up such systems on a large scale have failed in the past. Nevertheless, it is reasonable to believe that they will play an important role in improving healthcare, provided that relevant investment is undertaken.

Information and communication technologies also create the possibilities of improving surveillance and follow-up of chronic patients. For instance, a house may be equipped with sensors that detect the fall of a fragile patient and send an alarm, or measure blood pressure or other elements, the evolution of which may indicate that some action is needed. Again, such technologies are in their infancy, but their potential is huge.

Yet another area in which the digitalisation of health and healthcare creates new opportunities is the value assessment of drugs and medical devices. The producer of a new drug has to prove, in order to bring the drug to the market, that it is safe, and that it improves patients' health. This proof is usually produced in randomised clinical trials, which impose increasing development costs and delays. Whereas such procedures do increase safety and confidence in efficacy, these delays may be detrimental to patients who have to wait before being allowed to receive the treatment. Once the drug can be prescribed, it remains under strict surveillance, and eventual side effects, too rare to be observed in a clinical trial involving a few hundred or thousand carefully selected patients, can arise when the drug is prescribed *in real life* to much larger, and more heterogenous, groups of patients. Investing in health data systems that routinely collect information relevant to the evaluation of safety and efficacy of a drug may actually decrease substantially the relative costs of such "real life" experience vs *ex ante* (in an RCT) production of information.

This issue is particularly relevant for treatments of rare diseases. A disease is qualified as "rare" when it concerns a small number of patients, i.e., when its prevalence is very low, lower than one case per 2000 individuals (actual thresholds vary, but this value is commonly used in Europe). There are many rare diseases, 70 to 80% being genetic diseases, so that the total number of patients suffering from a rare disease is estimated to be around 250,000 in Europe.[3]

Rare diseases raise important issues in terms of innovation (see Section 8.3. below), and also in terms of health technology evaluation. First, the small number of patients in a given country makes it almost impossible to set up a standard randomised clinical trial with sufficient statistical power. Second, especially for gene therapies, the potential benefit to patients may last for many years, ideally for life, but at the time the therapy is discovered there is a high uncertainty about its duration, and therefore its expected overall value. Third, the unit production cost of such therapies is very high, usually larger than €1 m for the first cases, and given the small prevalence, the possibility to amortise research costs is limited. These elements raise specific issues in terms of pricing, financial risk-sharing between healthcare financing institutions and producers, and patients having access to promising treatments, as there is usually no therapeutic alternative.

A European perspective could bring important benefits: registers of all European patients could be created and maintained, gathering clinical and patient satisfaction data in a standardised way, matched with existing healthcare data such as reimbursement or cost data routinely collected by health insurance organisations. Given that such processes are currently defined and operated at each country's level, building a European platform will raise important technical, and political, issues.

---

3   https://ec.europa.eu/health/non_communicable_diseases/rare_diseases_en.

8.3 Hospital and Long-Term Care

Hospital care is a highly innovative industry. Surgeons can be assisted by surgical robots for many interventions, and sometimes such robots can be operated at long distance. Less invasive surgical procedures can treat patients who now need to stay hospitalised for a shorter period. Some surgical interventions can even be done in the outpatient section of the hospital patients can also be treated at home for illnesses that required full hospitalisation not long ago. Digitalisation offers opportunities to improve coordination of care by providing us with better circulation of information. A reasonable prediction is that fewer hospital beds will be needed in the future, but these beds may be occupied by patients receiving more intensive care.

Needless to say, all such innovations may lead to important changes in the role of hospitals within the healthcare system. Such transformations may require important investment. Identifying the relevant investments which are needed in Europe would go far beyond the scope of this brief, in part because the current state of hospitals varies a lot across, and within, European countries. Relevant innovations may be quite different across, say, northern Italy, Switzerland, and Scandinavian countries, or across southern Italy, Greece, or the United Kingdom. But what is quite clear is that no country will be prepared to face the challenges raised by the transformation of hospital care without important investment.

Population ageing has been associated with some medical progress, but the reduction in mortality at older ages is not necessarily associated with a gain in quality of life in the last years of life, especially for women. Given the sharp increase in the number of elderly people, especially in countries with a low fertility rate and very limited immigration flows, more long-term care homes will need to be built, equipped with medical facilities, and staffed with medical and paramedical personnel. This can be a highly profitable investment, since as stated above, the alternative is to rely on family or informal care to provide long-term care, which in most cases leads to relying on women, some of whom may have to withdraw, temporarily or permanently, from the labour force.

8.4 Industry: Pharmaceuticals

Along with the information technology industry, the pharmaceutical industry is the most intensive in research and development, and about 10% of firms' revenue is devoted to it on average. It is a key player in a system which articulates fundamental research, usually undertaken in publicly-funded universities; start-ups which often originate from such universities; patent law which grants temporary monopolies to inventors; big pharmaceutical firms which may conduct their own R&D, invest in start-ups, and buy (and sell) patents; health authorities which assess the safety and efficacy of new treatments; healthcare financing institutions which reimburse treatments; and patients who may benefit from new treatments. Research and development by private firms is often subsidised by governments, and innovative financing mechanisms, such as advanced market commitments (Kremer et al. 2020), also contribute to the evolution of cost- and risk-sharing between different bodies.

Public funding of R&D in health technologies varies substantially across countries in Europe, and shows divergence between countries (Figure 3). Public investment in universities, by financing fundamental research in life sciences, also varies substantially. There is high potential in investing more in R&D, both at the fundamental stage of research and in supporting and incentivising private firms.

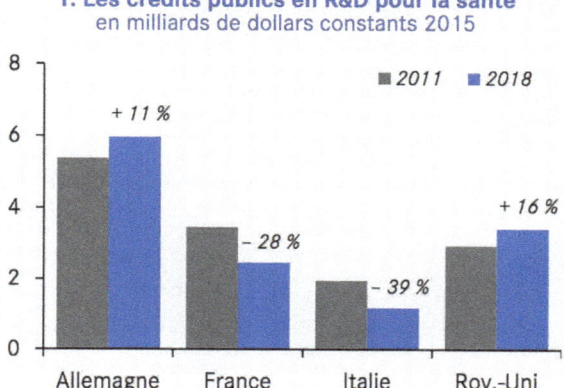

Fig. 3 Public Investment in Healthcare R&D.

Source of data: OECD, Government Budget Allocations for R&D, https://stats.oecd.org/Index. aspx?DataSetCode=GBARD_NABS2007.

Patent protection and drug pricing are also important drivers of innovation. The question seems, at first, not to be related to investment, but it is in fact closely linked. Patent protection and adequate pricing guarantee profits over ten or more years, and this perspective of profits stands as a strong incentive to innovate—and to put more effort into—therapeutical areas in which the number of patients is large and the negotiated price, at least partly based on therapeutic added value, is high. However, patents are also an artificial barrier to competition, which prevents other firms from producing a similar drug, and discourages process innovation to produce it at the lowest cost. An alternative to patents would be innovation prizes (Geoffard 2020), in which financing authorities commit to pay a high lump-sum payment to the inventor of a socially desirable drug to buy out its patent; this allows *ex post* competition, reduces costs for health insurance, and requires an upfront investment which is a substitute to future profits paid during patent protection.

As stated above, some recent innovations, and others in the pipeline, have a very high production cost. Some gene therapies may cost more than €1 m for a single treatment, which has to be tailored to each patient. However, when they concern only a very small number of patients each year, even such sky-rocketing prices do not threaten health insurance budgets. Investing in such innovations is important to attract localisation of R&D units in Europe, as well as to reduce the delay patients experience before being able to access the treatment.

Innovation is not everything. Production also matters, and requires investment in production lines. This fact is highly visible for vaccines against COVID-19, for which limited production capacities reduce the speed at which populations could be vaccinated throughout the world. And though we do not know when a new virus will strike, we know it will happen again, some time in the future. However, we do not know its features, and of course we do not have treatments nor vaccines on the table for these future viruses. New technologies such as mRNA have shown their ability to offer a fast and efficient response to new viruses, and seem particularly powerful in a situation with a high uncertainty, as they can be adjusted to the specific characteristics of the still-to-come virus.

In that sense, setting up large production lines (which can be mobilised rapidly whenever a new pandemic hits the world) now is also an investment that could enable us, in the future, to respond much more rapidly and to avoid the health, economic, and social crises that we witnessed in 2020 and 2021. Investing in flexible, adjustable, vaccine production lines could be worth considering.

Finally, the COVID-19 crisis has also shown how the whole supply chain for certain pharmaceutical drugs can be very fragile, as it relies on a very small number of upstream producers of active ingredients, mostly located outside Europe. Relocating the production of some of these components in Europe could indeed be an answer to this fragility, but it will also require important investment.

8.5 Prevention

Preventing, at the individual or societal level, the occurrence of a future illness, or reducing its severity, is a textbook example of investment in health. As an old proverb attributed to Erasmus says, "Prevention is better than cure". Is it really? The answer is a typical economist one: "It depends". Some preventive actions, like vaccination, come at a small cost, and may produce high health benefits in the future. However, some other preventive actions do improve future health or reduce future mortality, but the cost per life saved, or per year in good health gained, is out of range with other, preventive or curative, interventions (Tengs et al. 1995).

Preventive care also typically represents a small share of total healthcare expenditure (Figure 4), and varies a lot across countries, ranging from 5.1% in the UK to less than 0.8% in Slovakia.

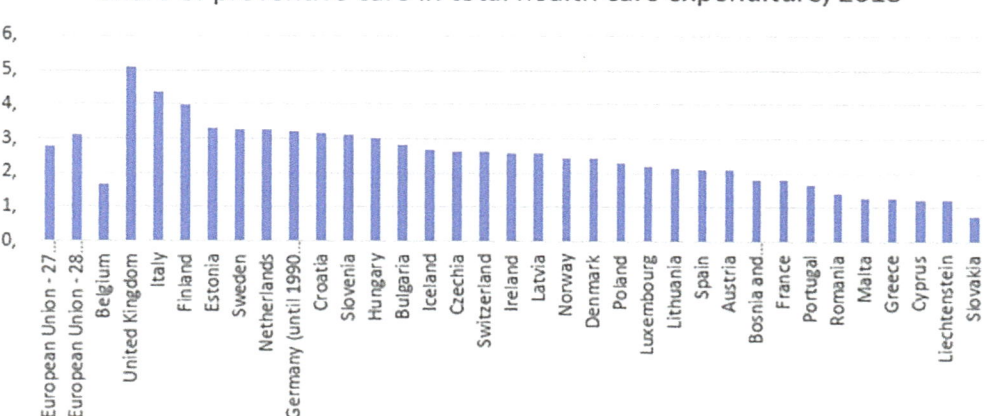

Fig. 4 Share of Preventive Care in Total Healthcare Expenditure, 2018.

Source of data: Eurostat, https://ec.europa.eu/eurostat/databrowser/view/HLTH_SHA11_HC__custom_423640/bookmark/table?lang=en&bookmarkId=5a8bfe63-5f2d-475c-b221-d7480f54fba3.

Notice that the average share of healthcare expenditure devoted to prevention dropped from 3.12% to 2.77% when the UK left the EU. This points out how much the UK National Health Service is rooted in prevention. Physicians, or more precisely group practices made up of several healthcare professionals, are partly financed according to their involvement in prevention. The health indicators in the UK are comparable to other countries of similar per capita GDP (e.g., same life expectancy at birth for men as in France), but the UK devotes a substantially lower share of GDP to healthcare expenditures (9.8% in 2019). In addition, whereas economic inequality is large in the UK, the association between socioeconomic status and health, at the individual level, seems weaker than in other comparable countries. In most countries, shifting from a healthcare system mostly centred on hospital care towards a more decentralised system, where general practice is the entry point into healthcare and tackles prevention as well as reduction of health inequalities, is an option to consider. Would such a shift require huge investment? Not necessarily, but such a reorganisation would be so disruptive to many healthcare professionals that it would surely need to be accompanied by important investment in organisation strategy, information systems, and training.

More generally, in the era of evidence-based medicine, prevention suffers from a disadvantage with respect to curative medicine: it is less often evaluated, impact evaluation being more difficult to assess due to the multiplicity of causes for any disease, the unknown duration before effects materialise, and the huge heterogeneity of situations. Better evidence on the costs and benefits of disease prevention across the board could yet be produced. Another similar investment in knowledge would also be welcome, to better understand the causal mechanisms underlying the strong socioeconomic inequalities witnessed in all countries.

To conclude on prevention, the ongoing COVID-19 crisis has shown a major weakness of health systems in Europe and elsewhere. Epidemiological surveillance failed to detect early diffusion of the virus in certain European countries or regions, at a time where it would have been possible to break, or at least to delay, the epidemic. This, also, needs to be strengthened in the future, if we want to be better prepared for the next pandemic.

8.6 Conclusion

The healthcare sector is, in essence, a very innovative industry in all its components. In conclusion, it should be reminded that if the years to come are associated with attempts to reduce public expenditure in order to repay the debt inherited from the COVID-19 crisis, such budget cuts should be contemplated with great prudence if they affect healthcare expenditure. In a sector where the main input is labour, budget cuts often lead to delayed or foregone capital investment, not because they are less efficient, but because they are easier to reduce.

However, demographic trends, digitalisation, and an increased role of prevention are the structural drivers of transformation in healthcare, and such changes will require important investment in the future.

References

European Commission (2014) *Investments in Health: Policy Guide for the European Structural and Investment Funds 2014–2020*, https://ec.europa.eu/health/sites/default/files/health_structural_funds/docs/esif_guide_en.pdf.

Geoffard, P. Y. (2020) *Covid-19: Speeding up Vaccine Development*, https://voxeu.org/article/accelerating-development-covid-19-vaccine.

Kremer, M., J.D. Levin, M. Christopher and C.M. Snyder (2020) *Designing Advance Market Commitments for New Vaccines*, NBER wp 28168, https://www.nber.org/papers/w28168.

OECD (2019) *Health at a Glance 2019: OECD Indicators*. Paris: OECD Publishing, https://doi.org/10.1787/4dd50c09-en.

Tengs, T. O., M.E. Adams, J.S. Pliskin, D.G. Safran, J.E. Siegel, M.C. Weinstein and J.D. Graham (1995) "Five-Hundred Life-Saving Interventions and Their Cost-Effectiveness", *Risk Analysis*, 15(3): 369–90.

9. Education, Human Capital, and Social Cohesion

Lieve Fransen, Romano Prodi, and Edoardo Reviglio

Introduction

The pandemic has speeded up many of the great transformations that are taking place in society. Pervasive digitalisation, green transition, major changes in job markets due to the new industrial revolution, the ageing society, growing inequalities and poverty, geo-political changes—the list goes on. In this sense, the pandemic has become an unexpected "experimental laboratory" for what may become our new world. The evolution of this new world can still be directed in one way or another, and it represents both risks and opportunities. We must be careful to think through and design the most effective policies and investments that leave no-one behind and protect us from the risks inherent in such transitions.

Indeed, it is of paramount importance that we invest massively in our human and social capital—and especially in education and lifelong learning.

In the 1950s and 1960s, scholars like Jacob Mincer, Theodore Schultz, and Gary Becker documented and explained the close connection between human capital (i.e., the stock of skills, abilities, and knowledge an individual possesses) and economic returns. Their groundbreaking studies stimulated a growing research agenda, which is still contributing to our knowledge concerning the relationship between the educational system and the economy. For example, we know that education, combined with other variables, significantly affects an individual's social mobility, earnings, employability, and health too. But we also know that a better educated society is correlated with economic growth and prosperity.

However, the mere focus on the economic effects of human capital should not let us forget about the social and political "returns" of education. Indeed, not only is education one of the main drivers of economic growth, but it is also one of the great equalisers within and across societies. Social justice, intended as equality of opportunities, begins in the classroom, and gaps in the educational systems are gaps that we find in society. In order to go beyond the rhetorical commitment to inclusion

https://doi.org/10.11647/OBP.0280.09

and equality of opportunities, there is now, more than ever, a need to invest in an open and collaborative education, based on information-sharing where students are active contributors in connection with teachers.

Moreover, in a world where the spread of democracy cannot be taken for granted anymore, the goals of educating thoughtful citizens of and for a democratic society should permeate how we think about the classroom of the future. Indeed, education is not only about increasing knowledge and skills for personal and social growth, but it is also about the attempt to foster in pupils those values and ideas that make democratic life possible, such as critical reflection, the capacity to balance individual rights and responsibilities, the ability to judge and evaluate ideas on the basis of their intrinsic value rather than their popularity, etc.

In this chapter, we discuss the impact of digital distance learning during COVID-19, along with the need to transform our education and learning models and to invest in physical and intangible infrastructure, based on new needs. We discuss recent data on expenditures on education in the EU, make concrete proposals for a change in the Growth and Stability Pact (GSP)—especially with regard to social investment and infrastructure—and propose new models for financing social infrastructure. We show that the new expansionary policy will increase the demand for "safe assets", which includes financial instruments for social and green infrastructure. We also stress the role of multi-lateral and national promotional banks and institutions in becoming new "market makers" by increasing "patient capital" going into the real economy. Finally, we look at the InvestEU programme and the Next Generation EU (NGEU) fund and discuss their potential contribution to education investment.

9.1 Digital Learning: A Boost During the Pandemic but and Increaser of Inequality and Stress on Public Investment

Twelve years after the financial and economic crash, Europe seemed to have passed the worst of the recession and the austerity response, only to find itself in the midst of a major health crisis with the COVID-19 pandemic. The response to the pandemic illustrates how austerity measures and a lack of investment in health and human capital left Europe poorly prepared—and how distance learning, tele-medicine, tele-working, and tele-education were boosted at great speed, while the growth and stability rules were upended in 2020.

For many years, the world has tried to reimagine education and lifelong learning for the digital age (Camara, Biglia, Van Looy et al. 2020), but nobody predicted that the greatest transformation would be caused by communicable disease spreading globally. While historically, crises have often been at the origin of major changes in social systems, COVID-19 changed socializing, learning, working, and parenting globally and at a scale never seen before. By mid-April 2020, more than 90% of Europe's students had been locked out of classrooms for months, and teachers and parents were confronted with teaching, supervising, and guiding young people during a radically changed situation for all. The pandemic demonstrated that investing in human capital in the digital age is essential, while the socialising role of schools and peer groups has been highlighted as never before.

Digital learning received an enormous boost during the pandemic, forcing education professionals and learners to rapidly adapt their competences. It had a positive impact by limiting the loss of human capital for some (The World Bank Group 2020). But for others, adaptation has been slower and not well managed due to multiple factors including the lack of or asymmetric distribution of infrastructure and connectivity; inadequate preparation of teachers, parents, and pupils; some students' low motivation for learning; social isolation; cyber risks; technical incompatibilities among the learning systems available; technology dependency; and higher costs for the institutions and the families involved.

Estimates for France, Italy, and Germany suggest that students suffered a significant learning loss (time spent on formal learning) when switching from offline to online learning. Using PISA 2006 data, it was demonstrated that one additional weekly hour of instruction over the school year increases test scores by about 6%. Therefore, the loss reported in France, Italy, and Germany reflects the reduction in test score students would be experiencing because of less time spent in learning compared to the amount of time they typically invest when they are in school (Di Pietro, Biagi, Costa, Karpinski, and Mazza 2020).

Learning loss does not impact all students in the same way. An analysis of learning loss during the COVID-19 school closures shows a substantial divergence by socioeconomic status. Therefore, addressing learning loss and implementing large-scale catch-up programmes should be a top priority of the recovery in Europe (Algan, Brunello, Goreichy, and Hristova 2021). Investment in targeted interventions for the most vulnerable could limit the inequality between rich and poor children—which widened during the months of school closure (Nugroho, Pasquini, Reuge, and Amaro 2020; Ionescu, Paschia, Nicolau, Stanescu, Stancescu, Coman, and Uzlau 2020).

Data collected by OECD in 2018, prior to the pandemic, speak for themselves: on average, less than 40% of educators across the EU felt ready to use digital technologies in teaching, with divergences between EU member states (Tiven, Fuchs, Bazari, and Quarrie 2018).

More than one third of 13–14 year old who participated in the International Computer and Information Literacy Study (ICILS) in 2018 (European Commission 2018) did not possess the most basic proficiency level in digital skills. A quarter of low-income households have no access to computers and broadband, with divergences across the EU affected by household income (Eurostat 2019).

The Global Survey on Youth and COVID-19 by the International Labor Organization in 2020 (ILO 2020) found "the impact of the pandemic on young people to be systematic, deep and disproportionate." The report mentions that COVID-19 left 13%

of young people without access to learning; 65% reported having learned less since the pandemic began, and 51% believe their education will be delayed. The pandemic has also had a heavy impact on young workers: 17% stopped working and 42% reported a reduction in income.

The pandemic is clearly far more than a health crisis alone: it is affecting human capital formation and retention, affecting societies and economies, and will have long-term consequences.

To foster the consolidation and the resilience of education, training, and employment in Europe, the European Commission adopted a renewed Digital Education Action Plan, reflecting on the lessons learned from the crisis.

However, soon there will be even fewer resources and potentially lower investment in education and learning. Large debt and slower growth mean that education budgets will not rise in absolute terms as needed. Education budgets as a share of national spending are likely to be squeezed.

When the World Bank analysed education spending after the Global Financial Crisis in 2008, in lower-middle-income countries (LMICs) it observed a large dip in education spending in the immediate aftermath of the crisis that did not recover for several years (The World Bank Group 2020).

Despite high hopes that technology and connectivity would be the answer to learning continuity and reskilling during the crisis, there is not yet any evidence that those can replace teachers or reduce inequality. This isn't surprising, because we are depending on technologies that many households around the world do not have access to or have not developed the skills to use or to help the students use. In low- and lower-middle-income countries, only 20% of households have access to the internet (The World Bank Group 2020). Even in the EU, stark digital divides along lines of income, race, and geography characterised distance learning experiences, particularly for low-income households.

9.2 Reforming Education and Lifelong Learning, and Ensuring Adequate Investment

Reform of education and lifelong learning is essential to raise and preserve human capital, facilitate life course transitions, provide a buffer against risks such as unemployment and disease, and guide long-term investors (Vandenbroucke, Hemerijck, and Palier 2011; Hemerijck and Santoni 2019; Fransen, Prodi, and Reviglio 2018).

The world today and the society our children will work and live in are very different to the world our schools and universities were designed to serve decades ago. Formal education was implemented around the time of the first Industrial Revolution; schools

Box 1. on definitions

Formal learning takes place in the education and training system, in universities and in the high-level arts education institutions. It leads to a certification or a vocational qualification that can also be obtained through an apprenticeship.

Non-formal learning is an intentionally chosen learning that takes place outside the formal education and training system. It takes place in any organization with educational and training purposes, also in voluntary bodies, national civil service organizations, organizations of the private social sector or enterprises.

Informal learning refers to activities carried out in every-day life, at work, at home and in leisure time, even without an intentional choice.

Source: European Commission 2018

then were less about improving children's human capital than producing a punctual and obedient workforce for the factories. This concept is no longer fit for purpose and reforms are long overdue.

The main drivers for education and lifelong learning reforms are:

- Changing work patterns (the need to work longer and on consecutive careers requiring a high degree of flexibility) and societal realities (new lifestyles) requiring regular upskilling.

- Opportunities offered for the creation of a large learning ecosystem because of the availability of new technologies.

- The need for transformation to adapt to demographic realities (ageing populations, low fertility rates, and economic and political migrations) and location changes (rural-urban movements).

Schools are now only one part of a far bigger learning ecosystem. In the digital age, learning can and must become a lifelong experience. We should aim to improve learning opportunities not only in schools but also in homes, community centres, museums, and workplaces. The internet has created new learning opportunities, enabling online learning communities in which children and adults around the globe collaborate on projects and learn from each other (Resnick 2020).

The unexpected boost for tele-education provided by the COVID-19 pandemic should now require major of structural reforms, and help boost and guide larger long-term investment in those areas. The Economist in January 2021 reported that: "Lots of children could benefit if the pandemic raises awareness that not all pupils are well-served by a one-size-fits-all approach to schooling, and if it directs attention and funding to improving alternative models."

The content of learning activities, as well as how learning is organised, needs drastic transformation and adaptation. For example, digital native students simply search the internet for information, while many teachers and parents have not grown up with the same digital skillset. With information more widely available and theoretically more accessible, learners could take more ownership and initiative, and educators could provide mentorship, context, and more individualised guidance.

Providing equal opportunities and adequate attention to social and gender inclusion and participation implies that access to quality childcare and education should also be ensured from an early age, including for those children and students with special needs, migrants, minorities, those who are low-income, etc. (Muraille 2020).

Education in the future should be founded on multifunctional community learning centres that provide virtual and actual space, have reliable connectivity, and mobilise teachers/trainers and learners. The future community learning centre focuses on including all potential learners, with greater inclusion of pupils with socioeconomic disadvantages and special educational needs, equipping them with appropriate skills to improve their chances of finding rewarding work, leading independent lives, and actively contributing to society.

Transformation will require re-envisioning the spaces where learning takes place and changing how people learn by using multiple physical and virtual spaces in and outside of formal settings. This would see full individual personalisation of content and pedagogy enabled by leading-edge technology, and drawing on body information, facial expressions, neural signals, and AI (Khan, Ihalage, Ma, Liu, Liu, and Hao 2021).

As the distinction between formal and informal learning blurs and eventually disappears, individual learning can advance by taking advantage of collective intelligence being rapidly accessible through new technologies, helping us to solve real-life problems.

Technologies are changing not only what students *should* learn, but also what they *can* learn. Fresh ideas are now accessible through creative use of digital technologies. For example, you can now use simulations to explore ecosystems, economic systems, and immune systems in ways that were previously not possible.

In terms of bricks and mortar, the community learning centres should be constructed as passive buildings, with sustainable design working in two ways. First, because of low energy costs, additional costs will be earned back in the long run. Second, such designs trigger children to reflect on environmental and sustainability issues. Spaces can be used for different purposes, and areas such as sports facilities and libraries could be used by third parties in the evening or weekends. Investment must be made in digital and ICT facilities and connectivity, such as digital whiteboards and programmable robots.

The returns on investing (ROI) in such centres could include savings on welfare and assistance, in addition to economic returns.

Universities could become hubs for advanced learning, research, and innovation for a larger geographical area, and facilitate the provisions for a learning society. These hubs would be interconnected with local businesses, public bodies, and other research institutes, attracting private capital to develop innovative technologies, incubate startups, and develop new business models.

ROI from such advanced learning hubs would need to include the wider economic benefits of innovation and impacts on productivity and on competitiveness.

Current expenditure may not need to increase significantly everywhere, but instead be reallocated towards the new approaches. However, some geographic areas do have critically underfunded education and lifelong learning. This is especially the case in regions that cut investment in social sectors drastically with austerity measures after the financial crisis. This lack of investment in health, human capital, and connectivity left Europe poorly prepared for the COVID-19 pandemic.

Capital expenditure for education and lifelong learning in the EU was approximately €65 bn in 2015 (national accounts data from Eurostat), with the UK, Germany, France, and the Netherlands accounting for around two thirds of the total (Fransen, del Bufalo, and Reviglio 2018).

- Spain, Italy, Austria, Denmark, Ireland, and Slovakia invest 0.3 % of their GDP or less

- Czechia, Latvia, Lithuania, Estonia, Finland, and the Netherlands invest 0.8 % or more

Per pupil, Spain spends €183 and the Netherlands €1,283.

Box 2. On Education & lifelong learning

Total estimated at +/- €65 bn. Education infrastructure spending by:

- The **public sector** as a percentage of GDP: public investment in the EU-28 was €65 bn in 2015 including gross capital formation and capital transfers. This is equal to 0.43 % of GDP—€580 per student, ranging from €382 at primary level to €723 at third level.

- The **private sector** as a percentage of GDP: private investment in education is more difficult to gauge. The OECD says private expenditure represents 15 % of total expenditure. Almost all of this consists of household outlays for tuition and other current costs; private sector investment only makes up a small fraction.

Source: Fransen, del Bufalo, and Reviglio 2018.

It was estimated that a minimum additional capital investment is needed annually of 15 bn per annum (Fransen, del Bufalo, and Reviglio 2018).

The total average *public expenditures* for education also decreased constantly from a share of 5.5% of GDP in 2009 to only 4.7% in 2018, representing a 17% disinvestment since 2009. While the absolute amount of resources destined towards education and training has increased, it is the percentage over GDP that gives the real measure of the importance.

The breakdown of the data by countries in 2018 gives us an even grimmer image. Only three countries have increased their percentage of investment in education: Belgium (+0.1%), Sweden (+0.1%), and Croatia (+1.7%). On the other side of the scale, most countries have registered a decrease: Cyprus (-1.2%), Slovenia (-1.2%), Ireland (-1.5%), Portugal (-2.0%), and Lithuania (-2.6%).

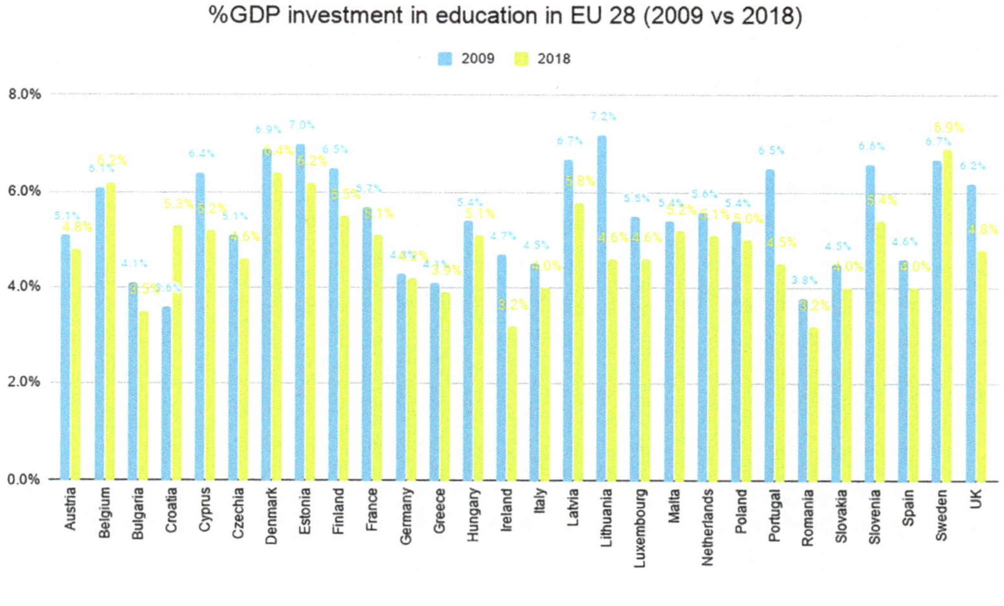

Fig. 1 % GDP Investment in Education in EU-28 (2009 vs 2018).

Source of data: Lifelong Learning platform 2021, *Europe's share of GDP for education and training has never been this low. A comparative analysis*, 23rd March 2020.

However, while investing sufficient long-term resources in reformed education and learning is critical, according to OECD, the relation between expenditure and learning outcomes breaks down after a certain threshold is passed: after reaching a minimum level of inputs, more resources do not necessarily imply an improvement (Canton, Thum-Thysen, and Voigt 2018).

It is important to note that the figures mentioned above refer to formal education and do not capture potential investment effort made in informal and non-formal education contexts.

9.3 New Models for Financing Social Infrastructure for Education

How shall we finance such great needs of education infrastructure within the huge transition which we tried to describe above, which will characterise our educational system and lifelong learning in the future, without weighing too much on high public debts across the EU?

Schools and related education infrastructure were traditionally financed directly by local authorities, eventually with contributions from the state, by raising long-term debt from public institutions. The interest rates of debt were very close the one paid on sovereign debt, because institutions providing the financing were using funding guaranteed by the state. The technical capacity of local authorities was much better than it is today, but the infrastructure was also simpler and more basic. Today, as we have seen above, much more complex education infrastructure is needed, and technical capacities to project, build, and manage must be much more sophisticated.

In this section, we will try to describe the new innovative schemes which are emerging across the EU in financing education infrastructure.

To accommodate this changing world, the model that is used to finance infrastructure in the EU is rapidly changing. With public budgets under stress and a huge demand for new infrastructure due to green and digital revolutions, we will see a growing involvement of private and institutional investors in public-private initiatives, including infrastructure for education.

Institutional long-term investors with more than $130 tn of assets under management at the global level are looking at "education infrastructure" as a new, fully-fledged asset class to invest in (OECD 2013; Garonna and Reviglio 2015; Inderst 2021). Moreover, as we shall discuss later, there is a growing demand for "safe assets" by long-term investors, to match long-term assets to long-term liabilities.

Economic infrastructure, such as energy, transport, and telecommunications, produces cashflows on its own that can repay the cost of construction. Such infrastructure involves construction, tariffs, and market risks, and this makes their yield higher. With social infrastructure mostly financed by public money and paid for by taxpayers, it does not have the same risks (Figure 4) and the risk/yield profile is lower. Both types of infrastructure investment are attractive to institutional investors who like to diversify the risk in their portfolios.

Social infrastructure investment has distinctive features that distinguishes it from economic infrastructure (EDHEC-Risk Institute, February 2012; Fransen, Prodi, and Reviglio 2018). Generally, it tends to be illiquid investment. This type of investment has long time horizons and, if equity is invested, it becomes difficult to exit. However, on the debt side, ever larger, deeper, and more liquid social and green bond markets are emerging and may overcome this problem, making it far more attractive for institutional and even retail investors to invest in education infrastructure. Moreover, default rates and recovery rates of infrastructure debt, in general, are relatively lower than high-rated corporate debt.[1]

Infrastructure projects in education (and health) are usually relatively small. According to EDHEC-Risk Institute (EDHEC 2012), roughly 99% of existing social infrastructure projects in Europe entail a total capital investment of less than €1 bn, with the great majority of projects below €30 m. The small-average size is good for spreading risk (portfolio diversification), but it reduces cost synergies during the structuring and arranging phase. Unlike many economic infrastructure projects, such as toll roads, ports, airports, or power generation plants, which usually collect revenue from end users, social infrastructure projects often rely on the availability of fees paid by the public sector. Therefore, from a financial (and financing) perspective, it is key to bear in mind that the cashflow streams to repay the financing of social infrastructure investment come ultimately from public budgets. This means that education infrastructure investment risk is only slightly higher than sovereign bonds' risk. To overcome the potential small-average capex size "bottleneck" while preserving the sought-after portfolio diversification, a solution could be the efficient "bundling" of similar education infrastructure projects. In fact, when bundled into a single, larger procurement, a beneficial structure can be implemented to address:

- A group of similar assets across multiple sites.
- An assortment of different assets at a single site.
- Different assets across multiple sites.

In addition, the bundling of similar assets can save on design and construction costs, as similar materials can be used and bought in bulk. More standardized design and construction processes also create the opportunity to save on long-term maintenance due to similar replacement parts and equipment used.

Availability payments from the public sector are usually agreed beforehand and tend to be inflation-linked. Predictable and steady real returns are attractive for investors.

The small-average capital investment size of social infrastructure projects, however, makes direct infrastructure investment unattractive to large long-term investors, as they face relatively high active management costs for such modest investment. Therefore, financial intermediaries are key to channeling institutional investors towards social infrastructure. Institutional investors have the possibility of investing in equity through listed infrastructure funds, unlisted intermediary funds, or directly at the SPV level.

Political and regulatory risks, often linked, are another key dimension of social infrastructure investment. Public policies might change over the extended life span of

1   See Moody (2017) *Default and Recovery Rates for Project Finance Bank Loans, 1983–2015*, Default Research, Moody's Investors Service, 6 March 2017; Moody (2017) *Addendum: Infrastructure Default and Recovery Rates, 1983–2015*, Default Research, Moody's Investors Service, 27 April 2017; and Moody (2016) *Infrastructure Default and Recovery Rates, 1983–2015*, Default Research, Moody's Investors Service, 18 July 2016.

an asset. Governments may renege on commitments and regulators may change the regulatory framework.

Even so, innovative solutions for financing education, health, and social housing at a sustainable cost for European public finances are becoming more widespread. In the main, direct contracts by the public authority to a private enterprise are financed by long-term loans. Quantitative easing means the spreads between EU member states have been reduced significantly, but this will not last forever, and local authority debt offers little room for maneuvering.

It will be important to crowd in as much institutional and private investment in social infrastructure financing as possible. The added value is not merely providing financing so much as the quality of the schemes required to attract investors and others. The public sector, generally, does not have the necessary technical competencies to effectively plan, build, and manage complex projects. If they had such skills, as we already mentioned, it would be cheaper to finance schemes directly through sovereign funding. The complexity of today's integrated and eventually bundled sets of infrastructures is typically handled by the many specialised players who are generally not within the public sector. To ensure that every single stakeholder play fair, promotional banks and the EIB, CEB, and other institutional regional platforms can play a crucial role in organising and giving technical assistance to public sector promoters. Moreover, other contributions from various sources can be "blended" to reduce direct costs to taxpayers (Prodi and Reviglio 2019).

In general, we need a clearer and friendlier system of rules by Eurostat to understand if a project is an on- or off-balance sheet (Fransen, del Bufalo, and Reviglio 2018).

Now consider, for instance, that a municipality, group of municipalities, or other public administration needs to invest in education or other social infrastructure. They can decide to implement it through innovative forms of institutional public-private partnerships or investment platforms:

1. The local administration will pay for the work through an availability fee that will affect expenditure year after year.

2. Costs can be kept down by a national or European grant, public guarantees, or tax incentives.

3. Fiscal space can be provided through a special clause for social investment.

4. Contributions in kind can be made using local public heritage assets, land, or buildings, for example.

5. An institutional "technical assistance" system can ensure risks and profits are well distributed between public and private sectors.

This solution, known as "blending", helps to contain the cost of public administration and increase the quality and timing of the construction of infrastructure (EPEC 2017; Fransen, Prodi, and Reviglio 2018; Inderst 2021). There is also the possibility of creating public-private-institutional vehicles that may bundle different projects to reach a critical mass for investors and to achieve similar high quality across several municipalities or regions involved in a bigger project.

Why are institutional investors so interested in infrastructure investment? Because infrastructure is a "safe asset", and there was a huge shortage of this type of financial instrument after the 2008 financial crisis. Indeed, the importance of safe assets has become central since that crisis.

Safe assets are a pillar of an ordered financial system. They are a store of value for institutions, including pension funds and insurance companies, as they allow them to match long-term assets to long-term liabilities. They are also structural elements of commercial bank balance sheets (Reviglio 2020).

More generally, they are used by financial institutions to meet regulatory requirements and provide collateral for borrowing additional funds. These stores of value come in many forms: cash, bank deposits, US Treasury bills, European government bonds, projects bonds, recovery bonds, infrastructure bonds, green and social bonds, and bonds raised by the EIB and by national promotional banks and institutions. They can include high-rating corporate bonds, stocks, and equity in infrastructure funds and/or projects.

There is another reason why education and social infrastructure in general are considered good investments for institutional investors. They are generally "green" and/or come with strong social externalities at a point when markets' short-termism has not yet priced upcoming taxation on polluting investment.

To hedge climate risks, investors can either divest polluting investment in their portfolio, invest in low-carbon indices, or invest in green and social bond companies.[2] Indeed, investing in properly constructed decarbonised investments, such as those in education infrastructure, can allow long-term passive investors to hedge climate risk without sacrificing financial returns (Andersson, Bolton, and Samama 2015; see also Bolton, Depres, Pereira da Silva, Samama, and Svartzman 2020).

Now, with the Next Generation EU fund (2021–27), the American Rescue Plan Act (2021–31), and other recovery plans in many countries, the number of safe assets will grow at unprecedented levels. This is a unique opportunity to move to a more long-term finance approach that is oriented towards infrastructure and the real economy.

9.4 The Golden Rule for Social Investment, Reforming the Stability and Growth Pact, and Next Generation EU

For many years, it was argued that investing in education and health should be an investment and not a cost in budgetary terms, and it was vital to boost investment in

---

2   There exist two main types of low-carbon indices: "pure-play" indices, including stakes of green (and social) companies, and "decarbonised" indices (or "green beta indices"), constructed by excluding the largest GHG emitters from a benchmark index.

social infrastructure. But despite fine words and new instruments doing some of this, the pandemic has shone a light on failings.

Because of the pandemic, the EU institutions suspended the Stability and Growth Pact (SGP) rules for government spending and debt reduction through activation of the General Escape Clause. This will remain in place until the end of 2022. The pandemic led to a remarkable consensus among EU member states on the need to provide fiscal stimulus beyond the levels allowed by the rules. As the recovery continues, different views on debt consolidation are likely to emerge and old differences to re-emerge. However, returning to pre-coronavirus rules would be counterproductive. The need to reform the EU's fiscal framework has, in the meantime, gained traction and could be an opportunity to introduce meaningful reforms to boost social investment and social infrastructure investment sooner rather than later.

The priority now should be to allow for more long-term public investment, including in social sectors. This raises the question of whether fiscal rules can be amended to encourage countries to step up their national social investment strategies while maintaining the overall integrity of a rules-based budgetary framework, including the Stability and Growth Pact (SGP) 3% deficit and 60% debt limits, and crowding in private sector investment at the same time.

Public investment in general, as a % of GDP, continued to decrease years after the Global Financial Crisis and only recently started picking up, slightly before the pandemic. However, the slight increase in public investment suffers from a pro-cyclical bias and a short-term orientation, while still insufficiently targeting social investment in human capital formation and in social infrastructure.

Investing in education and in social infrastructure in general should be given special consideration, and it is unclear if the new financing instruments of the EU will do so at all. In the 2021 *European Outlook on Public Investment*, in the chapter on Social Investment and Infrastructure (Hemerijck, Mazzucato, and Reviglio 2020), a Golden Rule was proposed to exempt human capital stock spending from the euro area fiscal rulebook for 1.5% of GDP for around a decade, as a flagship initiative of the new European Commission. Today, this move has become even more urgent.

The Next Generation EU fund comprises the Recovery and Resilience Facility and several other EU programmes. It is clearly a missed opportunity that social infrastructures did not receive a unique dedicated "window", but instead are spread across other missions and programmes. This is most likely because they include strong digital, green, and social cohesion components. However, this approach goes against EU best practices around highly integrated systems (school, health, housing, etc.). In InvestEU, for example, more than sixty-five guaranteed funds and twelve financial instruments are combined in only four policy windows, as also recommended in the 2018 "Prodi Report" on social infrastructure (Fransen, del Bufalo and Reviglio 2018). The policy windows in InvestEU are sustainable infrastructure, research, innovation and digitalisation, SMEs, and social investment and skills. From this perspective, Next Generation EU is a step backwards. Digital, green, and transport are undoubtedly essential elements of EU recovery, competitiveness, and social cohesion. However, integrated social infrastructure and investment will be as important, if not more so, especially early in the post-pandemic period. Next Generation EU does not have such an integrated view. As a result, education, health, and social housing are spread here and there without a coherent view, and with fewer resources directly dedicated to these sectors, including education. Therefore, we should aim to integrate more successfully the elements contained in the EU Plan, including digital and green, alongside renewed investment in education, health, and social housing.

9.5 Conclusion

Since the 2008 crisis, investment in education has been greatly reduced. The austerity policies which have characterised the EU have had a strong negative impact on education, health, and social housing. This is partially because social infrastructure is largely financed by local authorities, which have seen their budgets substantially reduced.

We demonstrated that the gap between the actual investment and the needs is large in most of the EU member states. Now, because of the suspension of the Growth and Stability Pact since the COVID-19 pandemic, more resources should be available, at least temporarily. Moreover, the Next Generation EU instrument provides substantial funds for digital and green transition, including education infrastructure.

The world today and the society our children will work and live in are very different. Our schools and universities were designed to serve the needs of a very different society. Formal education was implemented around the time of the first Industrial Revolution; schools then were less about improving children's human capital than producing a punctual and obedient workforce for the factories. This concept is no longer fit for purpose and reforms are long overdue.

The schools of the future are going to be very different from those of the past. Changing models of education, plus more pervasive digitalisation, will lead to the need to restructure and build new schools. Moreover, lifelong learning has become even more important than in the past due to the transformation of the job market. Much more mobility from one type of job to another is going to be required.

How will those great needs of education infrastructure be financed in the future?

We described innovative schemes which are emerging across the EU in financing school and other education infrastructure.

It will be important to crowd in as much institutional and private investment in education infrastructure financing as possible. The added value, we argued, is not merely providing financing so much as the quality of the schemes required to attract investors and others. The public sector, generally, does not have the necessary technical competencies to effectively plan, build, and manage complex projects. If they had such skills, it would be cheaper to finance schemes directly through sovereign funding. The complexity of today's integrated and eventually bundled sets of infrastructures is typically handled by the many specialised players who are generally not within the public sector. To ensure that every single stakeholder play fair, promotional banks and the EIB, CEB, and other institutional regional platforms can play a crucial role in organising and giving technical assistance to public sector promoters. Moreover, other contributions from various sources can be "blended" to reduce direct costs to taxpayers.

Institutional long-term investors are looking at "education infrastructure" as a new fully-fledged asset class to invest in.

Social infrastructures have interesting characteristics for private/institutional investors, such as low volatility of returns (payments from the public sector are generally agreed *ex ante* and tend to be linked to inflation) and low correlation with the resulting risks from other assets (the nature of a social infrastructure investment reduces exposure to market risk and capital market volatility), high value of physical assets that can act as collateral for loans, and a stable long-term investment prospect term (twenty to thirty years).

Institutional investors have the option of investing capital through infrastructure funds, investment platforms, or directly into projects.

Why are institutional investors so interested in infrastructure investment? Infrastructure is a typical "safe asset", and there was a huge shortage of this type of financial instrument after the 2008 Global Financial Crisis. Indeed, the importance of safe assets has become central since that crisis.

Public debt of advanced economies is projected to raise from 87% in 2019 to 109% in 2021 (IMF data 2021): in the US from 103% to 125%, in the Eurozone from 86% to 99%, in the UK from 84% to 111%, and in Japan from 232% to 258%.

The US has passed an Infrastructure and Job Bill worth \$1 tn (with a very large component in social investments); the Next Generation EU fund, at the level of current prices, is worth around €800 bn over the next six years.

Finally, COVID-19 may help capital markets overcome the so-called "safe asset trap" (i.e., the lack of long-term financial instruments that match the long-term liabilities and assets of institutional investors, such as pension funds and insurance companies).

Investment in education infrastructure should be as great as it ever has been in the history of the EU. So, it is time to be brave. Much of the future of our new generation depends on education systems which properly prepare students and workers for a changing world.

References

Khan, A.N., A.A. Ihalage, Y. Ma, B. Liu, Y. Liu and Y. Hao (2021) "Deep Learning Framework for Subject-Independent Emotion Detection Using Wireless Signals", *PLOS ONE*, 16(2): e0242946, https://journals.plos.org/plosone/article?id=10.1371/journal.pone.0242946 .

Algan, Y., G. Brunello, E. Goreichy and A. Hristova (2021) *Boosting Social and Economic Resilience in Europe by Investing in Education*, February 2021.

Arezki, R., P. Bolton, S. Peters, F. Samama and J. Stiglitz (2016) "From Global Savings Glut to Financing Infrastructure: The Advent of Investment Platforms", *IMF Working Paper* 16(18), https://www.imf.org/external/pubs/ft/wp/2016/wp1618.pdf.

Bassanini, F. (2012) "Financing Long Term Investment after the Crisis: A View from Europe', in *Sovereign Wealth Funds and Long-Term Investing*, ed. by P. Bolton, F. Samama, J. E. Stiglitz (New York: Columbia University), pp. 37–44, https://doi.org/10.7312/columbia/9780231158633.001.0001.

Bassanini, F. and E. Reviglio (2011) "Financial Stability, Fiscal Consolidation and Long-Term Investment after the Crisis", *OECD Journal: Financial Markets Trends* 1:37–75, https://doi.org/10.1787/fmt-2011-5kg55qw1vbjl.

Bassanini, F. and E. Reviglio (2015) "From the Financial Crisis to the Juncker Plan", in *Investing in Long-Term Europe. Fixed, Re-Launching Fixed, Fixed, Network and Social Infrastructure*, ed. by P. Garonna and E. Reviglio (Rome: LUISS University Press), pp. 59–80.

Bassanini, F., G. Pennisi and E. Reviglio (2015) "Development Banks: From the Financial and Economic Crisis to Sustainable and Inclusive Growth", in *Investing in Long-Term Europe. Re-launching fixed, Network and Social Infrastructure*, ed. by P. Garonna and E. Reviglio (Rome: LUISS University Press), pp. 312–16.

Bolton, P., M. Depres, L.A. Pereira da Silva and P. Samama (2020), *The Green Swan—Central Banking and Financial Stability in the Age of Climate Change*, January 2020.

Caballero, J. and E. Farhi (2017) "The Safety Trap", *The Review of Economic Studies Limited*. Harvard University and NBER.

Camara, A., A. Biglia, B. Van Looy, D. Guttieres, D. Tilbury, E. Artvinli, G. Kostakos, J. M. Hughes, K. Ohnishi, L. Fransen, L. Neves, M. Hartnett, M. van der Ree, M. Denis, N. Selwyn, N. De Smyter, N. Oliver, P. Seshaiyer, P. Bettelli, R. Linturi, S. Downes, V. Vandeweerd and W. Liu (2020) *Adapting Education Systems to a Fast Changing and Increasingly Digital World*. Covid 19 education alliance (Covidea), Website Platform for transformative technologies (P4TT).

Cantillon, B. and F. Vandenbroucke (eds) (2014) *Reconciling Work and Poverty Reduction. How Successful are European Welfare States?* Oxford: Oxford University Press.

Canton, E. A. Thum-Thysen and P. Voigt (2018) *Economists' Musings on Human Capital Investment Efficiency in Public Spending on Education in EU Member States*, Discussion paper 081, June 2018, European CommissionDella Croce, R. and J. Yermo (2013) "Institutional Investors and Infrastructure Financing", *OECD*, November 6 2013.

EDHEC-Risk Institute (2012) *Pension Fund Investment in Social Infrastructure. Insights from the 2012 Reform of the Private Finance Initiative in the United Kingdom*, https://www.edhec.edu/sites/www.edhec-portail.pprod.net/files/publications/pdf/edhec-publication-pension-fund-investment-in-social-infrastructure-f_1332412681078.pdfjpg.

Habib, Livio Stracca, L. and F. Venditti (2020) *The Fundamentals of Safe Assets*, Working Paper Series No 2355, January 2020.

Engel, E., R. Fischer and A. Galetovic (2020), *When and How to Use Public-Private Partnerships: Lessons from the International Experience*, NBER Working Papers Series 26766.

Ehlers, T. (2014) *Understanding the Challenges for Infrastructure Finance*, BIS Working Papers 454, https://www.bis.org/publ/work454.pdf.

EIB (2018) *EIB Investment Report 2018/2019: Retooling Europe's Economy.* Luxembourg: European Investment Bank, https://www.eib.org/attachments/efs/ economic_investment_report_2018_en.pdf.

EPEC (2016) *A Guide to the Statistical Treatment of PPPs*, https://www.eib.org/attachments/ thematic/epec_eurostat_statistical_guide_en.pdf.

European Commission (2016) *Report on Public Finances in EMU*, Institutional Paper 045, https:// ec.europa.eu/info/sites/info/files/ip045_en_0.pdf.

European Commission (2018) *The International Literacy Study (ICILS) Findings and Implications for Education Policies in Europe.* European Commission, Validation of Formal and Non formal learning, eacea.ec.europa.eu, https://ec.europa.eu/education/resources-and-tools/ document-library/the-2018-international-computer-and-information-literacy-study-icils-main-findings-and-implications-for-education-policies-in-europe_en.

European Commission (2020) *Macroeconomic Database*, Ameco.

European Expert Network on Economics of Education, EENEE (2020) *Analytical Report No.42*, prepared for the European Commission.

Eurostat (2019) *Digital Economy and Society Statistics—Households and Individuals.*

Foster, S. and C. Iaione (2016) "The City as a Commons", *Yale Law & Policy Review* 34: 281–349, https://digitalcommons.law.yale.edu/cgi/viewcontent.cgi?article=1698&context=ylpr.

Foster, S. and C. Iaione (2019) "Ostrom in the City: Design Principles and Practices for the Urban Commons", in *Routledge Handbook of the Study of the Commons*, ed. by D. Cole, B. Hudson and J. Rosenbloom (London: Routledge), pp. 235–55, https://doi.org/10.4324/9781315162782-19.

Fransen, L., G. del Bufalo and E. Reviglio (2018) *Boosting Investment in Social Infrastructure in Europe. Report of the HLTF Force on Investing in Social Infrastructure in Europe chaired by Romano Prodi and Christian Sautter.* Luxembourg: Publications Office of the European Union, https://www.fondazioneifel.it/notizie-ed-eventi/item/download/2376_ee5d868e16ae749 daced6f41cce3709c.

Garonna, P. and E. Reviglio (eds) (2015) *Investing in Long-Term Europe. Fixed, Re-Launching Fixed, Fixed, Network and Social Infrastructure.* Rome: LUISS University Press.

Gorton, G. (2017) "The History and Economics of Safe Assets", *Annual Review of Economics*, 9(1): 547–86.

Gourinchas, P.-O. and O. Jeanne (2012) *Global Safe Assets*, BIS Working Papers 399, Bank for International Settlements.

Hemerijck, A. (2013) *Changing Welfare States.* Oxford: Oxford University Press.

Hemerijck, A. (ed.) (2017) *The Uses of Social Investment.* Oxford: Oxford University Press, https:// doi.org/10.1093/oso/9780198790488.001.0001.

Hemerijck A. and M. Santoni (2019) *Rescue, Not Renewal: Social Investment for the Future Wellbeing for Social Europe.*

Hemerijck, A. and S. Ronchi (2020) "European Welfare States' Detour(s) to Social Investment", in *The Oxford International Handbook of Public Administration for Social Policy: Promising Practices and Emerging Challenges*, ed. by J. Boston, E. Ferlie, F. Filgueira, Y. Jing, E. Ongaro and V. Taylor. Oxford: Oxford University Press.

Hemerijck, A., M. Mazzucato and E. Reviglio (2020), "Social Investment and infrastructure", in F. Cerniglia and F. Saraceno (eds), *A European Public Investment Outlook.* Cambridge: Open Book Publishers, pp. 115-34, https://doi.org/10.11647/obp.0222.07.

Inderst, G. (2017) "Social Infrastructure Investment: Financing Sources and Investor Perspective", *HLTF SI*, Draft for discussion, June 15.

Inderst, G. (2020) "Lessons learned from the United Kingdom and Europe" in *Innovation in Infrastructure Delivering: How Government and Institutional Investors Can Lead an Infrastructure Renaissance"*, in *Institutional Investing in Infrastructure*, A Supplement to the November 2020 i3, a publication of Institutional Real Estate, Inc.

Ionescu, C.A., L. Paschia, N.L.G. Nicolau, S.G. Stanescu, V.M.N. Stancescu, M.D. Coman and M.C. Uzlau (2020) "Sustainability Analysis of the E-Learning Education System during Pandemic Period—COVID-19 in Romania," *Sustainability, MDPI, Open Access Journal*, 12(21): 1–22, October.

Di Pietro, G., Biagi, F., Costa P., Karpiński Z., Mazza, J. (2020) *The Likely Impact of Covid 19 on Education*, 30275 EN Publication office of the European Union, Luxemburg.

ILO Global Report on Youth & COVID-19 (2020) *Impacts on Jobs, Education, Rights and Mental Well-being*.

Lifelong Learning Platform (2021) *Europe's Share of GDP for Education and Training Has Never Been This Low: A Comparative Analysis*, 23rd March 2020.

Luna-Martinez, J. and L. Vicente (2012) "Global Survey of Development Banks", *World Bank Policy Research Working Paper* 5969, http://documents.worldbank.org/curated/en/313731468154461012/pdf/WPS5969.pdf.

Marjorie, B., E. Tiven, R. Fuchs and A. MacQuarrie, *Evaluating Global Digital Education: A Student Outcomes Framework*, OECD.

Muraille, M. (2020) *From Emergency Remote Learning to a New Digital Education Plan: An EU Attempt to Mainstream Equality into Education"*, European Policy brief No 66.

Mazzucato, M. and C. Penna (2016) "Beyond Market Failures: The Market Creating and Shaping Roles of State Investment Banks", *Journal of Economic Policy Reform* 19(4): 305–26, https://doi.org/10.1080/17487870.2016.1216416.

Nugroho, D., C. Pasquini, N. Reuge and D. Amaro (2020) *COVID-19: How Are Countries Preparing to Mitigate the Learning Loss as Schools Reopen? Trends and Emerging Good Practices to Support the Most Vulnerable Children*, an Innocento Research Brief, UNICEF.

OECD (1998) *Human Capital Investment: An International Comparison*, OECD Publishing, Paris.

Prodi, R. and E. Reviglio (2019) *A New Fund for Europe. The Creation of a New European Social Bond Would Help EU Member States Meet their Infrastructure Needs*, OMFIF Bulletin.

Resnick, M. (2020), *Rethinking Learning in the Digital Age*, Cambridge, Mass.: MIT Press.

Reviglio, E. "Exacerbating Public Debt", in *OMFIF Global Public Investor*, ed. by Danae Kyriakopoulou (London: OMFIF Ltd), pp. 132–33.

Schmid, G. (2015) "Sharing Risks of Labour Market Transitions: Towards a System of Employment Insurance", *British Journal of Industrial Relations* 53(1): 70–93, https://doi.org/10.1111/bjir.12041.

The Economist (2021) *How Covid 19 Is Inspiring Education Reform*.

The Economist (2021) *Closing the World's Schools Caused Children Great Harm*.

The World Bank Group (2020) *The Human Capital Index 2020 Update*. Washington DC.

10. COVID-19 and the Corporate Digital Divide[1]

Désirée Rückert, Reinhilde Veugelers, Antilia Virginie, and Christoph Weiss

Introduction

The COVID-19 crisis is likely to play a dual role in digital technology adoption. On the one hand, the crisis has led to wider recognition of the importance of innovation and digital transformation. According to the 2020 results of the EIB Investment Survey (EIBIS), a majority of firms in the EU and the US expect COVID-19 to have a long-term impact on the use of digital technologies (EIB 2021a). On the other hand, many firms have experienced a falloff in revenue and liquidity during the pandemic. This may force firms to focus on short-term survival strategies (Revoltella, Maurin, and Pal 2020), leading them to delay or cancel investment. Therefore, whilst the need to adopt digital technologies is more salient than ever, a collapse in firm investment may impede the creation, transfer, and adoption of new digital technologies.

The benefits associated with digital adoption have long been established. Digital technologies, such as advanced robotics, 3D printing, artificial intelligence, or the internet of things, are associated with higher firm productivity and innovation activities (Gal et al. 2019; Rückert, Veugelers, and Weiss 2020; EIB 2021a). Policymakers should pay particular attention to digital technology adoption as its impacts extend beyond firms' productivity and competitiveness to also include labour markets effects (Frank et al. 2019; Acemoglu and Restropo 2020; EIB 2021a).

Until recently, the implementation of digital technologies was usually associated with the largest, most innovative and modern companies. However, the pandemic has placed issues of digital transformation at the heart of many firms' survival. Digital technologies were indispensable to preventing business disruption, organising work remotely, improving communication with customers, suppliers and employees, and

---

1   The views expressed in this paper are those of the authors and do not necessarily reflect the views of the European Central Bank or the European Investment Bank.

https://doi.org/10.11647/OBP.0280.10

selling products and services online. Businesses that had adopted digital technologies were therefore better able to cope with the disruption unleashed by the COVID-19 pandemic and better able to forge ahead with digital technology adoption. Due to the pandemic, digitally laggard firms were exposed ever more clearly to the need for change, whilst simultaneously being less able to move into a higher digital gear. Will the pandemic turn out to be a momentum for catching up and closing the digital divide? Or in contrast, will it lead to a more polarised economic structure, with the benefits concentrated in a few "superstar" firms leaving many firms and workers on the losing side?

Several recent studies provide evidence of polarisation and of "winner-takes-all" market dynamics linked to the use of digital technologies, especially on a global scale. Andrews, Criscuolo, and Gal (2016) show an increasing productivity gap between firms at the global frontier and laggard firms.[2] Debates surrounding "winner-take-all" markets have been particularly strong in the EU, as the winners are most associated with "Big Tech" firms coming from the US, South Korea, or China. EU firms are hardly present among the Big Tech giants or the leading digital R&D investors that push the frontier of digital technology (Veugelers 2018; EIB 2021a). This growing digital polarisation in the global corporate landscape has implications for the rising polarisation of firm productivity and performance. If EU firms are unable to integrate new digital technologies into their business models, they will lose out, even in the sectors where they are currently still global leaders such as the automotive sector.

Even though these are first-order concerns, recent large-scale firm-level evidence about digital technology adoption across EU countries and the US is scant. Measuring digital adoption by firms and assessing the extent to which digitalisation may be transforming and affecting different economies can be challenging due to the lack of comparable firm-level data across countries.

To foster an evidence-based debate on the impact of digitalisation, this chapter relies on annual EIBIS data on more than 13,000 companies from twenty-nine countries. In 2020, the survey was conducted between May and August, several months after the outbreak of the COVID-19 pandemic. The survey monitors firms' use of various advanced digital technologies, allowing us to capture digital adoption rates and assess the impact of digital transformation on different economies. In 2020, EIBIS also asked firms about their future digital perspectives.

Our main contributions are as follows. First, we identify digitalisation profiles based on firms' current use of digital technologies and their perspectives on the expected long-term impact of COVID-19 on digitalisation. Using these profiles, we first show a growing digital polarisation. Second, we show that this digital polarisation matters

---

2   Andrews, Criscuolo, and Gal (2016) define global frontier firms as the top 5% of firms in terms of labour productivity levels, within each two-digit sector and in each year, across all countries since the early 2000s. All other firms are defined as laggards.

by investigating the relationship between digital profiles and various measures of firm performance—including innovation activities, labour productivity, and employment growth. Our survey data also allow us to provide evidence that firms along the digital divide grid face different obstacles to investment. The findings suggest that addressing barriers to digital infrastructure and skills, which are both major impediments to digital technology adoption, should be a priority if policymakers want to support digital transformation and redress the digital divide. Addressing the regulatory burden and the uncertainties regulations can create should also be high on the digital policy agenda.

10.1 Adoption of Digital Technologies and Their Increased Use after COVID-19

The analysis presented here relies on data from EIBIS, a firm-level survey administrated annually to senior managers or financial directors of a representative random sample of firms in each of the twenty-seven countries of the EU, the UK and the US.[3] EIBIS is designed to be representative of the business population in each country for different sectors and firm size categories.[4] Importantly, the design and implementation of the survey is consistent across countries, which is critical for understanding differences in the adoption of digital technologies. In addition, the survey does not only cover firms in the manufacturing sector but also firms in services, construction and infrastructure.

In EIBIS, firms are surveyed about the use of four advanced digital technologies that are specific to their sector.[5] They are asked the following question: "Can you tell me for each of the following digital technologies if you have heard about them, not heard about them, implemented them in parts of your business, or whether your entire business is organised around them?" A firm is identified as "digital" if at least

---

3   Eligible respondents are senior persons with responsibility for investment decisions and how investments are financed. This person can be the owner, the finance manager, finance director, head of accounts, Chief Financial Officer (CFO), or Chief Executive Officer (CEO).

4   See Ipsos (2020) for a description of the sampling methodology. The sample is stratified by country, sector, and size class. Brutscher et al. (2020) provide evidence on representativeness of the data for the business population of interest (namely enterprises above five employees) by comparing distributions in EIBIS with the population of firm-level data available in Eurostat's Structural Business Statistics (SBS).

5   The state-of-the-art digital technologies considered are different across sectors. Firms in *manufacturing* are asked about the use of: (a) 3D printing: also known as additive manufacturing; (b) robotics: automation via advanced robotics; (c) IoT: internet of things, such as electronic devices that communicate with each other without human assistance; (d) big data/AI: cognitive technologies, such as big data analytics and artificial intelligence. Firms in *construction* are surveyed about the use of: (a) 3D printing; (b) drones: unmanned aerial vehicles; (c) IoT; (d) virtual reality: augmented or virtual reality, such as presenting information integrated with real-world objects presented using a head-mounted display. Firms in *services* are surveyed about the use of: (a) virtual reality; (b) platforms: a platform that connects customers with businesses or customers with other customers; (c) IoT; (d) big data/AI. Firms in *infrastructure* are surveyed about the use of: (a) 3D printing; (b) platforms; (c) IoT; (d) big data/AI.

one digital technology is implemented in parts of the business and/or if the entire business is organised around at least one digital technology.

The survey thus provides us with unique information on the adoption of digital technologies in the EU and the US compared to other databases. Eurostat data used in the Digital Economy and Society Index (DESI) do not include US firms, which is paramount information for the analysis of the digital divide discussed in this paper.[6] Similarly, OECD statistics on ICT access and usage by businesses provide data on two indicators for the US, but only in 2007 and 2012.[7]

10.1.1 Taking Stock of Digital Adoption

The results of EIBIS show that digital technology adoption is spreading rapidly (Figure 1): the share of digital firms has increased by 5 pp compared to 2019, both in the EU and in the US. However, the EU is not closing its digital gap with the US. EU firms are and continue to be lagging behind the US in terms of digital adoption. In 2020, only 63% of EU firms have implemented at least one digital technology, compared to 73% in the US (Figure 1).

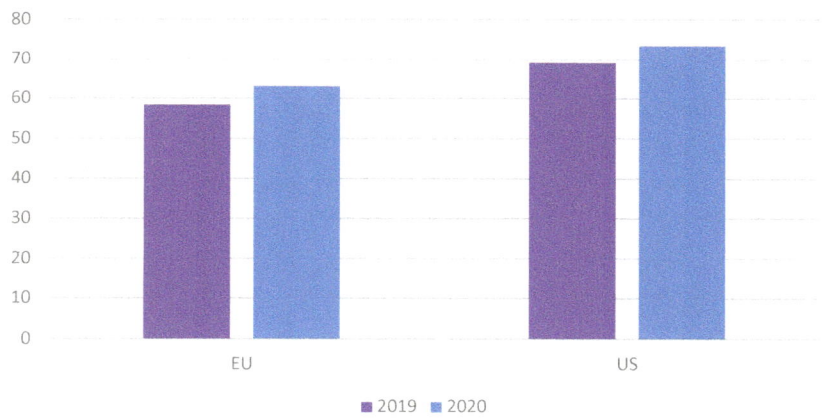

Fig. 1 Adoption of Digital Technologies (% of Firms).

Source of data: EIB Investment Survey (EIBIS wave 2019 and 2020).

Note: A firm is identified digital if at least one advanced digital technology was implemented in parts of the business. Firms are weighted using value added.

---

6   For example, Eurostat provides data on the share of enterprises (with more than ten employees) using industrial robots (17% of the enterprises in manufacturing) in the EU in 2020, which is very similar to the share of manufacturing firms that have implemented automation via advanced robotics according to EIBIS in 2020 (18%). However, there are larger differences between Eurostat data and EIBIS in the use of other digital technologies (such as 3D printing or IoT).

7   For the US, the ICT Access and Usage by Businesses Database provides data on (i) the share of business with a website or home page (in 2007 and 2012) and (ii) the share of business placing orders (i.e., making purchases) over computer networks (in 2007).

The differences between the adoption rates in the EU and the United States are mainly driven by the lower use of technologies related to the internet of things (IoT), i.e., electronic devices that communicate with each other without assistance (Figure 2). On average, 34% of European firms have adopted this technology, compared to 53% of US firms. EU firms also fall short when it comes to the adoption of drones in the construction sector. For the other digital technologies captured in the survey, the differences in adoption rates between EU and US firms are less pronounced.

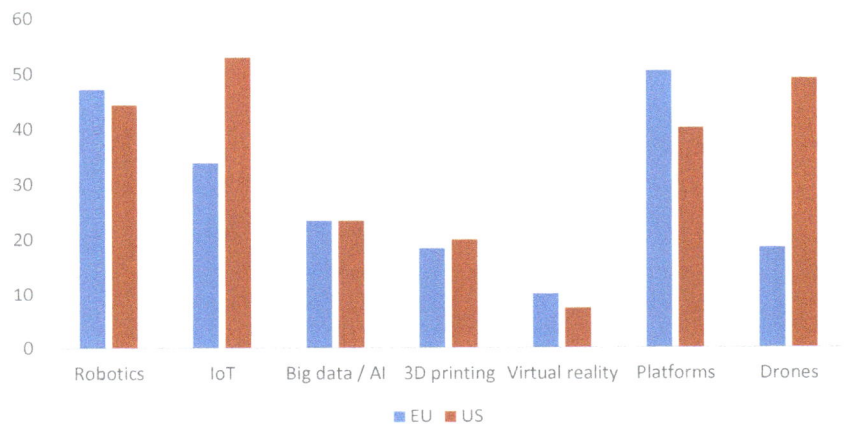

Fig. 2 Adoption of Different Digital Technologies (% of Firms).

Source of data: EIB Investment Survey (EIBIS wave 2020).

Note: A firm is identified digital if at least one advanced digital technology was implemented in parts of the business. Firms are weighted using value added.

10.1.2 The Dual Impact of COVID-19 on Digital Adoption

Throughout 2020, firms were faced with acutely high levels of uncertainty as the COVID-19 crisis weighed on the economic outlook. Uncertainty about the future became a severe constraint to investment activities with half of EU firms considering it to be a major obstacle to investment, up from 34% in 2019 (Figure 3).[8] These higher levels of uncertainty jeopardising investment also hold for US firms, albeit less intensely than for EU firms: 42% of US firms consider that uncertainty about the future limit their investment, up from only 18% in the previous year. As a result, we may expect future investment in digital technologies to be postponed or abandoned altogether.

---

8   In 2020, the survey was conducted between May and August, several months after the outbreak of the COVID-19 pandemic.

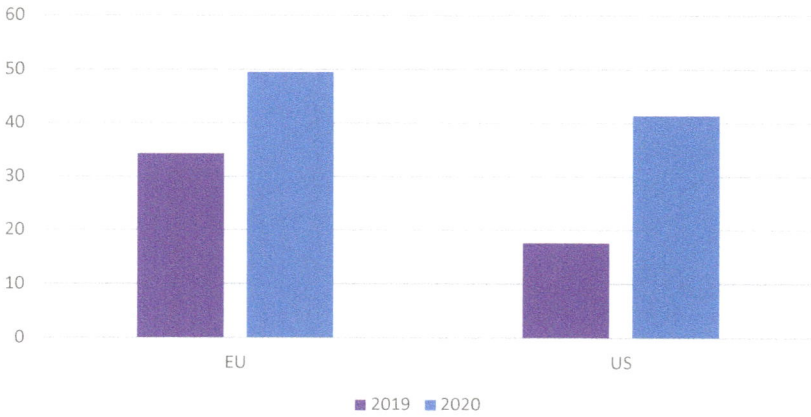

Fig. 3 Uncertainty as a Major Obstacle to Investment (% of Firms).

Source of data: EIB Investment Survey (EIBIS waves 2019 and 2020).

Note: Firms are weighted using value added.

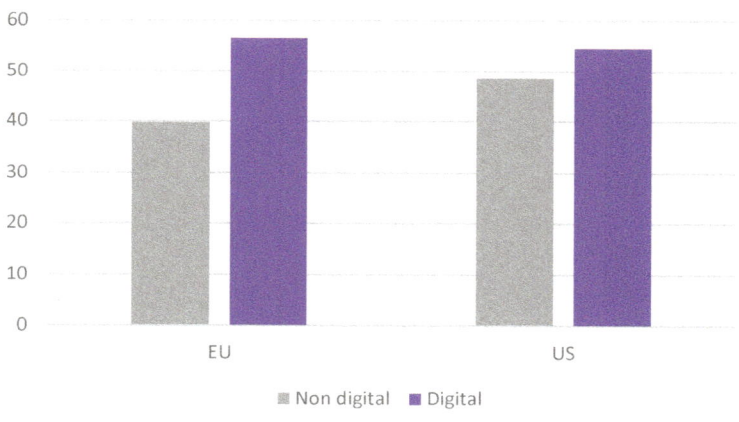

Fig. 4 Firms Reporting that COVID-19 Will Lead to an Increased Use of Digital Technologies (% of Firms).

Source of data: EIB Investment Survey (EIBIS wave 2020).

Note: A firm is identified digital if at least one advanced digital technology was implemented in parts of the business. Firms are weighted using value added.

At the same time, a majority of firms report that they expect COVID-19 to increase the use of digital technologies in the long term (50% in the EU and 53% in the US).[9] What is more, those firms that are already digitally active are more likely than non-digitally

---

9   The relevant survey question reads: "Do you expect the coronavirus outbreak to have a long-term impact on the increased use of digital technologies (e.g., in order to prevent business discontinuity or improve communication with customers, suppliers and employees)?"

active firms to report that COVID-19 will lead to an increased digitalisation, both in the EU and the US: 57% of EU digital firms think COVID-19 will lead to an increased use of digital technologies, compared to 40% of non-digital firms (Figure 4). This is evidence suggesting that the COVID-19 shock further deepens the corporate digital divide, with leading firms pushing ahead whilst laggards are further falling behind (Rückert, Veugelers, and Weiss 2020).

This divide in the perceived long-term importance of digital technologies is observed both in the EU and in the US, across different sectors and in multivariate regression analysis.[10]

10.2 Who Are the Firms Falling Behind? Who Is Forging Ahead?

The previous section has identified a corporate digital divide. A next step is to identify and characterise the firms on each side of the divide. To address this question, firms are classified into four categories based on the combination of their current digital status and their digital outlook: potential frontrunners, digitally stagnant, potential catch-up, and persistently non-digital. Figure 5 positions firms on the digital divide grid according to these categories.

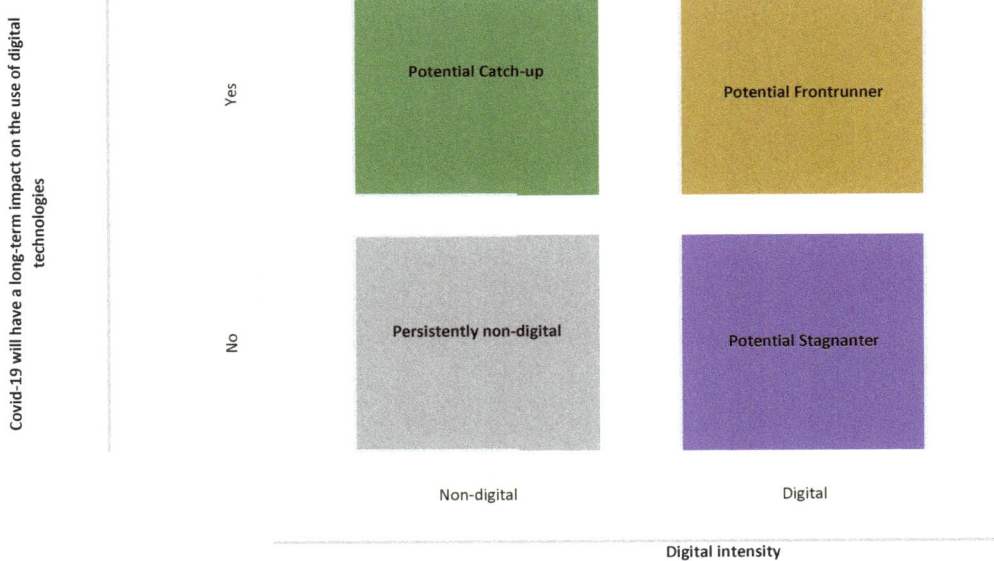

Fig. 5 Corporate Digital Divide Profiles

---

10   The multivariate regression analysis uses the expected long-term impact of COVID-19 on digitalisation as the dependent variable and the interactions of firm size and firm age, sector, and country as explanatory variables. Marginal effects from Probit estimation show that digital firms are 11% more likely to report that they expect COVID-19 to have a long-term impact on digitalisation.

Firms that have not implemented any digital technology and do not expect digitalisation to become more important in the long term due to COVID-19 years face the threat of falling behind on the digital divide grid. We categorise them as potentially "persistently non-digital". Companies that are currently non-digital but expect COVID-19 to increase the use of digital technologies are categorised as potential "catch-up". Among firms that have already implemented digital technologies, some firms do not expect COVID-19 to have a long-term impact on digitalisation: we categorise them as potentially digital "stagnaters". Finally, already digitally active firms that are expecting an increase in the use of digital technologies are categorised as potential digital "frontrunners".

Figure 6 displays the share of firms in each of these categories in the US and the EU. The most worrisome part of the digital divide lies with the share of "persistently non-digital" firms in the EU (22%), which is significantly higher than in the US (14%). These firms likely do not intend to take steps to invest in digital transformation, and a policy response may be necessary to prevent them from falling further behind. Perhaps unsurprisingly, given the lower share of digitally active firms in the EU, the share of potential "frontrunners" is slightly lower in the EU than in the US (36% and 40%).

In contrast to this stern outlook for the digital divide in the EU, the share of potential digital "stagnaters" is lower in the EU than in the US (27% and 33% respectively), and the share of non-digital firms that intend to potentially "catch-up" is similar (15% in the EU and 13% in the US).

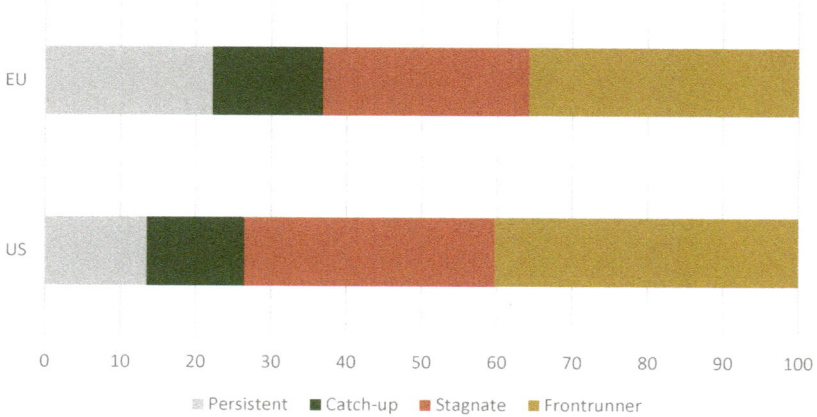

Fig. 6 Corporate Digital Divide Profiles (% of Firms).

Source of data: EIB Investment Survey (EIBIS wave 2020).

Note: See Fig. 5 of the definition of the corporate digital divide profiles. Firms are weighted using value added.

Which companies are falling behind, and which are forging ahead? Grouping the firms along the size dimension, it is clear that size plays an important role in the corporate digital divide. Consistently across the EU and the US, smaller firms are much more likely to be on the wrong side of the corporate digital divide: they are more likely to be "persistently non-digital" and less likely to be potential digital "frontrunners" (Figure 7). Within every size category, EU-US difference are less pronounced, suggesting that the EU-US digital divide differences are due to differences in size composition of the firm population. An exception holds for small firms (of ten to forty-nine employees). The share of small EU firms that are "persistently non-digital" in the EU is higher than in the US (34% and 27%, respectively), while the share of small EU firms that are potential digital "frontrunners" is lower (only 23%, compared to 30% in the US). This lack of investment in digital technologies by small EU firms is an area of concern because there are many more small firms in the EU than in the US (EIB 2021b). The fact that EU firms are smaller on average than those in the United States is likely to be a major disadvantage for accelerating the adoption of digital technologies (Revoltella, Rückert, and Weiss 2020). If EU policymakers want to close the gap in digital adoption with the US, they need to particularly address what is holding back small firms.

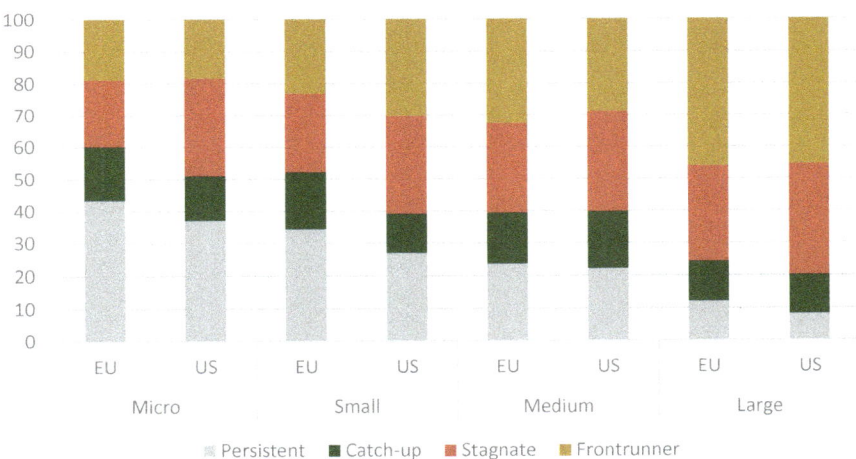

Fig. 7 Corporate Digital Divide Profiles (% of Firms), by Firm Size.

Source of data: EIB Investment Survey (EIBIS wave 2020).

Note: See Fig. 5 of the definition of the corporate digital divide profiles. Micro firms: 1 to 9 employees, small firms: 10 to 49 employees, medium-sized firms: 50 to 249 employees, large firms: 250+ employees. Firms are weighted using value added.

Differences between the EU and the US in corporate digital divide profiles are also associated with firm age (Figure 8). In the US, young firms (less than ten years old) are taking digital technologies much more seriously: the share of young firms that are "persistently non-digital" is smaller than for old firms. In the EU, the share of young firms that are "persistently non-digital" is larger than for old firms, and the share of young firms that are potential digital "frontrunners" is lower.

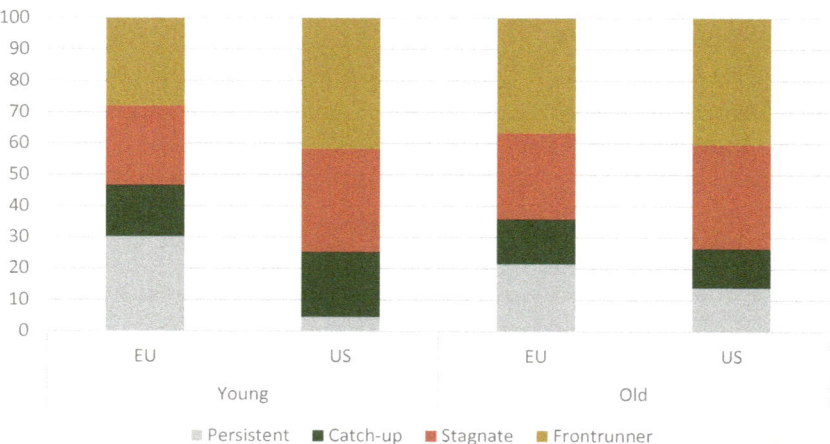

Fig. 8 Corporate Digital Divide Profiles (% of Firms), by Age.

Source of data: EIB Investment Survey (EIBIS wave 2020).

Note: See Fig. 5 of the definition of the corporate digital divide profiles. Young: less than ten years. Old: ten+ years. Firms are weighted using value added.

10.3 Firm Performance along the Digital Divide Grid

It is concerning that a large share of non-digital firms that do not take digital transformation seriously. This persistent lagging behind could have serious long-term repercussions, especially regarding their performance and long-term success. In the following, we look at how firms with different digitalisation profiles perform with regards to employment growth, skills and training of employees, and innovation activities. This analysis is purely correlational and cannot be interpreted as causal.

By comparing the current number of employees with the number of employees in the same firm three years ago, Figure 9 shows that "persistently non-digital" firms are less likely to increase employment. This holds both in the EU and in the US. Firms' positioning on the corporate digital divide thus matters for employment growth: firms forging ahead with digital transformation are more likely to be dynamic than those that do not invest in digital technologies and are left behind. Multivariate regression analysis confirms the positive association with employment growth: potential digital "frontrunners" are 10% more likely to report positive employment growth over the past three years than "persistently non-digital" firms.[11]

As argued by many economists, digital technologies—such as artificial intelligence, machine learning and industrial robots—can have an impact on shifting demand for skills, creating winners and losers among employees, impacting job polarisation

---

11   Marginal effects from Probit estimation, using positive employment growth as the dependent variable and the interactions of firm size and firm age, sector, and country as explanatory variables.

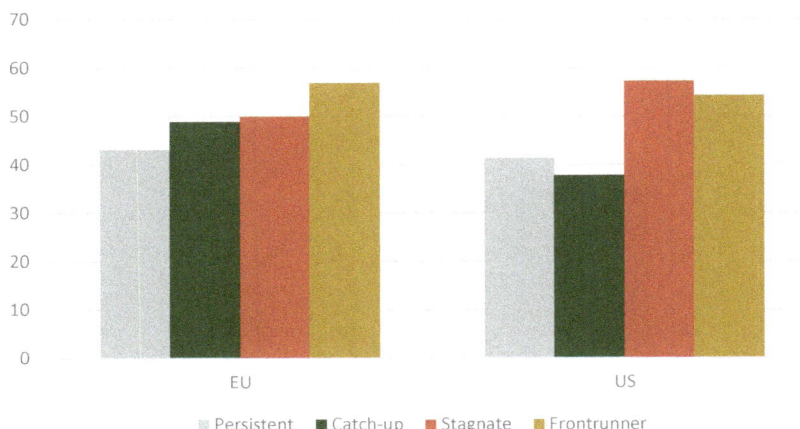

Fig. 9 Share of Firms with Positive Employment Growth over the Past Three Years (% of Firms), by Corporate Digital Divide Profiles.

Source of data: EIB Investment Survey (EIBIS wave 2020).

Note: See Fig. 5 of the definition of the corporate digital divide profiles. Firms are weighted using value added.

(Acemoglu and Autor 2011; EIB 2018; Frank et al. 2019; Acemoglu and Restrepo 2020). We find that there are significant differences in the average wage paid by firms to their employees across the corporate digital divide profiles (Figure 10). Potential digital "frontrunners" grow faster and tend to pay higher wages to their employees, both in the EU and the US. Assuming that average wage per employee can be a proxy for the level of the skills of the workers employed by the firm, this suggests that the jobs created by the potential digital "frontrunners" tend to be for more skilled workers.

However, the pattern across the other corporate digital profiles differs between the EU and the US. In the EU, average wages are higher for more advanced corporate digital divide profiles, the highest wages paid by potential "frontrunners", the lowest by "persistently non-digital" firms. For the US, we find a U-shaped relationship. US firms that intend to invest in digital transformation (the "catch-up") or those that are already implemented some digital technologies but do not intend to forge ahead (the potential digital "stagnaters") are paying lower wages on average. This may support evidence of wage polarisation due to digital technologies in the US labour market.

There are also significant differences in investment in employee training across the four corporate digital divide profiles (Figure 11): "persistently non-digitally" active firms are less likely to invest in human capital of their employees, which might further exacerbate the digital job polarisation. This result holds both in the EU and the US and in multivariate regression analysis.[12] Investment in digital skills—and an environment

---

12   The multivariate regression analysis uses positive investment in training of employees as the dependent variable and the interactions of firm size and firm age, sector, and country as explanatory variables. Marginal effects from Probit estimation show that potential digital "frontrunners" are 16% more likely to invest in employee training than "persistently non-digital" firms.

that is conducive to learning about them —is more likely to come from companies that take digital technologies seriously.

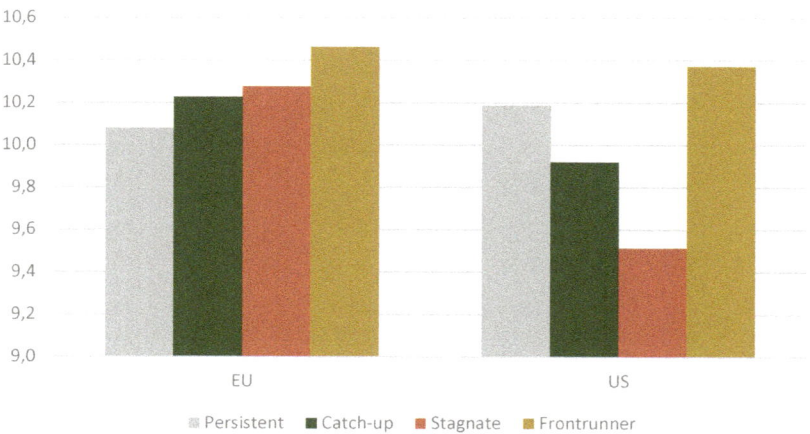

Fig. 10 Log Average Wage per Employee (in EUR), by Corporate Digital Divide Profiles.

Source of data: EIB Investment Survey (EIBIS wave 2020).

Note: See Fig. 5 of the definition of the corporate digital divide profiles. Firms are weighted using value added.

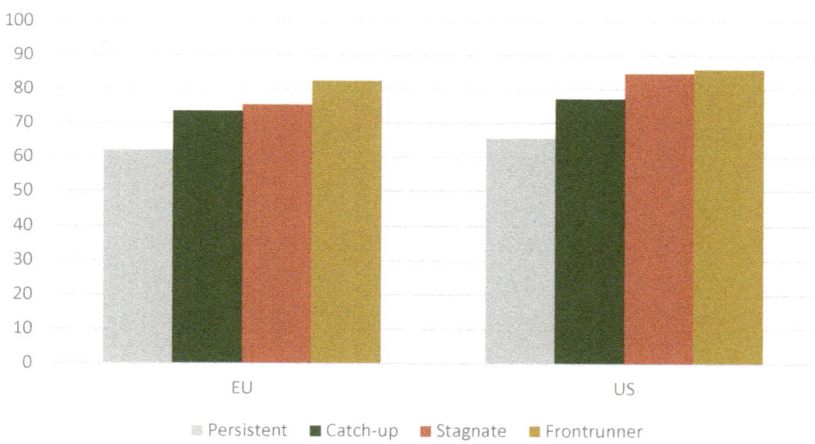

Fig. 11 Firms Investing in Training of Employees (% of Firms), by Corporate Digital Divide Profiles.

Source of data: EIB Investment Survey (EIBIS wave 2020).

Note: See Fig. 5 of the definition of the corporate digital divide profiles. Firms are weighted using value added.

Investment in innovation and digital transformation are closely intertwined. Following Veugelers et al. (2019), we identify companies as active innovators if they invest in

R&D and introduce new products, processes and services. We would expect digital technologies to empower innovation and therefore non-digitally active firms to also be less likely innovation active. Figure 12 confirms this: "persistently non-digitally" active firms are less likely to be active innovators. This result holds both in the EU and the US and is confirmed in multivariate regression analysis.[13]

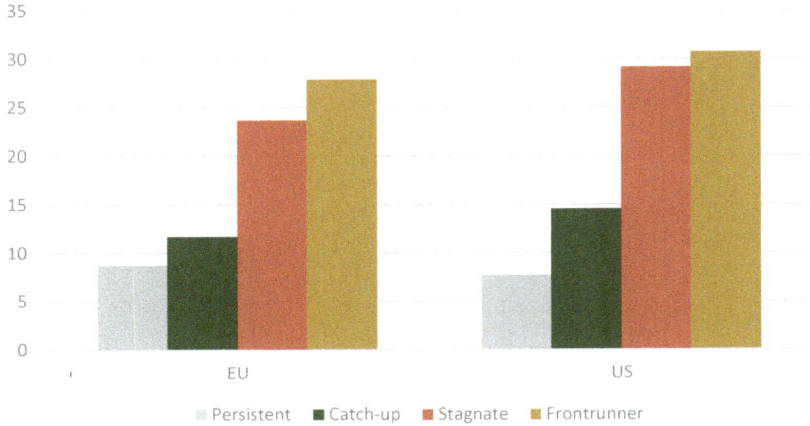

Fig. 12 Active Innovators (% of Firms), by Corporate Digital Divide Profiles.

Source of data: EIB Investment Survey (EIBIS wave 2020).

Note: See Fig. 5 of the definition of the corporate digital divide profiles. Active innovators are firms that invest in R&D and invest to develop or introduce new products, processes or services. Firms are weighted using value added.

10.4 Obstacles to Investment in the EU

EIBIS data also allow us to look at the different barriers and incentives firms perceive when contemplating investment decisions. Identifying any barrier to investment activities that specifically impedes firms that are left on the wrong side of the digital divide is relevant for the identification of policy levers to help move these firms away from of their "persistently non-digital" status, addressing the digital divide. Similarly, identifying the obstacles faced by digital investors will allow EU policymakers to better understand and fast-track investment in digital transformation.

Uncertainty about the future is the most important constraint to corporate investment in the EU, with 50% of EU firms reporting it as a major obstacle (Figure 13). Labour market regulations appear to be a more important obstacle for "persistently non-digital" firms than for other firms, whereas business regulation and taxation is a

---

13 The multivariate regression analysis uses active innovator as the dependent variable and the interactions of firm size and firm age, sector and country as explanatory variables. Marginal effects from Probit estimation show that potential digital "frontrunners" are 18% more likely to be active innovators than "persistently non-digital" firms.

major concern for roughly 30% of firms, independently from the profile. At the same time, the availability of staff with the right skills is a more severe obstacle for firms that consider that COVID-19 will have a long-term impact on the use of digital technologies. 54% of potential "catch-up" and 47% of potential digital "frontrunners" see it as a major obstacle, compared to 42% of "persistently non-digital" firms and 40% potential "stagnaters". Access to digital infrastructure is on average less often reported as a major obstacle to investment, but it differs along the digital profile of companies. While 20% of potential "catch-up" and "frontrunners" report this as a major barrier, this only holds for 10% of the "persistently non-digital" firms and 13% of potential "stagnaters".

Fig. 13 Major Obstacle to Investment (% of EU Firms), by Corporate Digital Divide Profiles.

Source of data: EIB Investment Survey (EIBIS wave 2020).

Note: See Fig. 5 of the definition of the corporate digital divide profiles. Firms are weighted using value added.

Fig. 14 Download Speed Faster than 1/Gbs (% of Households) and Digital Infrastructure as an Obstacle to Investment (% of Firms), by Country.

Source of data: EIBIS (2020) and Eurostat.

Note: Firms in EIBIS are weighted using value added.

The level of access to digital infrastructure is converging across the EU, with the vast majority of households having access to broadband, but more needs to be done to accelerate the spread of fast connections. There is a negative correlation across countries between the share of households having access to download speeds faster than 1/Gbs and the share of firms reporting digital infrastructure as an obstacle to investment (Figure 14). This indicates that many EU countries have the potential to unlock investment in the digital transformation of businesses by making access to faster broadband speeds more widespread.

10.5 Conclusion

The analysis presented in this chapter confirms the trend towards a digital divide in the EU and US corporate sector. A substantial share of firms does not implement any state-of-the-art digital technology and does not consider that COVID-19 will have a long-term impact on digitalisation. This share of "persistently non-digital" firms is larger in the EU than in the US, in particular for small firms.

Our results show that dynamics along the digital divide matter for firm performance and employment. "Persistently non-digital" firms are less likely to create new jobs, tend to pay lower wages and invest less in training of employees. They are also less likely to invest in innovation activities.

Lifting firms out of persistent digital non-activity by incentivising them to invest in digitalisation should be a top priority on the policy agenda. Digital transformation is notably a core element of the EU and national recovery and resilience plans to address the COVID-19 crisis.

Effective policy guidance and implementation for digitalisation is especially needed since the COVID-19 crisis may exacerbate the digital divide between firms. Some firms will realise the benefits of implementing digital products, switching to robotic production, using internet of things applications or harnessing the power of big data and artificial intelligence. However, others that fail to innovate and invest in digital transformation are at risk of being left behind. Unprecedented changes in workforce arrangements make the crisis a unique opportunity to raise awareness and encourage non-digital firms to reassess their management strategies and start taking digital transformation seriously before it is too late.

Looking at the major obstacles to investment perceived by firms in the EU also allows us to identify the bottlenecks to unlock further digital transformation. The findings suggest that addressing digital infrastructure and barriers to skills should also be a priority for policymakers to support firms in their digitalisation efforts. Similarly, addressing the regulatory burden and its associated uncertainties should also be high on the digital policy agenda.

To recover from the long-term impact of COVID-19, the EU will need to rapidly create better conditions to foster investment in digital transformation. To ensure that EU firms do not lose ground compared to their US peers, policymakers should strive to preserve a well-functioning, competitive, and integrated EU market environment that will push firms to invest more in the most advanced digital technologies. For example, EU members need to review labour and product market regulations that prevent firms from growing and reaching the size needed for the successful adoption and integration of multiple technologies within their businesses. Policy action should also develop measures to improve the digital skills of workers through training.

References

Acemoglu, D. and D. H. Autor (2011) "Skills, tasks and technologies: Implications for employment and earnings", in *Handbook of Labor Economics,* ed. by O. Ashenfelter and D. E. Card, Amsterdam: Elsevier, 1043–171.

Acemoglu, D. and P. Restrepo (2020) "Robots and jobs: Evidence from US labor markets", *Journal of Political Economy* 128(6): 2188–244.

Andrews, D., C. Criscuolo and P. Gal (2016) "The best versus the rest: The global productivity slowdown, divergence across firms and the role of public policy", OECD Productivity Working Paper No. 5.

Brutscher, P.-B., A. Coali, J. Delanote and P. Harasztosi (2020) "EIB Group survey on investment and investment finance—A technical note on data quality", EIB Working Paper 2020/08.

EIB (2018) *Investment Report 2018/19: Retooling Europe's economy.* Luxembourg: European Investment Bank.

EIB (2021a) *Investment Report 2020/21: Building a smart and green Europe in the Covid-19 era.* Luxembourg: European Investment Bank.

EIB (2021b) *Digitalisation in Europe 2020: Evidence from the EIB Investment Survey.* Luxembourg: European Investment Bank.

Frank, M. R., D. Autor, J. E. Bessen, E. Brynjolfsson,M. Cebrian, D. J. Deming, M. Feldman, M. Groh, J. Lobo, E. Moro, D. Wang, H. Youn and I. Rahwan (2019) "Toward understanding the impact of artificial intelligence on labor", *Proceedings of the National Academy of Sciences* 116(14): 6531–539.

Gal, P., G. Nicoletti C. von Rüden, S. Sorbe and T. Renault (2019) "Digitalization and productivity: In search of the Holy Grail—firm-level empirical evidence from European countries", *International Productivity Monitor* 37: 39–71.

Ipsos (2020) "EIB Group Survey of Investment and Investment Finance", Technical Report, October 2020.

Revoltella, D., L. Maurin and R. Pal (2020) "EU firms in the post-COVID-19 environment: Investment-debt trade-offs and the optimal sequencing of policy responses", *VoxEU.org*, 23 June 2020.

Revoltella, D., D. Rückert and C. Weiss (2020) "Adoption of digital technologies by firms in Europe and the US", *VoxEU.org*, 18 March 2020.

Rückert, D., R. Veugelers and C. Weiss (2020) "The growing digital divide in European and the United States", EIB Working Paper 2020/07.

Veugelers, R. (2018). "Are European firms falling behind in the global corporate research race?", Bruegel Policy Contribution 2018/06.

Veugelers, R., A. Ferrando, S. Lekpek and C. Weiss (2019) "Young SMEs as a motor of Europe's innovation machine." *Intereconomics* 54(6): 369–77.

11. EU Investment in Energy Supply for Europe

Carlo Jaeger, Diana Mangalagiu, and Jonas Teitge

Introduction

A central element of the European Green Deal is the commitment of the EU to become climate neutral by 2050. Against that backdrop, the European Commission promises a "shift from strategy to delivery" in 2021, and the 2021 EU climate law states that the EU will reduce greenhouse gas emissions by at least 55% by 2030 compared to 1990. The "Fit for 55 Package" is wide-ranging in scope, encompassing renewables, delivering on the "energy efficiency first" principle, energy performance of buildings, land use, energy taxation, effort sharing and emissions trading.[1] It goes without saying that this requires the multiannual financial framework (MFF) 2021–27 to allocate resources accordingly.

The unprecedented measures taken in the spring of 2020 by the EU to counter the unprecedented crisis triggered by the spread of the coronavirus SARS-CoV-2 have been designed in the spirit of "building back better": they shall not simply get the EU economy back on the trajectory it was on before the crisis, rather they shall help switch this huge economy to an ambitious trajectory that realises the European Green Deal.

One of many aspects of this endeavour is the allocation of public investment resources for the energy supply for Europe. Such resources fall into three categories. First, there are those mobilised in the 2021–27 MFF. Second, there are the exceptional resources made available through what Olaf Scholz, the German minister of finance, labelled as a Hamilton moment for Europe (more about this below): the decision that the EU would raise €750 bn (at 2018 prices) on the international financial markets. Eventually, these resources were grouped under the label Next Generation EU (NGEU). And third, there are the resources that the European Investment Bank, EIB, by its mandate, can regularly raise on the same markets.

---

1   "Energy efficiency first" is one of the key principles of the Energy Union, intended to ensure secure, sustainable, competitive and affordable energy supply in the EU. The adaptation of the EU ETS, covering 40% of Europe's emissions, is seen as the central instrument for reducing GHG emissions in the "Fit for 55" package.

          https://doi.org/10.11647/OBP.0280.11

With regards to investment for the energy supply for Europe, estimates for the resulting numbers in 2021 are collated in Tables 1a, 1b, and 1c (see the Annex for sources and explanations).

a) MFF

Budget items	ITER	Euratom	Energy facility	InvestEU	Life	Horizon EU	Total
€ (2021) Amount	0.8 B	0.3 B	0.8 B	0.2 B	0.2 B	1.1 B	3.4 B

b) NGEU

Budget items	InvestEU	Recovery & Resilience	Regional Development	Horizon EU	Total
€ (2021) Amount	0.2 B	30 B	3 B	0.2 B	33.4 B

c) EIB

Budget item	Climate Action	Total
€ (2021) Amount	10 B	10 B

Table 1a, 1b, 1c: EU Investment in Energy Supply for Europe in 2021

For sources and supplementary information, see the Annex.

The total over the three budgets is €46.8 bn. The three totals come with leverage rates for investments of various kinds that will be discussed in more detail below. For the MFF, a reasonable leverage ratio is 1.2, leading to an enhanced amount in the order of €4.1 bn. For NGEU, a reasonable leverage ratio is 1.5, leading to an enhanced amount in the order of €50.1 bn. For the EIB, a reasonable rate is 2, yielding €20 bn. All three together then amount to an investment flow of €74.2 bn. To put these numbers in perspective, one needs to consider some implications of the 55% reduction goal of the EU for 2030.

11.1 The 2030 Challenge

Several studies (EEA 2020; Agora Energiewende & Ecologic Institute 2021) based on EU Long-Term Strategy and European Green Deal project at least a 10% gap for EU emissions reductions in its current baseline scenarios for 2030. They also estimate that in the 2021–30 period the EU will need to invest €35–88 bn per year more for buildings and transport alone. Despite significant climate financing allocated in the European Green Deal, EU financing alone will not close the projected investment gap. McKinsey & Company (2020) state that an average incremental investment of €160 bn per year is needed for the 2021–30 period. Of this amount, 31% (€50 bn) is allocated to buildings and 12% (€19 bn) is allocated to transport.

In 2019, 69.3% of all energy in the EU was produced from fossil fuels, namely coal (11.6%), oil and petroleum products (34.5%), and natural gas (23.1%) (all numbers from Eurostat 2021a). Renewable energies made up 15.8% of the total, nuclear accounted for 13.5%. A 55% reduction of emissions implies a reduction of fossil fuels in the order of 30% of total energy use (38% if the fossil fuel mix should stay unchanged). To replace this with renewables, the EU would have to triple the present production of renewable energy within ten years. Alternatively, one might double the amount of both renewables and of nuclear. The contribution of renewable energy sources showed a stable growth, having already surpassed coal in 2018 and further increasing in 2019. Coal decreased by 19.7% in 2019 and reached the record lowest value since 1990.

One may try to boost this process by importing renewable energy from outside the EU. Presently, about 60% of fossil fuels used in the EU are imported (Eurostat 2021a). In principle, large scale imports of renewable energy are feasible, e.g., as green hydrogen or via high-voltage direct power transmission. But this presupposes the establishment of large infrastructures and institutional arrangements that are hardly feasible before 2030.

A different option is the reduction of energy use, often labelled as increasing energy efficiency (European Commission 2020). A reduction of energy use by one third in the nine years remaining until 2030 is not impossible, but hard to achieve and definitely harder without increasing the EU's current energy efficiency target (32.5% for 2030). The 55% reduction could then be achieved by doubling renewable energy generation. Clearly, this requires massive investments in wind and solar power plants, combined with similarly massive investments in power grids. Green hydrogen may play an increasing role, but it will hardly reach a sufficient volume to make a huge difference by 2030.

In view of the energy supply for Europe, the upshot of this analysis is that the 2030 goal will require unprecedent investments in renewables. So far, the highest investment in Europe in wind energy alone took place in 2016, when it reached €46.8 bn for a total new capacity of 20.2 GW, followed by 2020 with 42.8 for 19.6 GW (Figure 1).

With the previous, less ambitious targets for 2030, total annual investment needs for wind, solar, transmission, distribution, and storage were estimated in the range

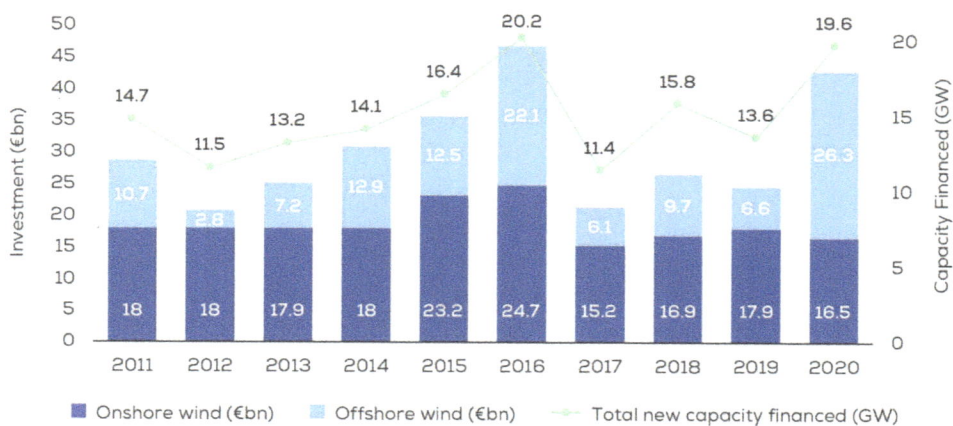

Fig. 1 New Asset Finance in Wind Energy 2011–20 (GW and € bn).

Source of data: Wind Europe (2021).

of €95–145 bn (Trinomics 2017). With the raised ambition of the -55% target, €150 bn is more realistic. The leveraged figure of about €75 bn from Tables 1 a, 1b, and 1c may give the impression that the door for those investments is wide open. However, these numbers are for the envisaged disbursements from the EU to member states, the actual investments will come with a delay. What is more, the grant allocations last for three years only, allocation of loans for two years. Front loading these financial flows is appropriate for the purposes of economic recovery, but for the needed changes in energy supply up to 2030 they cannot suffice.

Of course, additional investments for renewable energy supply can and will be induced by specific regulation and increasing CO_2 prices. The political, economic, and technological obstacles to be overcome EU-wide, however, are substantial. And without further measures to stimulate effective demand, these politically induced investments will crowd out other investments, putting a drag on growth and thereby employment in other sectors.

The macroeconomic impact of EU investments in energy supply must not be overestimated. In 2019, gross investment in the EU was 22.1% of GDP, i.e., €3.1 bn. Of these, energy supply investments of €150 bn would make up 1% of EU GDP. As long as they are mainly shifted from other sectors and lasting only two or three years, the overall economic impact will be limited.

A substantial positive effect, however, can be reached if EU energy supply investments will be additional and steady until 2030 or later. We are well aware of how contentious the debate about such possibilities is (Amato et al. 2020; Arnold et al. 2018; Bini-Smaghi 2021; Schäuble 2021). Unfortunately, the debate is still rather obsessively focused on the volume of public debt. But the historical breakthrough of the original Hamilton moment, the compromise struck between Hamilton, Jefferson, and Madison in 1790, was not about an increase of public debt (public debt was only shifted from single states to the US), but about the creation of an effective market for US bonds. Without this market, the US would never have achieved its impressive successes. Nowadays, the financing and possible success of the European Green Deal are tied to an analogous challenge.

Whether the Franco-German compromise of 2020 will usher in a Hamiltonian dynamic for the European Green Deal remains to be seen. It will critically depend on whether Germany will develop the will and competence to become the benevolent catalyst of a European Renaissance, or whether it will stick to a mercantilist interpretation of its national interest.

11.2 Employment and Geography

In terms of economic variables, the energy sector is a small part of the economy (Taylor 2021). We have seen this by comparing investment in the energy sector with overall investment. The same holds when considering employment. However, the effects of decarbonisation on employment are a big topic, especially as decarbonisation is being pursued in a global context of digitalisation. A closer look at employment is warranted, especially in view of the European Green Deal.

Table 2 shows a breakdown of employment in the energy sector, broadly defined, for EU28 from 2010 to 2018. Taking Brexit into account, employment in the EU27 by now is somewhat below 2 million people. The number of employees in the EU27 in turn is in the order of 220 million: the energy sector amounts to less than 1% of total employment. Table 2 also suggests that the bulk of energy sector jobs is in electricity, gas, steam and air conditioning supply. An emissions reduction of 55% by 2030 is unlikely to reduce the number of jobs in this domain; quite the opposite: the transformation of the energy system will require more craftspeople and professionals able to handle the new devices and technologies to be introduced.

Table 2: Employment of the EU28 Energy Sector, 2010–18 (Czako 2020).

Thousands	2010	2015	2016	2017	2018
Mining and Coal Lignite	331.2	294.5	274.1	258.9	247.6
Extraction of Crude Petroleum and Natural Gas	103.8	88.9	81.4	70.0	60.7
Extraction of Peat	11.1	11.1	9.9	9.7	9.7
Support Activities for Petroleum and Natural Gas Extraction	47.7	56.8	48.0	41.4	41.4
Manufacture of Coke and refined Petroleum Products	218.7	190.0	186.5	188.6	193.6

Thousands	2010	2015	2016	2017	2018
Electricity, Gas, Steam and Air Conditioning Supply	1645.3	1550.5	1553.0	1546.0	1569.1
Broad Sector Total Employment	**2357.9**	**2191.8**	**2152.9**	**2114.5**	**2122.0**

Of course, things may look very different in other sectors. But as far as the energy sector is concerned, the challenge at the scale of the EU labour market as a whole concerns about 0.25% of the total labour force. Regular fluctuations on the labour market are much larger than this. However, here we are faced with half a million people concentrated in regions where the fossil fuel-based energy sector plays a prominent role. Whether employment in a coal-mining region can turn into jobs focused on generating wind and solar power is far from obvious. How to address the challenge these regions are faced with is a hard problem that needs and deserves in-depth research (for an example of research in this direction, see https://tipping-plus.eu).

When looking at employment, geography matters. In the EU and especially the Eurozone, this is particularly relevant with regard to the divergence of the Eurozone (Gräbner et al. 2020). In the Next Generation EU package, this divergence is addressed by allocating the largest budget to Italy and the second largest to Spain.

Looking first at Italy, one of the most pressing problems is indeed the one of employment (the following numbers are from https://tradingeconomics.com): at the time of writing, the unemployment rate is larger than 10% for Italy as a whole, with youth unemployment higher than 30%. Moreover, unemployment is heavily concentrated in the south of Italy. The plan for how the Italian government, led by former ECB president Mario Draghi, intends to use the money from the EU pandemic recovery funds reflects this challenge (MEF 2021; Johnson and Fleming 2021). The priority is on digitalisation and high-speed rail. These technological investments shall help increase productivity across the whole of Italy, including both the private and the public sector. They are explicitly planned in the perspective of the European Green Deal, but with an emphasis on energy renewal of the—private and public—buildings more than on expanding renewable energy generation. This makes perfect sense, as construction has a much larger potential for job creation than the energy sector. And according to the European Commission (2020) the contribution of energy efficiency to the -55% reduction goal for 2030 is as important as the expansion of renewables generation. Last but not least, by improving train connections across Italy, explicitly aiming at sustainable mobility at the local scale, and strengthening the health sector shattered by the pandemic, tourism can rebound as a key sector of the Italian economy.

The details of the Italian plan are sound, and the argument from the previous section applies here, too: it will be crucial to avoid the temptation of a new austerity cycle in the coming years and instead stabilise the measures undertaken as a reaction to the pandemic at least until the 2030 goal has been reached.

The situation in Spain is similar in many respects, although internal tensions are presently making the task of forming a common will even more difficult than in Italy. At the time of writing, the unemployment rate is in the order of 15%, with youth unemployment at nearly 40% (numbers from https://tradingeconomics.com). For good reasons, the goals are similar to those in Italy: strengthen employment and foster growth (Gobierno de España 2021; Lázaro Touza 2020). Given the structure of the Spanish economy, including its tourist sector, the plan has a strong focus on supporting SMEs. Again, digitalisation is high priority, as is sustainable mobility. Generation of renewable energy is included, but not at a scale that would change the energy supply for the EU or the growth rate of the Spanish economy. However, a long-term strategy in the direction of green hydrogen production is embedded in the plan, as is an emphasis on science, technology, and education.

When it comes to renewable energy supply for Europe, the big difference in the present decade will not come from the countries prioritised by Next Generation EU, but from countries like Germany and Denmark, who can expand renewable generation with domestic means if they avoid a return to austerity.

11.3 "There is No Alternative" or Experimentalist Governance?

When thinking about a historical project like the European Green Deal, one may be forgiven for imagining it as defined by necessities that are as inevitable as they are foreseeable. The whole process is then governed by "TINA": there is no alternative.

Once this perspective is embraced, the transition to a climate neutral Europe starts looking like a journey on trains with well specified timetables, clearly foreseeable transfers from one train to another, and a sense of safety strengthened by smoothly running organisations. Expanding the generation of renewable energies can be envisaged with such a mindset, too, and in many contexts this is the way to go. But there is danger in ignoring the fact that contexts change, and often in unexpected ways.

An important example is the idea of leveraging large private investments with small public ones. As we have seen, the public investment in renewable energy financed through the combination of MFF, NGEU, and EIB is quite small; first, because the largest annual budget, the one of NGEU, is designed for no more than three years, and second, because for perfectly understandable reasons the main recipients of NGEU funds, while determined to use them for a broad ecological transition, don't focus on large-scale expansion of renewable energy generation. In this situation, the idea of leveraging large private investment through small public ones is comforting. In fact, there is overwhelming evidence to the effect that there are contexts where such leverage is considerable, but there is also evidence for contexts where the effect is much smaller (Boitani and Perdichizzi 2018). Moreover, while some of the relevant contexts are known (economic recessions vs economic booms), many of them defy easy definition (e.g., through output gaps; see Heimberger and Kapeller 2016).

In the case of NGEU, the leverage ratio boils down to the multiplier linking government expenditure to effective demand. As NGEU funds are disbursed in situations of economic crisis, high unemployment, capacity underutilisation, and strong incentives for investing in renewable energy, the leverage of 1.5 used in Section 1 is a conservative estimate. The same holds for those MFF expenditures that go into investment for expanding capacity of renewable energy generation. ITER and Euratom are not in this category (if some day nuclear fusion should really work, the whole analysis about renewables might have to change—but that's certainly irrelevant for the present decade). That's why for MFF a leverage of 1.2 is more appropriate.

The EIB presents a fundamentally different situation. First, the EIB engages in co-financing of investments. From the point of view of the investor, alternative co-financing is usually available, although often at somewhat less advantageous conditions. Many profitable investments co-financed by the EIB would still take place with other co-financing partners. Simply using the ratio of the total investment volume to the EIB contribution as a leverage factor is misleading. On the other hand, the EIB does encourage and sometimes trigger investments—especially by public authorities— that would not take place otherwise. That's why a leverage factor of 2, i.e., somewhat higher than for NGEU, is a reasonable estimate in this case.

In the past two decades, the EU economy, like smaller and even bigger economies, has experienced diversity of contexts and their often unforeseen changes on two dramatic occasions: the Global Financial Crisis and the COVID-19 pandemic. Perhaps no surprises of that scale will happen during the transition to climate neutrality, but for sure surprises will happen. This is where the concept of experimentalist governance (Sabel and Zeitlin 2012; see also Foray and Woerter 2021) matters for the expansion of renewable energies as well as for other dimensions of the European Green Deal.

Experimentalist governance can build on the diversity of regional contexts by creating conditions that allow and enable different regions to implement different strategies. For this purpose, regions need a safety net to engage in risky endeavours. And if they succeed, they need to share their learning experience with others without trying to impose a simplistic recipe. In this spirit, a Spanish region may aggressively explore the options for green hydrogen, while a region in Italy may gather experience with methanol gained from air capture of CO_2 in a circular economy perspective (Olah et al. 2018).

Public and private investments in expanding renewable energy generation offer scope for strategic leadership, e.g., in expanding offshore wind wherever it is possible and reasonable. And they offer scope for complementary approaches in different regional contexts as illustrated above. What matters is to combine the diversity of experiences needed to navigate future surprises with the perseverance of pursuing the opportunity created by the near-Hamilton moment in the midst of the COVID-19 pandemic.

ANNEX: Background for Tables 1a, 1b, 1c

MFF	Link https://ec.europa.eu/info/sites/default/files/about_the_european_commission/eu_budget/mff_2021-2027_breakdown_current_prices.pdf						:
Budget items	ITER	Euratom	Energy facility	InvestEU	Life	Horizon EU	**Total**
Full Name	International Thermonuclear Experimental Reactor	Euratom Research and Training Programme	European Strategic Investments - Connecting Europe Facility - Energy	InvestEU Fund	Programme for Environment and Climate Action	Research and Innovation - Horizon Europe	
Calculation	From MFF (rounded)	From MFF (rounded)	From MFF (rounded)	Minimum of 30% for support of Green Deal. We assume that 2/3 of this will flow into energy Investments. 1 B * 0.3 *2/3	We assume that from the 0,7 B an average of 30% will be used for energy investments	We assume that 10% of the funding for research will be spent energy investments. 11 B * 0.1	
€ (2021) Amount	0.8 B	0.3 B	0.8 B	0.2 B	0.2 B	1.1 B	3.4 B

NGEU	Link https://ec.europa.eu/info/sites/default/files/about_the_european_commission/eu_budget/mff_2021-2027_breakdown_current_prices.pdf			:
Budget items	InvestEU	Recovery & Resilience	Horizon EU	**Total**
Full Name	InvestEU Fund	Recovery and Resilience Facility	Research and Innovation - Horizon Europe	
Calculation	Additional 1,7 B according to calculation in MFF 1,7 B * 0.3 *2/3	300 B from which 30% are also meant to be spent supporting Green Deal. We assume that 1/3 of those will be spent in energy investments 300B *0.3 *1/3	According to MFF estimation: 1.8 B * 0.1	
€(2021) Amount	0.34 B	30 B	0.2 B	30.54 B

EIB	Link : https://www.eib.org/en/about/priorities/climate-action/index.htm#	
Budget item	Climate Action	**Total**
Full Name	European Investment Bank spending on Climate Actions	
Calculation	The average spending on general climate action of EIB was around 20B. We assume that 50% of that money is used to fund energy investments. 20B* 0.5	
€ (2021) Amount	10 B	10 B

References

Agora Energiewende (2019) *European Energy Transition 2030: The Big Picture. Ten Priorities for the next European Commission to meet the EU's 2030 targets and accelerate towards 2050,* https://www.agora-energiewende.de/en/publications/european-energy-transition-2030-the-big-picture/.

Agora Energiewende and Ecologic Institute (2021) *A "Fit for 55" Package Based on Environmental Integrity and Solidarity: Designing an EU Climate Policy architecture for ETS and Effort Sharing to Deliver 55% Lower GHG Emissions by 2030,* https://www.agora-energiewende.de/en/publications/a-fit-for-55-package-based-on-environmental-integrity-and-solidarity/.

Amato, M., E. Belloni, P. Falbo and L. Gobbi (2020) *Transforming Sovereign Debts into Perpetuities through a European Debt Agency,* http://dx.doi.org/10.2139/ssrn.3579496.

Arnold, N. G., B. B. Barkbu, H. E. Ture, H. Wang and J. Yao (2018) *A Central Fiscal Stabilization Capacity for the Euro Area,* IMF Staff Discussion Note, 18/03.

Bini-Smaghi, L. (2021) "The eurozone must not return to its pre-crisis 'normality'", *The Financial Times,* June 14, 2021.

Calhoun, G. (2020) "Europe's Hamiltonian Moment—What Is It Really?", *Forbes,* May 26, 2020, https://www.forbes.com/sites/georgecalhoun/2020/05/26/europes-hamiltonian-moment--what-is-it-really.

Czako, V. (2020) *Employment in the Energy Sector Status Report 2020.* Publications Office of the European Union, JRC120302, https://doi.org/10.2760/95180.

European Commission (2020) *Greenhouse Gas Emissions—Raising the Ambition,* https://ec.europa.eu/clima/policies/strategies/2030_en.

European Commission (2021) *Multiannual financial framework,* https://ec.europa.eu/info/sites/default/files/about_the_european_commission/eu_budget/mff_2021-2027_breakdown_current_prices.pdf.

European Environment Agency (2020) *Trends and projections in Europe 2020 Tracking progress towards Europe's climate and energy targets,* https://www.eea.europa.eu/publications/trends-and-projections-in-europe-2020.

Eurostat (2021a) *Energy statistics—an overview,* https://ec.europa.eu/eurostat/statistics-explained/index.php?title=Energy_statistics_-_an_overview.

Eurostat (2021b) *Data Explorer,* https://appsso.eurostat.ec.europa.eu/nui/show.do?dataset=nama_10_a64_e&lang=en.

Eurostat (2020), *National Accounts and GDP*, https://ec.europa.eu/eurostat/statistics-explained/index.php?title=National_accounts_and_GDP.

Foray, D. and M. Woerter (2021) "The formation of Coasean institutions to provide university knowledge for innovation: a case study and econometric evidence for Switzerland", *The Journal of Technology Transfer*, 46(5), 1584–610.

Gobierno de España (2021) *Plan de Recuperación, Transformación y Resiliencia*, https://www.lamoncloa.gob.es/temas/fondos-recuperacion/Documents/160621-Plan_Recuperacion_Transformacion_Resiliencia.pdf.

Gräbner, C., P. Heimberger, J. Kapeller and B. Schütz (2020) "Is the Eurozone disintegrating? Macroeconomic divergence, structural polarisation, trade and fragility", *Cambridge Journal of Economics* 44: 647–69, https://doi.org/10.1093/cje/bez059.

Heimberger, P. and J. Kapeller (2016) *The performativity of potential output: Pro-cyclicality and path dependency in coordinatingEuropeanfiscal policies*, ICAE Working Paper Series—No. 50, June 2016, https://www.boeckler.de/pdf/v_2016_10_21_heimberger.pdf.

Johnson, M. and S. Fleming (2021) "Draghi plans €220 B overhaul of Italy's economy", *The Financial Times*, April 21, 2021, https://www.ft.com/content/29d4b262-fb4a-46be-b504-6689e0eec994.

Lázaro Touza, L., G. Escribano Francés and F. Steinberg (2020) *Spain's Recovery, Resilience and Transformation Plan: key challenges for implementation*, https://www.iddri.org/en/publications-and-events/blog-post/spains-recovery-resilience-and-transformation-plan-key-challenges.

McKinsey & Co. (2020): *Net-Zero Europe. Decarbonization Pathways and Socioeconomic Implications*, https://www.mckinsey.com/~/media/mckinsey/business%20functions/sustainability/our%20insights/how%20the%20european%20union%20could%20achieve%20net%20zero%20emissions%20at%20net%20zero%20cost/net-zero-europe-vf.pdf.

MEF (Ministry of Economy and Finance of Italy) (2021) *The Recovery and Resilience Plan: Next Generation Italia*, https://www.mef.gov.it/en/focus/The-Recovery-and-Resilience-Plan-Next-Generation-Italia.

Olah, G. A., A. Goeppert and S. Prakash (2018) *Beyond Oil and Gas: The Methanol Economy* (Wiley).

Sabel, C. F. and J. Zeitlin (2012) "Experimentalist Governance", in *The Oxford Handbook of Governance*, ed. by Levi-Faur (Oxford: Oxford University Press), pp. 169–83.

Saraceno, F. (2021) "Europe After COVID-19: A New Role for German Leadership?", *Intereconomics* 56: 65–69.

Schäuble, W. (2021) "Europe's social peace requires a return to fiscal discipline", *The Financial Times*, June 2, 2021, https://www.ft.com/content/640d084b-7b13-4555-ba00-734f6daed078.

Statista (2021) *Wind energy investment outlook in Europe 2010–2022*, https://www.statista.com/statistics/858972/wind-energy-investment-outlook-europe.

Trinomics (2017) *European Energy Industry Investments*, trinomics.eu/wp-content/uploads/2018/05/European-energy-industry-investments.pdf.

Wind Europe (2021) *Financing and investment trends. The European wind industry in 2020*, https://windeurope.org/intelligence-platform/product/financing-and-investment-trends-2020/.

12. Environmental Impact Evaluation of a European High-Speed Railway Network along the "European Silk Road"

Maximilian Zangl (CEU), Katharina Weber (CEU),
Muhammad Usman Zahid (CEU),
and Mario Holzner (wiiw)

Introduction

The EU aims to be climate neutral by 2050, which includes the goal of a 90% reduction in greenhouse gas emissions from transport (EC 2019). The transport sector alone accounts for around 25% of the global carbon (CO_2) emissions and consumes more than half of the global demand for fossil fuels (IEA 2019). The Agenda 2030 specifically states that "more freight should be transported by rail" (EC 2019). With a study published in 2018 proposing the construction of a European Silk Road, the Vienna Institute for International Economic Studies (wiiw) proposed a contribution to achieve this envisioned shift to rail, suggesting *inter alia* a high-speed rail network along the envisaged routes. It would extend around 11,000 kilometres on a northern route from Lisbon to Uralsk on the Russian-Kazakh border, and on a southern route from Milan to Volgograd and Baku, also including other modes of transport and a string of logistic centres and ports. A central part is the route from Lyon to Moscow (Figure 1). The idea for a trans-European high-speed rail network is not necessarily new. Such a network was defined by the European Council Directive 96/48/EC of 23 July 1996. However, as noted in ECA (2018), a European high-speed rail network is not a reality but an ineffective patchwork of a few national lines. So far, the political will of the EU member states was lacking to build a network across national borders. However, in the current circumstances, when joint climate action gains support in all European societies, chances are increasing that consensus over cross-border high-speed railway infrastructure construction can be reached.

https://doi.org/10.11647/OBP.0280.12

Fig. 1 European Silk Road Routes including the Proposed Trainline from Lyon to Moscow *Source of data*: Holzner et al. (2018).

The wiiw report sets out the economic effects and advantages of a European Silk Road. In Europe, connecting the West with the East will generate growth and employment in the short- and long-term. Conservative estimations found a potential of 3.5% economic growth on average as well as an increase of employment of around two million over an investment period of ten years, due to the construction efforts in the countries concerned (Holzner et al. 2018). Under favourable circumstances and at continued low interest rates, an employment creation of over seven million can be expected in greater Europe. Furthermore, such large-scale investments into infrastructure projects can reduce the economic disparities around various regions and have long term productivity and trade gains. They can not only remove economic divergence but also create a move towards political integration, offering a new narrative for Europe. This is specifically important in the context of inequalities that persist between Western and Eastern European countries, as well as the European disintegration process, that culminated for the time being with Brexit.

Specific extra-budgetary financing models were proposed for the European Silk Road, which was estimated to cost in total about €1 tn, or roughly 7% of the EU's GDP (Holzner 2019). In order to conduct and finance the project, the establishment of a European Silk Road Trust owned by the euro area countries, other EU countries and third countries wishing to join the construction of the European Silk Road was suggested. The trust could rely on a public guarantee when it came to issuing long-term bonds (at currently zero or even negative real interest rates). It would formally be part of the private sector, especially as it would have sufficient income of its own from private customers (tolls).

As a strong core guarantor for the trust, the gradual development of a European Sovereign Wealth Fund by the euro area member states was suggested, following the structure of the Norwegian oil fund, for instance sourced from a part of the profits of the ECB. Other options, which would make use of existing institutions, would include, for instance, a substantial increase in the European Fund for Strategic Investments and/or a larger capital injection in the European Investment Bank (EIB), in order to finance the European Silk Road.

Recently, the proposal by the wiiw has gained significance as the idea of a European high-speed railway (HSR) network is also being considered as a mechanism for economic recovery after the COVID-19 pandemic. The Macroeconomic Policy Institute (IMK) in Düsseldorf, the Observatoire Français des Conjonctures Économiques (OFCE) in Paris and the wiiw have jointly proposed to dedicate a part of the EU's Recovery Fund *inter alia* to the development of a pan-European HSR network—an Ultra-Rapid-Train connecting EU capitals (Creel et al. 2020). Apart from the economic recovery, an HSR network could also be an important step towards achieving the announced goal of reducing greenhouse-gas (GHG) emissions in the Paris Agreement and the Agenda 2030. While the economic analysis as well as the financing of the project have been studied comprehensively, the environmental effects of constructing a European Silk Road, specifically the HSR network, have not been examined, so far. This study closes the gap by conducting an environmental impact evaluation of the proposed European HSR network. Given that this is about a hypothetical railway line, the calculations must remain rough and based on the results of studies on similar existing lines. Nevertheless, the goal is to determine in various scenarios the possible range of net GHG emissions of constructing and operating an HSR network and to provide a crude estimation of how many tonnes of CO_2 could be saved as compared to road and air travel, over the life cycle of sixty years. The analysis will focus only on the northern, proposed core HSR line from Lyon to Moscow, the cost of which was estimated at €200.4 bn. By comparison, this is approximately the amount that Italy receives in pandemic-related EU grants and loans from the Next Generation EU fund. However, it has to be noted that the assumptions about the unit costs were extremely conservative in the sense that the highest possible costs were assumed, i.e., for a new two-track railway line with a tunnel system. Thus, these cost estimates (and other economic estimates made in Holzner et al. (2018)) cannot be used for tying back the emission calculations. Instead, a range of potential GHG emissions based on the literature will be employed in the following exercises.

12.1 Life-Cycle Assessments—Calculating the Environmental Burden of HSR Networks

Generally, an LCA is defined as an analysis that evaluates the environmental impact of a product. In our case, this is the entire life cycle of the proposed HSR line from Lyon to Moscow. Input factors are compared and quantified and contain construction, operation, maintenance, and waste disposal in a period of sixty to one hundred years.

The output is the total burden the line will impose on the environment, measured in CO_2 or rather CO_2-eq. (Asplan Viak 2011).

Many studies focus on the Life-Cycle Assessment (LCA) of railways but are very specific to pre-existing train line infrastructures. While these studies give good insights on how to assess the CO_2 or CO_2-eq. of existing infrastructures, the study at hand is conducted for a hypothetical line from Lyon to Moscow, rather than an existing project. The aim of the literature review was therefore to find reliable data as a baseline on which to build our model.

This is possible because LCAs are standardised under the International Organization for Standardization (ISO). The ISO requires adherence to certain norms, namely ISO 14040 and ISO 14044, to allow a comparison and quantification of different studies. Despite the comparability through the framework of the ISO standards, a review of the literature revealed significant differences in results. Decisive factors for the differences turned out to be mostly geographical location, including the share of bridges and tunnels, materials used for construction and various energy mixes among the different countries. To use reliable data for our calculations, we consider twelve studies to incorporate into our model (Table 1). These are mainly European studies, from Germany (von Rozycki et al. 2003), Scandinavia (Åkermann 2011; Grossrieder 2011), Portugal (Jones et al. 2016) and Spain (Kortazar et al. 2021). Outside of Europe studies from the United States (Chester and Horvath 2012) and China (Yue et al. 2015) were considered. Relying on studies covering a broad geographic area as well as different methods will ensure a balanced approach and a realistic estimation of the range between possible outcomes.

12.2 Methodology for the Environmental Impact Evaluation

While HSR infrastructure already exists in some parts of the route and other networks would need updating, the analysis builds on the assumption that the entire route Lyon-Moscow of 3434 kilometres would need to be constructed. This implies that our results for CO_2-eq. emission savings—all GHG emissions are expressed as CO_2-equivalent—are per definition lower-bound estimates.

Drawing on the literature, our study has been developed based on an LCA methodology. We calculate the net CO_2-eq. emissions of the proposed HSR line from Lyon to Moscow considering the phases of construction, maintenance, operation, and disposal. While the construction of new HSR infrastructure will create new CO_2-eq., the environmental benefit lies in the modal shift of passengers from more polluting modes of transport such as air and road travel (Kortazar et al. 2021). Mathematically this can be represented as:

$$NetCO_2eq. = \sum CO_2eq._{HSRConstruction} + \sum CO_2eq._{HSROperation} - \sum CO_2eq._{aToHSR} \quad [1]$$

Table 1: Comparison of LCA Studies

Project	Country	Reference	km	Operations kg- CO_2/pkm	Construction tCO_2/km
Hannover - Wuerzburg	Germany	von Rozycki et al. (2003)	325		8,923.1
Europabanan line	Sweden	Akerman J. (2011)	740		5,405.4
Oslo-Trondheim	Norway	Grossrieder (2011)	486		
LGV Med	France	Baron et al. (2011)	251		5,760.0
South Europe Atlantic	France	Baron et al. (2011)	302		4,735.1
Taipei-Kaohsiung	Taiwan	Baron et al. (2011)	345		16,202.9
Bejing-Tianjin	China	Baron et al. (2011)	117		12,478.6
California HSR (CASHR)	USA	Chester and Horvath (2012)	1100	0.05883	8,818.2
California HSR (CASHR)	USA	Barnes E. (2014)	1100		5,477.3
Madrid-Barcelona	Spain	Sanz et al. (2014)	621		11,111.1
Beijing-Shanghai	China	Yue et al. (2015)	1318	0.0429	28,224.6
Turkish HSR	Turkey	Banar and Özdemir (2015)	888	0.0120	
Lisbon and Porto	Portugal	Jones et al. (2016)	297	0.0070	
UK HS2	UK	Cornet et al. (2018)	530		10,547.2
Botniabanan/Bothnia Line	Sweden	EPD (2019)	190	0.0130	
Y Basque	Spain	Kortazar et al. (2021)	180		15,055.6
			mean	0.0267	11,061.6
			σ	0.0228	6,606.8
			-1σ	0.0039	4,454.8
			+1σ	0.0496	17,668.3

where *a* denotes the alternative passenger modes of transport to the HSR and the emissions are summed over sixty years, which is a common period analysed in the literature.

Simplifying the equation provides:

$$NetCO_2eq. = \sum CO_2eq._{HSRConstruction} - \sum CO_2eq._{Avoided}$$
[2]

The following analysis takes a two-step approach according to the two parts of this equation. First, the life cycle emissions from HSR infrastructure are estimated. Second, avoided CO_2-eq. emissions compared to aviation and road transport are calculated. This provides an indication on how much CO_2-eq. could be saved if an HSR network was constructed.

12.2.1 Calculating Emissions from Construction

The emissions for constructing 3434 kilometres of line are estimated according to emission factors deduced from the existing life-cycle assessment studies for railway infrastructure. Hence, the emission factor includes all inputs for construction of rails, maintenance, operation and disposal of the infrastructure. Some studies also include vehicle manufacturing, maintenance, operation and disposal (Akerman 2011; Chester and Horvath 2010; Yue et al. 2015).

The CO_2-eq. emissions per kilometre of constructed railway vary widely among the different studies (Figure 2). This is due to two reasons. First, as explained above, some LCA include more input factors than others. Second, the complexity of construction varies widely among different studies. Bridges and tunnels account for the highest emissions during construction (Asplan Viak 2011). As the share of bridges and tunnels ranges from under 30% to over 80%, these differences lead to emission factors ranging from 4,735 tCO_2/km (Baron et al. 2011) to 28,224.6 tCO_2/km (Yue et al. 2015) (Figure 2). For the trainline from Lyon to Moscow, the number of bridges and tunnels required can hardly be estimated within the scope of this study. The analysis therefore covers three models: an optimistic, a moderate, and a conservative model. The moderate approach uses the mean of the available data on railway construction emission factors. The optimistic and conservative approaches rely on values of one standard deviation from the mean, covering the upper and lower bounds of available data (Table 1).

12.2.2 Calculating Avoided GHG Emissions

To estimate avoided CO_2-eq. emissions the modal shifts from aviation to train as well as road to train are determined. This is calculated as:

$$CO_2eq._{Avoided} = \sum_{Aviation} CO_2eq._{AviationToHSR} + \sum_{Road} CO_2eq._{RoadToHSR}$$
[3]

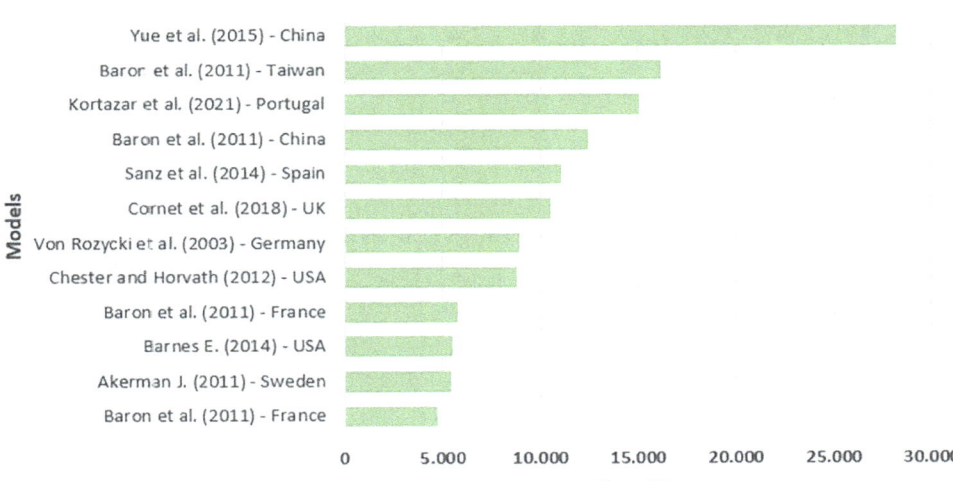

Fig. 2 Construction Emission Models.

Source of data: Bueno et al. (2017).

The avoided CO_2-eq. depends on three factors: one, the difference between the emission factors for operation of the mode of transport expressed in tonnes per passenger kilometre (pkm); two, the number of passengers shifting to train as a mode of transport; and three, the average distance travelled by passengers. Multiplying those three aspects will provide the sum of avoided GHG due to modal shifts over sixty years. Mathematically expressed this means:

$$\sum_{Aviation} CO_2 eq._{AviationToHSR} = \Delta CO_2 eq._{Aviation/HSR} \times pax\ shifted \times \frac{distance}{travelled}$$ [4]

12.2.3 Factor 1: Difference in Emission Factors

Emission factors for operation of the different ways of transport are relatively consistent across studies and literature. Trains have the lowest CO_2 emissions per passenger kilometre with a European average emission factor of 0.027 kg CO_2/pkm (Jones et al. 2016). Travelling by plane produces 4.5 times the emissions per passenger kilometre, with an emission factor of 0.126 kg CO_2/pkm (Fraunhofer ISI 2020). Passenger cars travelling on the highway emit 0.132 kg CO_2/pkm (Fraunhofer ISI 2020). Consequently, for every passenger shifting from aviation to train 0.099 kg CO_2/pkm can be avoided and for every passenger shifting from road to train 0.105 kg CO_2/pkm can be saved.

12.2.4 Factor 2: Passenger Shifts from Road and Air Travel

Estimating the expected passenger flows is one of the most important aspects of determining the environmental impact of the proposed HSR network. Only if enough passengers substitute their current mode of transport for travelling by train can the emissions from construction be offset. Estimations are based on current passenger flows of which a certain share is expected to shift.

The chosen data is based on values from the year 2019, as the COVID-19 pandemic has impacted passenger flows between countries significantly and thus data from 2020 is not representative. The number of passengers for air could be determined by passengers travelling between airports and reporting countries along the proposed route from Lyon to Moscow. In 2019, total passenger flows on this route amounted to 93.5 million (own calculations based on Eurostat 2021a; Eurostat 2021b; IATA 2019).

The number of passengers by road is estimated according to the average traffic flow on the nine core network corridors of the Trans-European Road Network (CEDR 2019). This amounts to 58,952 vehicles per day in 2019. Assuming an occupancy rate of 1.6 for cars (Fraunhofer ISI 2020) we can estimate 34.4 million passengers using the corridor from Lyon to Moscow within one year. Using these passenger flows as a baseline, an annual growth rate of 2% for aviation and a growth rate of 0.75% for road travel is assumed (Eurocontrol 2018; Alonso Raposo et al. 2019).

To determine a substitution rate, there are several factors that need to be considered. The main factors determining the choice of travel are price, travel time, travel time reliability, frequency of the connections and other factors such as convenience, comfort, and safety (EEA 2020b). Several studies have shown that trains can substitute aviation transport for a travel time of up to four hours (ÖBB 2021). With an average velocity of 250km/h for HSR (EIM 2008) this means that the train would be a good substitute for routes of up to 1000 km. Substitution rates range from 10% up to 90% (Steer Davies Gleave 2006) depending on the line length, and availability of other means of transport within origin and destinations, which makes it difficult to predict an accurate rate. The study therefore looks at three possible scenarios, which are based on the study on the California HSR by Chester and Horvath (2010). For air travel a shift of 25%, 50%, and 75% of passengers to railway is assumed, and for road transport a shift of 2%, 2.25%, and 2.5% of passengers is assumed. Taking the three models for construction emissions together with these three models provides nine models which are explored (Table 2).

12.2.5 Factor 3: Average Distance Travelled

As the emission factors are expressed in passenger kilometres (pkm), the distance travelled also plays an important role in calculating the total emissions. As discussed above, HSR travel has a cut-off point of around 1000 km. This means it will be used as a mode of transport for medium-distance travels which ranges from 300–1000 km

Table 2 Conceptual Depiction of Emissions Models.

Passenger Shift Models	Construction Models		
	Conservative (C)	Medium (M)	Optimistic (O)
Conservative (C)	C/C	C/M	C/O
Medium (M)	M/C	M/M	M/O
Optimistic (O)	O/C	O/M	O/O

(Eurostat 2018). Comparing flight distances regularly used on the route confirms this assumption. Only flights to Russia significantly surpass the 1000 km mark. The model is therefore built on the median of the medium-distance-range, which is 650 km. A more thorough approach would be to look at the individual expected passenger flows for the different passages of the route from Lyon to Moscow and use the weighted mean distance. Due to limitations in available data, we chose the simplified assumption, for both aviation and road travel.

12.3 HSR Networks as a Step towards European Climate Goals

The results show that constructing an HSR network across Europe would be a step towards the goal set out by the EU for cutting emissions in the transport sector. All the explored models provide net negative CO_2-eq. emissions. This indicates that more CO_2-eq. emissions could be avoided by the modal shift of passengers compared to the emissions from the construction and operation of the HSR line. While the most conservative model only predicts avoidance of 37.4 million tCO_2-eq., the medium model calculates 155.7 million tCO_2-eq. in savings and the optimistic model implies possible savings of 273.9 million tCO_2-eq. (Figure 3). Further, in the most optimistic model, emissions would be offset already after 3.2 years of operation. In the medium model the breakeven would be reached after 11.8 years of operation, while the most conservative model construction emissions will be compensated only after thirty-seven years of operation (Table 3).

To put the results into perspective, the most optimistic model is comparable to approximately 10% of net emissions within the EU-27 in a year (EPA 2020; EEA 2020a). While this might not seem considerable, several aspects need to be taken into account. First, only passenger travel is included and avoided emissions from freight were not considered. An additional shift within the freight-transport sector will increase the environmental benefits of an HSR line. Second, the construction, maintenance, and disposal of the road and air infrastructure have not been considered, while all

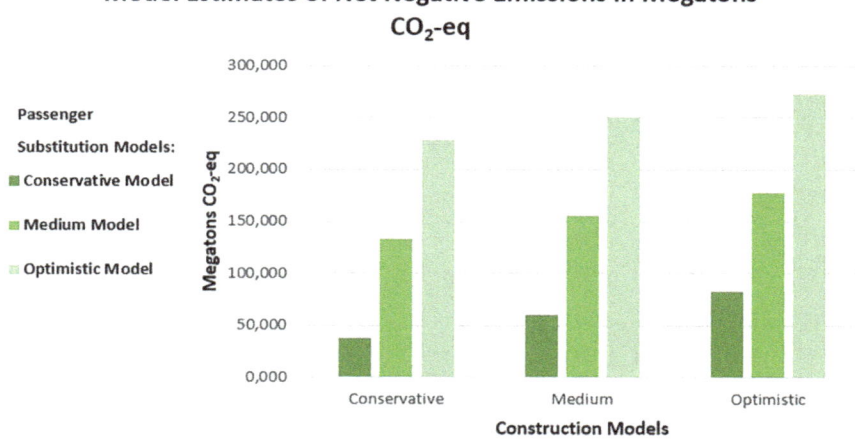

Fig. 3 Model Estimates of Net Negative Emissions

Source: own calculations (2021).

aspects for rail are included. This disadvantages rail compared to the other modes of transport. Third, the wiiw has shown the notable economic benefits of constructing a pan-European HSR network. The environmental benefits should thus not be evaluated independently but in addition to the economic advantages. Lastly, the examined passage of the line is only one part of the bigger network which has the potential to save further CO2-eq. emissions. Also, the costs of the Lyon-Moscow HSR, amounting to an estimated €200.4 bn euros, have to be taken into consideration.

Looking at the bandwidth of results between the nine models there is a need to discuss which model would be the most accurate. Therefore, in the following sections, the different models are examined more closely to provide an indication of which scenarios should be used as an estimate and as a basis for the impact evaluation.

Table 3 Net Negative Emissions by Model Type

Passenger Substitution Models	Construction Models		
	Conservative Model	Medium Model	Optimistic Model
Conservative	- 37,430,999.89	- 133,003,527.39	- 228,576,054.89
Medium	- 60,118,629.40	- 155,691,156.90	- 251,263,684.40
Optimistic	- 82,806,258.91	- 178,378,786.41	- 273,951,313.91

Table 4 Years to Offset Construction Emissions

Passenger Substitution Models	Construction Models		
	Conversative	Medium	Optimistic
Conservative	37.1	18.8	12.6
Medium	23.2	11.8	7.9
Optimistic	9.4	4.7	3.2

12.3.1 Impact of Sustainable Construction Practices

The conservative model is based on the mean plus one standard deviation from the considered literature, with 17,668 tCO_2-eq./km resulting in a total of 60.7 mil tCO_2- eq. for construction (Figure 4). The higher emission factor is mostly due to differences in construction (Yue et al. 2015). Specifically, the lack of light-weight metals and the usage of fly ash in concrete, as well as an unfavourable energy mix, lead to extremely high emission factors (Yue et al. 2015; Barnes 2014). As in Europe construction practices and materials used are more sustainable and have lower emissions, an emission factor as high as assumed in the conservative model is unlikely.

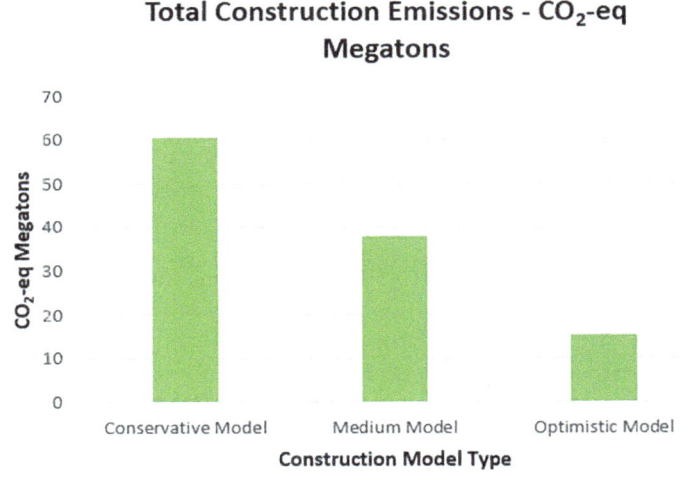

Fig 4 Construction Emissions by Model

Source: own calculations (2021).

The optimistic model, which utilises the mean minus one standard deviation of emissions found in the literature, is more plausible. France and Sweden have the lowest emissions during the life cycle of railways (UIC 2017). This is due to a less carbon-based energy mix, relatively more sustainable construction materials used and a lower share of bridges and tunnels. With an emission factor of 4,455 tCO_2-eq./km the total carbon emissions for construction amounts to 15.3 million tCO_2-eq (Figure 4). In comparison to the other two models this is only about 25% of the conservative model and 40% of the moderate model total emissions. Nonetheless, this could be achievable with a sustainable energy mix, sufficient numbers for passengers and freight, and sustainable construction practices, i.e., limiting or cutting out fly ash in concrete.

The medium model is based upon the average of twelve studies of tCO_2-eq./km emitted during construction. The emissions factor in this model is 11,062 tCO_2-eq./km and total emissions emitted from construction in this model amount to 38 million tCO_2-eq. (Figure 4). This correlates with other recent projects throughout Europe. For example, Spain has the second longest HSR network in the world and several LCAs have been conducted for different parts of the infrastructure (Kortazar et al. 2021). The quality of assessment is very reliable, because of the diversity of the sample studies used.

Additionally, the coherence found within the European studies shows that the medium model is the most realistic. Nevertheless, we see potential for outcomes according to the optimistic model, if sustainable construction practices are applied and cleaner energy mixes used.

12.3.2 Potential CO_2 Emissions Avoided through an HSR Network

For avoided tCO_2-eq. emissions, again a conservative, medium, and optimistic scenario have been examined, based on different expected substitution rates for aviation and road. While substitution rates range as wide as 10%-90% among the literature, several factors can indicate a more accurate expected substitution rate. As mentioned, the main factors determining the choice of travel are price, travel time, travel time reliability, and frequency of the connections (EEA 2020b). Linked to those factors are the density of population and competition by low-price airlines impacting the substitution rate (Steer Davies Gleave 2006).

The route from Lyon to Moscow encompasses many corridors where according to aforementioned factors a high substitution rate can be expected. Looking at routes within the 4 hour/1000 km distance, on the proposed lines this would for example include routes such as Lyon to Brussels (730 km), Paris to Berlin (1,050 km), Berlin to Warsaw (575 km), Warsaw to Minsk (545 km) and Minsk to Moscow (713 km). Duisburg to Warsaw would also only take about 4.5 hours. The data on passenger flows show that these routes are currently mainly covered by aviation. For example, in 2019, 1.8 million passengers travelled from Brussels' airport to Germany with an average flight distance of 383 km (Eurostat 2021a). If a reliable and fast railway system was in place, due to convenience and time of travel for such routes a substitution rate in line with the optimistic model can be expected (75%).

One factor which will constrain the substitution rates is the strong competition of low-price airlines, which cover most of the routes. From a cost perspective, it may be hard for an HSR network to compete with those airlines. However, with the emission trading system adapted by the European Union and possible further policies pushing for the reduction of GHG emissions, an increase of prices on flights can also be expected, which would benefit the substitution rates. Overall, we believe the substitution rate to lie on the upper end of the range, or in other words either the medium or the optimistic model, with substitution rates of 50% or 75%.

On the other hand, shifts from travel by car are expected to be very low. All factors such as price, reliability, and convenience of the car hinder significant shifts to train travel. On top of this, electric cars produce very low carbon emissions. This is an enticing alternative for the increasingly environmentally conscious European consumer market. For these reasons, the substitution rate can be estimated at only around 2–3% (Chester and Horvath 2010). The model does not depend on whether a 2%, 2.25%, or 2.5% substitution rate for cars is used. Therefore, for road travel it does not matter greatly whether the conservative, medium or optimistic model is chosen.

In conclusion, the medium-medium or medium-optimistic models seem to be the most likely (Table 2). This would result in total savings of emissions equivalent to the net tCO_2-eq. of the Netherlands (M/M) or Poland (M/O) for a year (EEA 2020a).

12.4 Limitations

Our study faces three major limitations. First, estimating outcomes over the next sixty years provides uncertainties, which could not be accounted for. Assumptions include a steady growth rate as well as a continuous substitution rate. Assuming the same substitution rate for sixty years may overestimate passenger flows. On the other hand, a relatively low growth rate was chosen to account for this aspect.

Second, it could not be considered that the continuous improvement of other modes of transport will reduce emissions as technology advances. Electrical cars are expected to cut emissions from road travel significantly in the future. Current targets set by the EU and member states regarding private car emission requirements aim at eliminating combustion engines within the next ten to fifteen years (Wappelhorst 2020). Similarly, airplane fuel efficiency has been increasing and is expected to reduce the emission factor for aviation (EESI 2019). However, it can be expected that the emissions by train will also reduce as the energy mix within the different EU countries moves towards renewable energies. Nevertheless, the shift to electric cars barely changes the results of our model.

Third, GHG savings from freight transport are not explicitly included in this study as their quantification would need further research. Qualitatively, though, we see strong grounds to expect a positive impact on emissions if freight transport shifts to rail are incorporated. A recent study by the European Environment Agency (EEA 2021) found that transport of freight via rail emits 43 times less CO_2 than transport via air. More specifically, a study by Bueno et al. (2017) on evaluating the environmental performance of a high-speed rail project in the Basque Country in Spain demonstrated that net CO_2 emissions improve by a factor of 1.3–2.1, depending on the model, when including freight in the calculations. Although the authors came to the conclusion that the Basque Y Line they studied will not reach a net negative CO_2-balance, with emissions dropping from 1.92 $MtCO_2$ net emissions if only passenger transport is considered to up to 0.9 $MtCO_2$ net emissions when including both passenger and freight transport. For our study, this is suggestive that the projected CO_2 savings could potentially double, when including freight into the calculations.

12.5 Conclusion

In conclusion, we could show that a construction of an HSR line between Lyon and Moscow along the "European Silk Road" provides not only economic advantages, as examined by Holzner et al. (2018), but also presents potential for a positive environmental impact. Based on calculations in the related literature, it could be determined that the most optimistic model projects an emissions avoidance equivalent to 10% net emissions of the EU-27 for a year for passenger transport alone. The bulk of the avoidance comes from an assumed reduction in air travel. The emissions from construction would be offset after eight to twelve years of operation, relying on the medium-medium and medium-optimistic models. Considering that freight transport was not incorporated in the calculations, the potential is in fact higher than portrayed by this study. Existing studies suggest that projected CO_2 savings could potentially double, when including freight in the calculations. We argue that the construction and operation of an HSR could significantly reduce passenger flows from aviation, contributing to the EU's goal to reduce emissions from aviation by at least 10% (EC 2019). While the idea, let alone the construction, of an HSR network seems radical, it certainly can have an extensive impact not only on the further economic integration of Europe but also contribute to a greener, more sustainable, more innovative and technologically advanced future. The estimated costs of the European Silk Road HSR line between Lyon and Moscow of more than €200 bn are substantial. However, as a share of 2020 EU GDP, this makes up only 1.5%. Considering that the investment would likely be spread out over at least a decade, the amount involved appears modest from a European perspective. Also, this has to be seen against the backdrop of the recent signals by the European Commission's President, Ursula von der Leyen, in her 2021 State of the Union Address, announcing the presentation of a new connectivity strategy called Global Gateway, with investments in quality infrastructure, connecting goods, people, and services around the world.

References

Åkerman, J. (2011) "The role of high-speed rail in mitigating climate change—The Swedish case Europabanan from a life cycle perspective", *Transportation Research Part D: Transport and Environment* 16(3): 208–17, https://doi.org/10.1016/j.trd.2010.12.004.

Alonso Raposo, M. and B. Ciuffo (eds) (2019) *The future of road transport—Implications of automated, connected, low-carbon and shared mobility* (Luxembourg: Publications Office of the European Union), https://doi.org/10.2760/668964.

Asplan Viak (2011) *New Double Track Line Oslo—Ski Life Cycle Assessment of the Follo Line—Infrastructure* (UOS-00-A-36100), Jernbaneverket.

Banar, M. and A. Özdemir (2015) "An evaluation of railway passenger transport in Turkey using life cycle assessment and life cycle cost methods", *Transportation Research Part D: Transport and Environment* 41: 88–105, https://doi.org/10.1016/j.trd.2015.09.017.

Barnes, E. (2014) *California High Speed Resilience to Climate Change*, https://repository.asu.edu/items/25239.

Baron, T., G. Martinetti and D. Pepion (2011) *Carbon Footprint of High-Speed Rail*, International Union of Railways, https://railroads.dot.gov/sites/fra.dot.gov/files/fra_net/15009/Carbon%20Foot print%20of%20High-Speed%20Rail%20UIC%202011.pdf.

Bueno, G., D. Hoyos and I. Capellán-Pérez (2017) "Evaluating the environmental performance of the high speed rail project in the Basque Country, Spain", *Research in Transportation Economics* 62: 44–56, https://doi.org/10.1016/j.retrec.2017.02.004.

CEDR (2019) *Trans-European Road Network, TEN-T (Roads): 2019 Performance Report* (October 2020), CEDR Working Group 3.5 Performance, https://www.cedr.eu/download/Publications/2020/CEDR-Technical-Report-2020-01-TEN-T-2019-Performance-Report.pdf.

Chester, M. and A. Horvath (2010) "Life-cycle assessment of high-speed rail: The case of California", *Environmental Research Letters* 5(1): 014003, https://doi.org/10.1088/1748-9326/5/1/014003.

Chester, M. and A. Horvath (2012) "High-speed rail with emerging automobiles and aircraft can reduce environmental impacts in California's future", *Environmental Research Letters* 7(3): 034012, https://doi.org/10.1088/1748-9326/7/3/034012.

Cornet, Y., G. Dudley and D. Banister (2018) "High speed rail: Implications for carbon emissions and biodiversity", *Case Studies on Transport Policy* 6(3): 376–90, https://doi.org/10.1016/j.cstp.2017.08.007.

Creel, J., M. Holzner, F. Saraceno, A. Watt and J. Wittwer (2020) *How to spend it: A proposal for a European Covid-19 recovery programme, wiiw Policy Note/Policy Report*, No. 38, https://wiiw.ac.at/publications-all-all-all-all-10-year-desc-0-how+to+spend+it.html.

EC (2019) *Sustainable Mobility—The European Green Deal*, European Commission, https://ec.europa.eu/commission/presscorner/detail/en/fs_19_6726.

ECA (2018) *A European high-speed rail network: not a reality but an ineffective patchwork*, European Court of Auditors, Special Report, No. 19.

EEA (2020a) *Approximated estimates for greenhouse gas emissions*, European Environment Agency, https://www.eea.europa.eu/data-and-maps/data/approximated-estimates-for-green house-gas-emissions-2.

EEA (2020b) *Transport and environment report 2020—Train or plane?* (19/2020), European Environment Agency, https://www.eea.europa.eu/publications/transport-and-environment-report-2020.

EEA (2021) *Rail and waterborne—best for low-carbon motorised transport*, European Environment Agency Briefing, No. 01/2021, https://www.eea.europa.eu/publications/rail-and-waterborne-transport.

EIM (2008) *European Railway Technical Strategy* (Version 1.2), European Rail Infrastructure Managers, https://ec.europa.eu/transport/sites/transport/files/themes/strategies/consultations/doc/2009_03_27_future_of_transport/20090305_eim.pdf.

Environmental and Energy Study Institute (EESI) (2019) *Fact sheet: The growth in greenhouse gas emissions from commercial aviation*, Environmental and Energy Study Institute Ideas, Insights, Sustainable Solutions, https://www.eesi.org/papers/view/fact-sheet-the-growth-in-greenhouse-gas- emissions-from-commercial-aviation.

EPA (2020) *Greenhouse gas equivalencies calculator*, US EPA, https://www.epa.gov/energy/greenhouse-gas-equivalencies-calculator.

EPD (International EPD Consortium) (2019) *Environmental Product Declaration for passenger transport on the Bothnia Line* (Reg. no. S-P-00194), Botniabanan AB, https://portal.environdec.com/api/api/v1/EPDLibrary/Files/3fa98013-e848-4dbc-ae38-ae496671833a/Data.

Eurocontrol (2018) *European Aviation in 2040*, European Organisation for the Safety of Air Navigation, https://www.eurocontrol.int/sites/default/files/2019-07/challenges-of-growth-2018-annex1_0.pdf.

Eurostat (2018) *EU Transport Statistics—Eurostat guidelines on Passenger Mobility Statistics* (December 2018), https://ec.europa.eu/eurostat/documents/29567/3217334/Guidelines_on_Passenger_Mobility_Statistics+%282018_edition%29.pdf/f15955e3-d7b4-353b-7530-34c6c94d2ec1?t=1611654879518.

Eurostat (2021a) *Air passenger transport between main airports in each reporting country and partner reporting countries*, Eurostat Data Browser, https://ec.europa.eu/eurostat/databrowser/view/avia_paoac/default/table?lang=en.

Eurostat (2021b) *Air passenger transport between reporting countries*, Eurostat Data Browser, https://ec.europa.eu/eurostat/databrowser/view/avia_paocc/default/table?lang=en.

Fraunhofer ISI (2020, March 24) *Methodology for GHG Efficiency of Transport Modes* (Final Report), https://www.eea.europa.eu/publications/rail-and-waterborne-transport/rail-and-waterborne-best/d3b-eea-ghg-efficiency-indicators/view.

Grossrieder, C. (2011) *Life-cycle assessment of future high-speed rail in Norway*, Norwegian University of Science and Technology.

Holzner, M., P. Heimberger and A. Kochnev (2018) *A 'European Silk Road'*, wiiw Research Report, No. 430, https://wiiw.ac.at/a-european-silk-road-dlp- 4608.pdf.

Holzner, M. (2019) *One Trillion Euros for Europe. How to finance a European Silk Road with the help of a European Silk Road Trust, backed by a European Sovereign Wealth Fund and other financing instruments*, wiiw Policy Note/Policy Report, No. 35, https://wiiw.ac.at/one-trillion-euros-for-europe-how-to-finance-a-european-silk-road-with-the-help-of-a-european-silk-road-trust-backed-by-a-european-sovereign-wealth-fund-and-other-financing-instruments-p-5106.html.

IATA (2019) *The Importance of Air Transport to The Russian Federation*, Russian Federation, https://www.iata.org/en/iata-repository/publications/economic-reports/russian-federation--value-of-aviation/.

IEA (2019) *Transport—Topics*, https://www.iea.org/topics/transport.

Jones, H., F. Moura and T. Domingos (2016) "Life cycle assessment of high-speed rail: A case study in Portugal", *The International Journal of Life Cycle Assessment* 22(3): 410–22, https://doi.org/10.1007/s11367-016-1177-7.

Kortazar, A., G. Bueno and D. Hoyos (2021) "Environmental balance of the high speed rail network in Spain: A life cycle assessment approach", *Research in Transportation Economics* 36(101035), 107006, https://doi.org/10.1016/j.retrec.2021.101035.

ÖBB Austrian Federal Railway (2021, January 21) Personal communication, Online interview.

Von Rozycki, C. V., H. Koeser and H. Schwarz (2003) "Ecology profile of the German high-speed rail passenger transport system, ICE", *The International Journal of Life Cycle Assessment* 8(2): 83–91, https://doi.org/10.1007/bf02978431.

Russian Federal Agency for Air transport and Aviation (2021) *Ob'emy perevozok cherez aeroporty Rossii*, Russian Federal Agency for Air transport and Aviation, https://favt.gov.ru/dejatelnost-ajeroporty-i-ajerodromy-osnovnie-proizvodstvennie-pokazateli-aeroportov-obyom-perevoz/.

Sanz, A., P. Vega and M. Mateos (2014) *Las cuentas ecológicas del transporte en España*, https://www.gea21.com/archivo/cuentas-ecologicas-del-transporte- en-espana.

Steer Davies Gleave (2006) *Air and Rail Competition and Complementarity*, https://ec.europa.eu/transport/modes/air/studies/internal_market_en.

UIC (2017) *Railway Handbook 2017*, International Union of Railways, https://uic.org/IMG/pdf/handbook_iea-uic_2017_web3.pdf.

Wappelhorst, S. (2020) *The end of the road? An overview of combustion engine car phase- out announcements across Europe*, International Council on Clean Transportation, https://theicct.org/sites/default/files/publications/Combustion-engine-phase-out-briefing-may11.2020.pdf.

Yue, Y., T. Wang, S. Liang, J. Yang, P. Hou, S. Qu, J. Zhou, X. Jia, H. Wang and M. Xu (2015) "Life cycle assessment of High-Speed Rail in China", *Transportation Research Part D: Transport and Environment* 41: 367–76, https://doi.org/10.1016/j.trd.2015.10.005.

13. Cohesion Policy and Public Investment in the EU

Giuseppe Coco and Raffaele Lagravinese

Introduction

The Cohesion Policy is certainly the most important policy area for the EU budget. Over the decades it has also progressively grown in size and relevance. The founding fathers' acute awareness of the centripetal forces that the Union would determine in the economic sphere, and consequently of the need for a policy to counteract the potential polarisation between central, high-growth regions and peripheral, lagging areas, determined the adoption of an EU-wide policy for territorial cohesion. The main funds of the policy are regional in nature, although nothing precludes their use in a coordinated manner at the national level. As such, the ERDF is the development policy fund, and the ESF, the social pillar fund. From 2007 on, due to the accession of new member states with lower per capita incomes, some resources have been allocated to a "national" fund, the Cohesion Fund (CF). This fund has mostly been used for infrastructure development in the new MS (as well, since 2013, as in some of the old MS whose per capita average income slipped below the 90% EU average threshold).

Discussing the relevance of the Cohesion Policy for investment in the EU is a difficult task as expenditure on EU programming is not categorised according to the current nature of its investment. A report (Prota et al. 2020) on last year's outlook mainly discussed the history of cohesion policy. It adopted a simple accounting view in reporting its size (only ERDF and CF) relative to the total public investment in each member state (a measure provided by Eurostat) and some *ad hoc* measures of investments financed by cohesion policy in specific fields like transport or energy. This idea is based on the implicit view that ERDF and CF are development policy funds, and therefore the whole expenditure on them can be attributed to investment. This view has also been used in the past to advocate in favour of cohesion policy as a tool for reducing the damage from decreasing capital expenditure in some countries. Brasili et al. (2021) in this handbook show clearly that most, if not all, of fiscal consolidation comes in the form of reduced capital expenditure and that this was particularly the case

https://doi.org/10.11647/OBP.0280.13

for Southern European member states of the EU during and after the Great Recession. The argument is that cohesion policy could have slowed this trend, although there is little evidence of that happening.

While the idea that much of the cohesion expenditure is capital is generally correct for many items, still the fact that some expenditure items refer for example to social infrastructure or better employment leaves many doubts about its integral use for this aim. This may also explain why in some countries the ratio of cohesion "development" expenditure to total public capital expenditure is extremely high (even unreasonably high).[1]

Cohesion policy probably contributes positively to public investment, but there are at least two open issues in using the total cohesion expenditure over public capital expenditure as a measure of its contribution. On the one hand, not all cohesion expenditure is an investment as it is stated to be, and therefore the ratio mentioned above is not normalised across countries to 100, as the numerator is not a part of the denominator. This makes it important to have a better measure of cohesion policy's real contribution to public investment expenditure. Our approach will consider the different "themes" in the EU budget (expenditure categorisation) to isolate the items that are, with a high probability, associated with capital expenditure, at least under a proper statistical definition.

However, this brings to the fore the issue of the correct definition of investment expenditure. The current statistical definition includes traditional items of physical capital and some items of intangible capital, notably R&D expenditure. Infrastructure expenditure and R&D expenditure, therefore, are certainly part of any capital definition. Also, most transfers to firms are probably finalised as investment and therefore can be accounted as capital account transfer (gross fixed capital formation).

On the other hand, a growing body of literature claims that a rising and increasingly unstable share of investment takes forms that were in the past less important and are more difficult to account for. Intangibles are becoming ever more relevant for defining the amount of capital embedded in a firm, for example (Haskel and Westlake 2018). The clearest way to understand this argument is to ask the value of the capital of firms like Microsoft or Google. The enormous divergence between an accounting measure of capital invested and the market value of these firms can be partly explained by their dominant positions. But, according to a stream of literature, this divergence is also down to the intangible (and therefore more difficult to evaluate) nature of the investment. According to this view, the value of a firm is equivalent to the value of the human capital working in it, and the network of relationships embedded in its organisation. In other terms value stems mostly from these forms of capital, rather than from traditional tangible items.

---

1   For some smaller countries, usually the beneficiaries of the highest per capita transfer, such as Hungary and Portugal, this ratio is close to 60% in the period 2015–17. It is very unlikely, however, that the whole of the Cohesion Policy expenditure is capital in a traditional accounting sense. The same proportions are negligible in larger and richer countries like Germany.

It can also be argued that a growing share of public capital is intangible, and therefore the traditional, narrow definition of capital can be misleading, particularly if we are examining a policy aimed at stimulating development in underdeveloped regions. It can be safely assumed for example that a large share of expenditure in education increases human capital and therefore should be accounted for as an investment. We will account for it separately. By the same token, we could claim that some types of social expenditure increase social capital and therefore constitute investments in an even broader sense. This would lead, however, to the view that all cohesion expenditure— and, in a more extreme view, also all of the public expenditure—is, one way or another, a form of capital expenditure. This would make the whole exercise of evaluating public capital expenditure, and specifically the cohesion policy contribution, meaningless. So we will adopt a more reasonable approach.

Based on this approach we will compare capital expenditure (traditional and human) in the wider context of cohesion policy and its share over time in different countries. In our opinion, this exercise may also shed some light on the recent literature on the effects of cohesion policy on growth. Several papers claim that the effects of cohesion policy are highly differentiated across countries and regions, not only in their overall effects on growth but also in the type of effects observed (see, for example, Crescenzi and Giua 2020; Fratesi and Perucca 2020). As suggested by Berkovitz et al. (2020) in a study about Greece, the key for understanding the differences may be to look at the composition of the expenditure.

The second interesting question we will tackle is whether cohesion policy actually increases capital expenditure in MS or whether it just substitutes national capital expenditure. Some investigations in member states have questioned the additionality of the public investment component of cohesion policy (for a recent example, see Psycharis et al. 2020, for Greece). In general, one would expect that if cohesion policy were able to increase capital expenditure then one should observe some correlation between its intensity at a regional level and public capital expenditure. But much of the anecdotal evidence does not confirm this view (see also in this volume, Barbieri and Cerniglia 2021, for the Italian case). To investigate this question directly we should ideally compare public investment at a regional level, but unfortunately, Eurostat does not collect such data. We will therefore look in particular at the regions receiving the largest contributions from cohesion policy. For these regions, we will compare the total gross fixed capital formation (GFCF) normalised by regional GDP to the national value of the same ratio. This comparison will give us information about the effectiveness of the EU cohesion policy in increasing investment (public and private) at the regional level and, indirectly, will also give us a clue on the additionality of public investment in different countries. Unfortunately, Eurostat does not provide a measure of public capital formation at the regional level, but gross fixed capital formation provides an interesting clue, in particular if one subscribes to the hypothesis of crowding in of public investments, convincingly put forward also in this volume by Durand et al. (2021).

A purely additional cohesion policy expenditure would increase capital formation in regions that receive more transfers relative to the national average. Of course, we expect some substitution effect, but the extent of this substitution is important information as it offers important clues on whether the policy really increases capital expenditure in the member states, and therefore if a European cohesion policy is really useful (at least for investment).

13.1 Disentangling Capital Expenditure from Other Cohesion Items

It is a generally held view that the EU cohesion policy increases capital expenditure. However, the claim is usually assumed away based on the view that most, or all, of the cohesion expenditure particularly in the "development" funds (notably the ERDF and the Cohesion Fund) are allocated to capital expenditure, while the ESF is allocated to current social expenditure. This is not necessarily the case, as we will see. National accounts (and the EU database on cohesion) do not provide a statistical measure of the amount of funds allocated to capital expenditure, and therefore only an indirect estimate is possible. An estimate of cohesion contribution to investment would be valuable for estimating the share of cohesion resources that generate investment. Even more importantly, we could identify which countries allocate a comparatively larger share of funds to capital expenditure. This information could be tentatively used to investigate the effects of the composition of expenditure on the success of cohesion policy in different countries and, ultimately, its effects on growth.

To allocate cohesion expenditure to current and capital expenditure, we will consider the items ("themes") identified in the Cohesion Policy Framework Budget for the period 2014–20 and isolate the items that are directly linked to capital formation in the statistical definition of fixed capital and R&D. We group these items in a High Content of Capital Expenditure (HCC) bundle and then calculate its share in each country. We then identify an intermediate content of capital expenditure (ICC) group of items, mostly linked to the Green Deal and Transition, that is likely linked to energy infrastructure and capacity, sustainable mobility, and therefore at least partially capital expenditure. The residual type of expenditure (low capital content) is generally social infrastructure expenditure. Within this group of items, special attention will be devoted to expenditure in "Education and vocational training". As discussed in the introduction, this item is linked to human capital formation and therefore can be considered a capital expenditure in a broader sense. It is useful to analyse its distribution in the context of capital formation. Table 1 shows the themes of the cohesion policy expenditure and their grouping in the above-named categories.

Table 1 European Structural and Investment Funds by Theme (2014–2020) (in billion euros, Current Prices)

High Capital Content	Competitiveness of SMEs	105.14
	ICT	18.14
	Network Infrastructures in Transport and Energy	66.20
	Research & Innovation	59.55
	Total HCC	249,03
Intermediate Capital Content	Environment Protection & Resource Efficiency	83.35
	Climate Change Adaptation & Risk Prevention	43.47
	Low-Carbon Economy	57.47
	Total ICC	184,29
Low Capital Content	Educational & Vocational Training	47.18
	Fostering crisis repair and resilience	5.86
	Social Inclusion	68.69
	Sustainable & Quality Employment	59.08
	Technical Assistance	20.42
	Efficient Public Administration	5.69
	Discontinued Measures	0.94
	Outermost & Sparsely Populated	0.69
	Total LCC	208,55

Source of data: Authors 'calculation on data, Open Data Portal for the European Structural Investment Funds—European Commission | Data | European Structural and Investment Funds (europa.eu), https://cohesiondata.ec.europa.eu/themes.

From the table above, it is easy to calculate that roughly 66.66% of cohesion expenditure is devoted respectively to the narrow category of "High Capital Content" expenditure and the broader category of "Intermediate Capital Content" (ICC). Of the remaining 33.34%, 7% is devoted to "Education and formation" and can be accounted for as a form of investment. On the whole, only 25% of cohesion expenditure at the EU level cannot be labelled as capital expenditure.

Table 2 shows the allocations to different "Capital Content" categories across member states in units of €1 bn. Of course, aside from the policy choices of member states, the amounts shown reflect both the size of the country and the overall allocation of cohesion funds. It is however worth noting the enormous allocation of expenditure to the "High Capital Content" category for Poland, €55 bn of the overall EU budget of €642 bn.

Table 3 reports the share of the different categories of expenditure for each member country, normalised to total cohesion expenditure by country. This table really highlights the policy choices of MS (which are, of course, coordinated and agreed with the EU Commission).

Table 2 MS Budget for 2014–20 by Level of Capital Content (Billion Euros, Current Prices)

EU MS	High Capital Content	Intermediate Capital Content	Low Capital Content	Total
Austria	3.13	5.47	2.45	11.05
Belgium	1.95	1.61	2.72	6.28
Bulgaria	3.99	4.24	3.76	12.00
Cyprus	0.35	0.57	0.34	1.26
Czech Republic	14.56	9.38	9.18	33.12
Germany	14.32	14.11	18.41	46.83
Danmark	0.48	1.48	0.82	2.78
Estonia	2.32	1.36	2.32	6.00
Spain	24.85	13.47	18.28	56.60
Finland	2.64	5.65	2.24	10.53
France	15.04	17.99	15.91	48.94
Greece	9.86	8.60	7.81	26.26
Croatia	5.36	3.60	3.70	12.66
Hungary	11.62	8.12	10.02	29.76
Ireland	1.32	4.70	1.58	7.60
Italy	28.82	17.44	26.16	72.42
Latva	2.93	2.10	1.88	6.91
Lithuania	3.82	2.85	3.60	10.27
Luxemburg	0.13	0.27	0.13	0.52
Malta	0.37	0.34	0.42	1.13
Netherlands	1.49	1.31	2.00	4.80
Poland	54.80	24.06	26.40	105.25
Portugal	9.45	7.56	16.19	33.21
Romania	13.93	11.04	11.80	36.77
Sweden	2.64	3.25	2.46	8.35
Slovenia	2.08	1.54	1.33	4.95
Slovakia	8.94	4.67	5.85	19.46
UK	7.84	7.52	10.81	26.17
Total	249.03	184.29	208.56	641.88

Source of data: Author's calculation on data, Open Data Portal for the European Structural Investment Funds—European Commission | Data | European Structural and Investment Funds (europa.eu), https://cohesiondata.ec.europa.eu/themes.

Table 3 MS Budget for 2014–20 (Daily Update) by Content of Capital (% Share of Country Allocation)

EU MS	High Capital Investments	Intermediate Capital Investments	Low Capital Investments	of which education and training (% on total budget)
Austria	28.3%	49.5%	22.2%	5.00%
Belgium	31.1%	25.6%	43.3%	11.20%
Bulgaria	33.3%	35.3%	31.3%	5.80%
Cyprus	27.8%	45.2%	27.0%	1.30%
Czech Republic	44.0%	28.3%	27.7%	8.00%
Germany	30.6%	30.1%	39.3%	8.70%
Denmark	17.3%	53.2%	29.5%	5.30%
Estonia	38.7%	22.7%	38.7%	9.80%
Spain	43.9%	23.8%	32.3%	6.90%
Finland	25.1%	53.7%	21.3%	4.20%
France	30.7%	36.8%	32.5%	5.90%
Greece	37.5%	32.7%	29.7%	5.90%
Croatia	42.3%	28.4%	29.2%	7.10%
Hungary	39.0%	27.3%	33.7%	6.90%
Ireland	17.4%	61.8%	20.8%	4.50%
Italy	39.8%	24.1%	36.1%	9.10%
Latva	42.4%	30.4%	27.2%	7.70%
Lithuania	37.2%	27.8%	35.1%	1.60%
Luxemburg	25.0%	51.9%	25.0%	8.70%
Malta	32.7%	30.1%	37.2%	7.00%
Netherlands	31.0%	27.3%	41.7%	0.80%
Polonia	52.1%	22.9%	25.1%	5.20%
Portugal	28.5%	22.8%	48.8%	17.00%
Romania	37.9%	30.0%	32.1%	3.50%
Sweden	31.6%	38.9%	29.5%	6.90%
Slovenia	42.0%	31.1%	26.9%	6.00%
Slovakia	45.9%	24.0%	30.1%	3.80%
UK	30.0%	28.7%	41.3%	11.50%
Total	38.8%	28.7%	32.5%	7.35%

Source of data: Author'calculation on data, Open Data Portal for the European Structural Investment Funds—European Commission | Data | European Structural and Investment Funds (europa.eu), https://cohesiondata.ec.europa.eu/themes.

Most new accession members, and particularly all eastern countries, allocate a very large share of cohesion funds to HCC Themes. This partly reflects the significance for these countries of the Cohesion Fund (CF), which is mostly allocated to infrastructure. However, note that there are important exceptions among "new" members, in particular Romania and Bulgaria, which allocate below-average shares to HCC expenditure. Most Nordic countries allocate larger-than-average shares to the intermediate category (ICC, the green transition section in Table 1), with a staggering share of 61.8% for Ireland. Older members allocate larger-than-average shares to non-capital expenditure, in particular Germany, Belgium, the Netherlands, and the UK. Also, some southern countries allocate a comparatively larger share to LCC expenditure, in particular Portugal and, to a lesser extent, Italy. Most of these countries however also allocate a large share of these resources to education and training, and are hence still investing, albeit in human capital. Particularly large are the shares of human capital investment of Portugal, Belgium, and the UK.

13.2 Does Cohesion Policy Increase Investment?

The last question we would like to address concerns the extent to which cohesion policy generates further net capital expenditure of potential crowding-out effects. It is indeed possible that cohesion funds are used to substitute for capital expenditure that would have been carried out with national funds anyway in the absence of an EU policy. Both at the EU level, and in certain individual countries, this possibility has generated heated debate about the real additionality of cohesion expenditure, and in particular of its investment.[2] To investigate this matter we will look at per capita capital expenditure in those regions that are more interested in cohesion policy: those that received the largest cohesion budgets over the last two budget cycles. We will therefore calculate at the regional level gross fixed capital expenditure (normalised to regional GDP) and compare this data to national gross fixed capital formation (again normalised to GDP). If cohesion expenditure adds value and contributes to the overall capital formation, we would expect to find that it exerts a significant positive effect on regional gross fixed capital formation. The gap between regional and national capital formation should be correlated with cohesion expenditure. A lower-than-the-national ratio of GFCF to GDP for a region receiving a large cohesion contribution would signal strongly that cohesion policy is ineffective in delivering investment. The next figure displays the transfers from cohesion policy over the last two programming periods to the largest recipient regions.

Table 4 compares the ratio of gross fixed capital formation to the region's GDP for these regions over the period 2007–20, with the national average of the same ratio. If

---

2   At the EU level, this originated a procedure for ex-post verification (see EU Commission 2017). For a description of the problem and the institutional attempt to tackle it in Italy, see Coco and De Vincenti (2020).

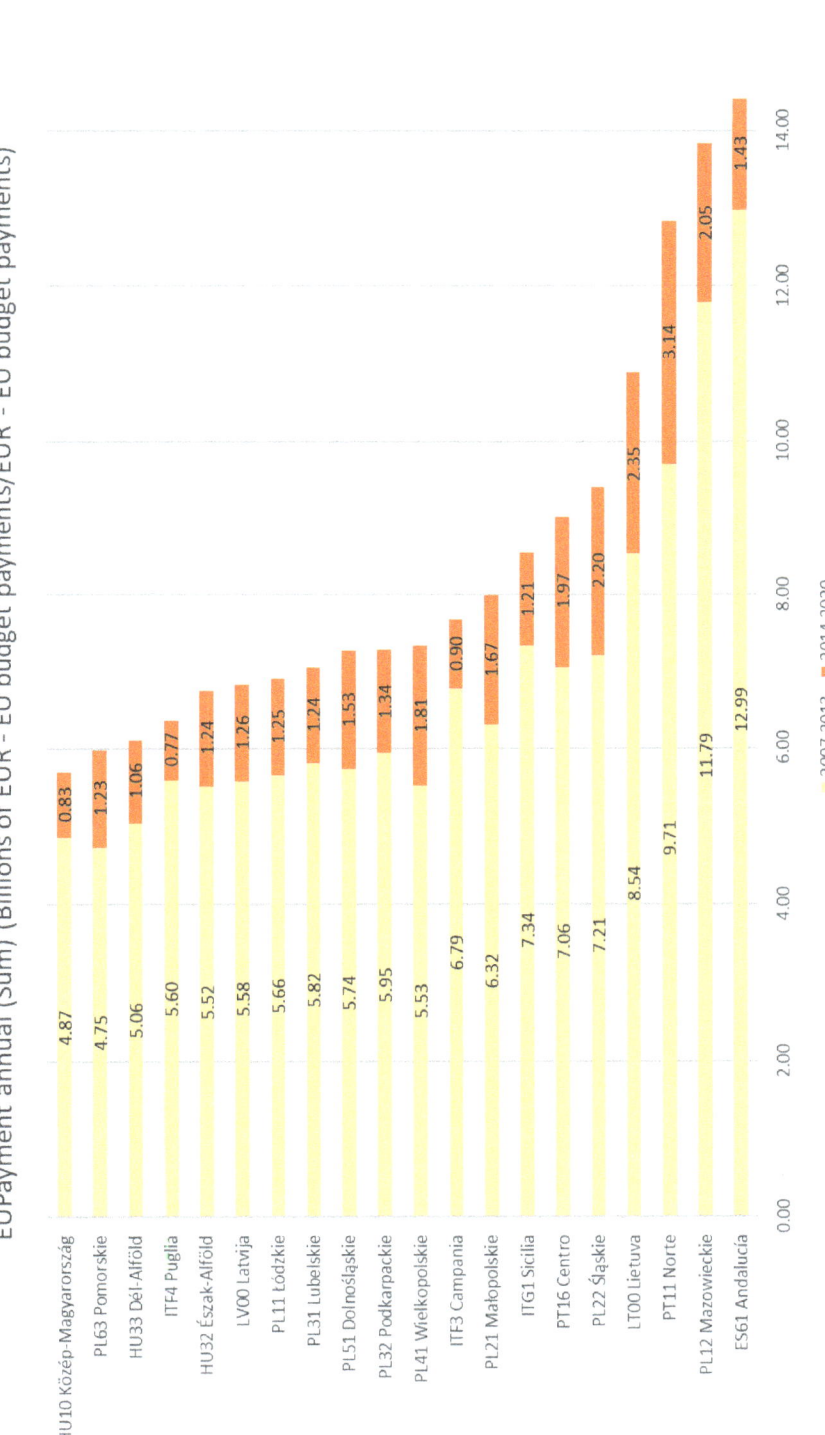

Fig. 1 Regions Receiving the Largest Contributions from Cohesion Policy (2007–20).

Source of data: https://cohesiondata.ec.europa.eu/EU-Level/Historic-EU-payments-by-MS-NUTS-2-region-filter-by/2qa4-zm5t.

cohesion policy significantly contributes to public (and private) investment we would
expect the regional ratio to be larger than the national one.

Table 4 Comparison of Ratio of GFCF to GDP with National Averages, Selected Regions, 2007–20
(Constant Price, 2015), %

NUTS 2 Regions	Regional GFCF/ Regional GDP	National GFCF/ National GDP
ES61 Andalucía	19.44	19.82
PL12 Mazowieckie	20.71	19.16
PT11 Norte	19.02	17.95
LT00 Lietuva	24.17	24.17
PL22 Śląskie	18.26	19.16
PT16 Centro	17.82	17.95
ITG1 Sicilia	16.56	18.88
PL21 Małopolskie	18.23	19.16
ITF3 Campania	17.08	18.88
PL41 Wielkopolskie	18.98	19.16
PL32 Podkarpackie	20.79	19.16
PL51 Dolnośląskie	19.49	19.16
PL31 Lubelskie	17.33	19.16
PL11 Łódzkie	19.29	19.16
LV00 Latvija	24.17	24.17
HU32 Észak-Alföld	24.33	22.68
ITF4 Puglia	17.67	18.88
HU33 Dél-Alföld	24.01	22.68
PL63 Pomorskie	21.26	19.16
HU10 Közép-Magyarország	27.24	22.68

Source of data: Author's elaboration on ARDECO database https://knowledge4policy.ec.europa.eu/
territorial/ardeco-online_en

Table 4 shows a complex picture, with different outcomes for different countries. While
the Hungarian regions (e.g., Közép-Magyarország, Észak-Alföld), some Polish regions
(e.g., Mazowieckie and Podkarpackie), and, to a lesser extent, the Portuguese regions
(e.g., Norte) display significantly higher-than-national GFCF ratios, the regions of Italy
and Spain display lower-than-the-national-average ratios of capital formation. This
certainly indicates that the cohesion policy has been ineffective in the main regions of
Italy in raising the level of total capital formation. Moreover, it may also indicate that
national public investment expenditure has been substituted by EU cohesion policy
funds in those regions. Certainly, there is no indication that public investment has been
increased significantly by cohesion policy in these countries.

13.3 Conclusion

In this paper, we explored data on Cohesion Policy expenditure to assess its real contribution, both directly and indirectly, to public capital formation in the EU. A significant proportion of Cohesion Policy, particularly in certain regions, is capital expenditure, although the standard approach of assuming that it is always entirely capital expenditure definitely appears wrong. We have tried to disentangle the likely share of capital expenditure in the budget cycle 2014–20 by exploring the themes of the policy. Some of them are mainly capital expenditures, others less so. By this method, we ascertained that some two thirds of cohesion expenditure has a significant investment nature. Another 7% is directed at increasing human capital (through education and formation). For 25% of the total, it is safe to assume that there is not an investment element. The composition of the expenditure according to the likely capital content is highly differentiated across countries. While some countries, notably Poland, spend a high proportion of funds on fixed capital formation, others spend considerably less. This may explain why cohesion policy is associated with very different outcomes (for example relating to productivity or employment without growth) in different countries (Crescenzi and Giua 2020).

In a second exercise, we explored the relationship between gross fixed capital formation at the regional level and cohesion policy, in an attempt to discover whether the latter has been able to increase investment and public investment in the regions receiving more transfers relative to the national average. The data show large differences between different regions and countries. In particular, the Italian regions seem not to benefit from cohesion policy in terms of overall investment.

Although this may also signal a lack of additionality of cohesion expenditure in some countries, a satisfactory test can only be conducted with public investment data at the regional level, which are currently not available in Eurostat. We believe it must be a priority for policy and statistical purposes to produce these data.

A final observation should be made on the effects of COVID-19 on cohesion investments. In 2020, the EU Commission launched two initiatives to allow the use of cohesion resources for a swift response to the coronavirus emergency, starting a large reprogramming of funds (EU Commission 2021). The use of cohesion funds for the emergency was necessary, but we must be aware that this may have an adverse impact on public investment. The initiatives allowed the transfer of funds across priorities and even among funds. Roughly €20 bn were transferred to health actions, emergency business support, and direct support of vulnerable groups of people. None of these actions are investments, hence we should to some degree expect a decrease in public investments in underdeveloped regions.

References

Berkowitz, P., P. Monfort and J. Pien´kowski (2020) "Unpacking the growth impacts of European Union Cohesion Policy: transmission channels from Cohesion Policy into economic growth", *Regional Studies* 54(1): 60–71.

Barbieri, G. and F. Cerniglia (2021) "The Relaunch of Public Investment in Italy", in *The Great Reset: 2021 European Public Investment Outlook*, ed. by F. Cerniglia, F. Saraceno and A. Watt (Cambridge: Open Book Publishers), pp. 63–78, https://doi.org/10.11647/obp.0280.04.

Brasili, A., A. Kolev, D. Revoltella and J. Shanz (2021) "Public Investment in the Pandemic— Europe at a Glance", in *The Great Reset: 2021 European Public Investment Outlook*, ed. by F. Cerniglia, F. Saraceno and A. Watt (Cambridge: Open Book Publishers), pp. 17–32, https://doi.org/10.11647/obp.0280.01.

Coco, G. and C. De Vincenti (2020) *Una Questione Nazionale—Il Mezzogiorno da problema a opportunità* (Bologna: Il Mulino).

Crescenzi, R. and M. Giua (2020). "One or many Cohesion Policies of the European Union? On the diverging impacts of Cohesion Policy across Member States", *Regional Studies*, 54(1): 10–20.

Durand, L., R. Espinoza, W. Gbohoui and S. Mouhamadou (2021) "Crowding In-Out of Public Investment", in *The Great Reset: 2021 European Public Investment Outlook*, ed. by F. Cerniglia, F. Saraceno and A. Watt (Cambridge: Open Book Publishers), pp. 107–26, https://doi.org/10.11647/obp.0280.07.

EU Commission (2017) *Communication on Ex-post Verification of Additionality 2007–13*, Brussels: European Commission, https://ec.europa.eu/regional_policy/en/information/publications/communications/2017/ex-post-verification-of-additionality-2007-2013.

EU Commission (2021) *European Structural and Investment Funds 2014–20, 2020 Summary Report of the annual implementation reports*, Brussels: European Commission, https://ec.europa.eu/regional_policy/en/information/publications/reports/2021/european-structural-and-investment-funds-2014-2020-2020-summary-report-of-the-programme-annual-implementation-reports-covering-implementation-in-2014-2019.

Fratesi, U. and G. Perucca (2018) "EU Regional Development Policy and Territorial Capital: A Systemic Approach", *Papers in Regional Science* 98(1), 265–81.

Haskel, J. and S. Westlake (2018) *Capitalism without Capital: The Rise of the Intangible Economy* (Princeton: Princeton University Press).

Prota, F., G. Viesti and M. Bux (2020) "The Contribution of the European Cohesion Policy to Public Investment", in *A European Public Investment Outlook*, ed. by F. Cerniglia and F. Saraceno (Cambridge: Open Book Publishers), pp. 175–92, https://doi.org/10.11647/obp.0222.10.

Psycharis, Y., V. Tselios and P. Pantazis (2020) "The contribution of Cohesion Funds and national funded public investment to regional growth: evidence from Greece", *Regional Studies* 54(1): 95–105.

List of Illustrations

Chapter 1

Chapter 2

Chapter 3

Chapter 4

Chapter 5

Chapter 6

Chapter 7

Chapter 8

Chapter 9

Chapter 10

Chapter 11

Chapter 12

Chapter 13

Fig. 1   Regions Receiving the Largest Contributions from Cohesion Policy 211
           (2007–20).
           Source of data: https://cohesiondata.ec.europa.eu/EU-Level/Historic-EU-
           payments-by-MS-NUTS-2-region-filter-by/2qa4-zm5t.

List of Tables

Chapter 1

Chapter 2

Chapter 3

Chapter 4

Chapter 5

Chapter 6

Chapter 11

Chapter 12

Chapter 13

About the Team

Alessandra Tosi was the managing editor for this book.

Melissa Purkiss and Rasalyn Sword performed the copy-editing and proofreading.

Anna Gatti designed the cover. The cover was produced in InDesign using the Fontin font.

Luca Baffa typeset the book in InDesign and produced the paperback and hardback editions. The text font is Tex Gyre Pagella; the heading font is Californian FB. Luca produced the EPUB, AZW3, PDF, HTML, and XML editions—the conversion is performed with open source software freely available on our GitHub page (https://github.com/OpenBookPublishers).

This book need not end here...

Share

All our books—including the one you have just read—are free to access online so that students, researchers and members of the public who can't afford a printed edition will have access to the same ideas. This title will be accessed online by hundreds of readers each month across the globe: why not share the link so that someone you know is one of them?

This book and additional content is available at:

https://doi.org/10.11647/OBP.0280

Customise

Personalise your copy of this book or design new books using OBP and third-party material. Take chapters or whole books from our published list and make a special edition, a new anthology or an illuminating coursepack. Each customised edition will be produced as a paperback and a downloadable PDF.

Find out more at:

https://www.openbookpublishers.com/section/59/1

Like Open Book Publishers

Follow @OpenBookPublish

Read more at the Open Book Publishers BLOG

You may also be interested in:

A European Public Investment Outlook

Floriana Cerniglia and Francesco Saraceno (eds)

https://doi.org/10.11647/OBP.0222

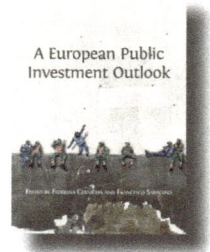

Infrastructure Investment in Indonesia
A Focus on Ports

Colin Duffield, Felix Kin Peng Hui, Sally Wilson (eds)

https://doi.org/10.11647/OBP.0189

The Infrastructure Finance Challenge

Ingo Walter (ed.)

https://doi.org/10.11647/OBP.0106

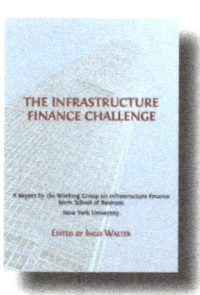

Lightning Source UK Ltd.
Milton Keynes UK
UKHW050301221221
396014UK00003B/46

9 781800 643505